Unveiling Pachacamac

UNIVERSITY PRESS OF FLORIDA

Florida A&M University, Tallahassee
Florida Atlantic University, Boca Raton
Florida Gulf Coast University, Ft. Myers
Florida International University, Miami
Florida State University, Tallahassee
New College of Florida, Sarasota
University of Central Florida, Orlando
University of Florida, Gainesville
University of North Florida, Jacksonville
University of South Florida, Tampa
University of West Florida, Pensacola

UNVEILING PACHACAMAC

NEW HYPOTHESES FOR AN OLD ANDEAN SANCTUARY

EDITED BY GIANCARLO MARCONE

UNIVERSITY PRESS OF FLORIDA

Gainesville / Tallahassee / Tampa / Boca Raton

Pensacola / Orlando / Miami / Jacksonville / Ft. Myers / Sarasota

27 26 25 24 23 22   6 5 4 3 2 1

Library of Congress Cataloging-in-Publication Data
Names: Marcone, Giancarlo, editor.
Title: Unveiling Pachacamac : new hypotheses for an old Andean sanctuary /
    edited by Giancarlo Marcone.
Description: 1. | Gainesville : University Press of Florida, 2022. |
    Includes bibliographical references and index. | Summary: "This volume
    synthesizes 25 years of new data and hypotheses on the sacred Andean
    site of Pachacamac, a sanctuary that has an enduring presence in
    Peruvian history and plays a pivotal role in the formation of current
    views about religion and thought in the pre-Hispanic period"— Provided
    by publisher.
Identifiers: LCCN 2021052461 (print) | LCCN 2021052462 (ebook) | ISBN
    9780813069333 (hardback) | ISBN 9780813070117 (pdf)
Subjects: LCSH: Excavations (Archaeology)—Peru—Lurín River Valley. |
    Temples—Peru—Lurín River Valley. | Indians of South
    America—Peru—Lurín River Valley. | Pachacamac Site
    (Peru)—Antiquities. | Lurín River Valley (Peru)—Antiquities. | BISAC:
    SOCIAL SCIENCE / Archaeology | SOCIAL SCIENCE / Anthropology / Cultural
    & Social
Classification: LCC F3429.1.P2 U68 2022 (print) | LCC F3429.1.P2 (ebook)
    | DDC 985/.01—dc23/eng/20211106
LC record available at https://lccn.loc.gov/2021052461
LC ebook record available at https://lccn.loc.gov/2021052462

The University Press of Florida is the scholarly publishing agency for the State
University System of Florida, comprising Florida A&M University, Florida Atlantic
University, Florida Gulf Coast University, Florida International University, Florida
State University, New College of Florida, University of Central Florida, University
of Florida, University of North Florida, University of South Florida, and University
of West Florida.

University Press of Florida
2046 NE Waldo Road
Suite 2100
Gainesville, FL 32609
http://upress.ufl.edu

Contents

Figures

Tables

Pachacamac in the Development of Andean Archaeology

GIANCARLO MARCONE

The Sanctuary of Pachacamac has been an enduring presence in Andean history. Early Spanish accounts portray the site as a center of wealth and prestige that played a key role in the dramatic events following the arrival of Spaniards in Peru, particularly in the capture of the Inca Atahualpa, and later the fall of the Inca Empire. These Spanish accounts, together with the striking monumentality of the site itself against the backdrop of the arid landscape of the Peruvian Central Coast, have captured the attention of scholars seeking to understand the pre-Hispanic past. Beginning in the sixteenth century, the site of Pachacamac was omnipresent in chronicles and descriptions of Peru.

The site has held a significant meaning for Andean archaeology at large: (1) Pachacamac played a pivotal role in the formation of current views about religion and ideology in pre-Hispanic times. Building on the ethnohistorical accounts, Pachacamac is envisaged as the archetypal pre-Columbian Andean sanctuary or shrine. The conceptual model of *sanctuary* and *oracle* was built in the classic pre-Hispanic historiography. (2) Pachacamac is meaningful for understanding chronology, trajectories, and time in Andean archaeology. The Pachacamac Sanctuary was an integrated part of the many early chronological sequences. Often, ceramics recovered from Pachacamac were part of the main Andean chronological sequences, such as the chronological sequence proposed by Rowe (1960) and later by Menzel (1964). (3) Pachacamac is the ultimate representation of the relationship between state, society, heritage, and population in Peru. In 1886, Max Uhle (1903; reprinted in Shimada 1991), a German scholar associated with several U.S. universities, started a large-scale project in the sanctuary that is believed by many to be the first stratigraphical and chronological excavation in Andean archaeology, and a landmark in the formation of archaeology as a scholarly discipline in the Andean region (for example, Rowe 1998; Schaedel 1993; Shimada 1991).

With the current controversy surrounding the construction of the new national museum inside the sanctuary, Pachacamac is still clearly a reflection of the changing conceptions of heritage and society, and the impact of current national discourses on the understanding of the ancient world.

Pachacamac: Geography and Chronology

The site of Pachacamac lies close to the shore on the northwest edge of the Lurín Valley, in the middle of the Peruvian Central Coast. The Peruvian Central Coast is a territory of geopolitical importance with a long trajectory of human occupation. The powerful social formations around what today is the city of Lima were central to the development of the Andes for centuries before the Spanish occupation. Geographically, the Peruvian Central Coast is a narrow desert strip located between the western chain of the Andes and the Pacific Ocean. This desert strip, less than 30 km wide, is cut by the presence of a series of narrow valleys.

Here, we consider the Central Coast as a region with a long shared cultural trajectory that includes the terrain from Huaura Valley in the north to Cañete Valley in the south. The central part of this territory is formed by the confluence at the mouth of the Chillón and Rímac rivers which, along with the mouth of the Lurín River to the southeast and the Villa Swamp (between Rímac and Lurín), form a fertile strip in the middle of the desert.

Toward the highlands to the east, the area that we can identify as the "coast" corresponds to the two lower zones of the valleys of the Pacific basins. These two zones are known as the *yunga* (basically the alluvial fans of the valleys of the western slope) and the *chaupiyunga* (between the alluvial fans and approximately 1,000 m above sea level). Although these limits are only referential and have varied through history in relation to specific political and social situations, the area maintains a relative cultural consistency (Marcone 2019).

The earliest traces of human occupation on the Central Coast go back at least to the Early Preceramic Period (circa 10,000–6000 BCE). The material evidence of this occupation is limited to accumulations of lithic materials found in what appear to be seasonal camps. Among the sites found during this period, the Chivateros lithic quarry stands out at the mouth of the Chillón River. Similar materials to those recovered in this quarry appear along the entire Peruvian coast (Kaulicke and Dillehay 1999).

During the Middle Preceramic Period (circa 6000–2500 BCE), the first villages appeared, such as Paloma, located in the foothills to the north of Chilca Valley, an hour from the city of Lima (Quilter 1989, 1991). By the Late Preceramic Period (circa 2500–1800 BCE), the first monumental sites emerged on the Central Coast at El Paraiso and Buena Vista (Benfer et al. 2007). This gradual process of centralization of people extended to the Initial Period (circa 1800–850 BCE), when ceremonial centers dominated by the architectural form known as the U-shaped temple appeared (Burger 2014; Burger and Salazar in this volume). Between 900 BCE and 700 BCE these ceremonial centers fell into disuse, and by the beginning of the Early Horizon (850–200 BCE) the U-shaped centers were abandoned and population collapse is suspected (Marcone 2019).

By the end of the Early Horizon, a new ceramic tradition began to develop. These ceramics are best known as the "white-on-red" style. By the start of the Early Intermediate Period (circa 200 BCE–AD 900) the white-on-red style was partially replaced by a tricolor style using red, white, and black which became known as the Lima style, giving its name to the best-known culture in the region for the early periods (Córdova 2003; Kaulicke 2000). It is around this time that the first evidence of organized and formal architecture appeared at the site of Pachacamac (Shimada 1991).

The appearance of Lima culture features in the Central Coast is also related to the expansion of the agriculture frontier (Canziani 2007; Silva 1996) and the appearance of irrigation networks that, by the end of the Early Intermediate Period, allowed the emergence of a state-level, multivalley polity or polities in the region (Marcone in this volume; Shady 1988).

For some researchers, the emergence of this state-level society in the central area was an expression of local trajectories (for example, Marcone 2010a, 2010b; Shady 1982, 1988; Stumer 1954). For others, it was the byproduct of Middle Horizon, intrusive highland Wari presence in the region (Menzel 1964; Patterson 1966). At Pachacamac, at the end of the Early Intermediate Period, local Lima structures increased in size and monumentality and the site began to have a clear regional presence, as my own chapter in this volume explores. In line with this discussion, understanding the nature and tempo of the increased presence of the Lima culture at Pachacamac is key to understanding the cultural/political formation of Lima traditions and their interaction with the Wari. This revisioning of Lima-Wari interaction calls for rethinking the interpretation of Wari-style ceramics (for example, the

Pachacamac ceramic style) recovered in Pachacamac—although with deficient contextual information. These ceramics have been used to support the imperial presence of Wari at the site (see discussion in Kaulicke 2000) even though there are no buildings at Pachacamac that can be assigned without doubt to the Middle Horizon.

The absence of Middle Horizon buildings at Pachacamac is congruent with the abandonment of domestic sites at the valley, which indicates not only the collapse of political institutions but also a decline in population. This phenomenon seems to be related to a series of alternating periods of drought and intense rainfall due to the ENSO phenomenon. Toward the second half of the Middle Horizon, the presence of southern, Wari-like styles declined and an increase in regional stylistic variations at the valley level could suggest a political fragmentation of the area, in which small elite groups sponsored new symbols of power to legitimize their authority (Kaulicke 2000). However, recent discoveries in the area of Huarmey suggest that some of these new elites may have been more powerful than suspected and closely linked to southern groups (Giersz 2014). This political fragmentation continued until the shaping of a new political polity in the later periods, a coastal group known as the Ychsma (Eeckhout 2004: 412–413). Dating to the Late Intermediate Period (AD 1100–1470), this new sociopolitical development has been characterized based not on ceramics (as were earlier periods), but on colonial records and other written sources (that is, Albornoz 1967 [1582]; de la Calancha 1639; Castro y Morejón 1974 [1558]; Cobo 1990 [1653]). According to these sixteenth-century sources, at the time of the Inca Conquest of the Lurín Valley, the region was populated by the Ychsma (Patterson 1985; Soriano 2014).

María Rostworowski's deep study of ethnohistoric sources suggests that the social order of the Ychsma society was based mainly around the cult of Pachacamac (Rostworowski 1972, 1973, 1999, 2002). The Ychsma do not appear to have been subject to a centralized hegemonic power until the arrival of the Incas in the Late Horizon. The Incas transformed the area into a subordinate province (Cornejo 2000; Soriano 2014). The site saw an increase of Inca presence, and Pachacamac was taught as an example of coexistence of Inca and local practices (Cobo 1990 [1653]). However, Makowski (this volume) has a different view: he proposes that the Inca presence was older and more important in terms of imposition than what is usually proposed. He suggests that Pachacamac underwent an intense reconstruction in Inca times. In this idea, the site that we can see on the surface is basically an Inca construction and not a local site with some Inca buildings. Other authors in this volume strongly disagree.

The open controversy existing in this volume between the articles of Makowski, Owens and Eeckhout, and Pozzi-Escot and Bernuy implies a challenge to the traditional understanding of the tempo and nature of the Inca expansion that could affect current ideas about Inca expansion at the pan-regional level.

Pachacamac Layout and Its Principal Buildings: Is There a Long Continuous Occupation?

The image of the site we see today represents the most recent occupation of the site, right before its abandonment and with the later intrusion of the archaeologist. Based on this latest image, the site has been seen as consisting of three concentric rings of walls and in the middle a superposition of temples, one over the other, in an onion-like layering. This reading of the site has become the most popular narrative of its organization (Ravines 1996). The present volume challenges the idea of a long continuity and that this Late Period picture is projectable to the deeper past. For example, Shimada and his collaborators propose a completely different arrangement, even of the orientation of the site during the Early periods.

The traditional interpretation of Pachacamac is clearly influenced by our expectation of what a religious pilgrimage center should be, with controlled access to the main temples. This traditional reading divides the site into three main sectors, each of which represents a different level of access.

At the north and the northeast ends of the sanctuary, it is possible to identify two gateways that are linked with the Inca Road and are usually referred to as the Third Wall, although it is not a wall in the exact sense. This Third Wall is followed by an open space with little surface evidence of construction, although excavation in this area shows several transitory or temporary structures (Jiménez 2014).

After this first area, which supplies a more general access, comes an area composed of several buildings known as Pyramids with Ramp (PWRs), which are circumscribed by a second wall. These buildings are organized in two axes or main streets (Pozzi-Escot and Bernuy in this volume). The functions of these PWRs are still under debate. Some researchers propose that the PWRs belong to the Late Intermediate Period and are embassies of a sort for the different valley-level local lords (Bueno 1982; Jiménez Borja 1992). Others propose that they correspond to successive palaces of regional lords (Eeckhout 2008, 2010). Makowski (this volume) questions these ideas and introduces the hypothesis that these buildings were also constructed, not by the local societies, but for the Incas.

After this area, in the innermost sector of the site, the principal temples of the site are surrounded by the First Wall. First is an early complex composed of two late Lima buildings (the so-called Old Temple and a Lima temple that was later covered by an Inca Sun temple) linked by a platform (Shimada 1991). This first complex was progressively covered by new temples that were added laterally to the Old Temple: first by Uhle's Red Temple (supposedly belonging to the Early Middle Horizon), and later—by the second part of the Middle Horizon—by the Painted Temple (Marcone 2005; Shimada 1991). The Painted Temple is proposed as the main Pachacamac temple (Ravines 1996). With the arrival of the Incas, a new temple, the Sun Temple, was constructed covering an old Lima temple. The survival of the Painted Temple at the same time as the Sun Temple is usually taken as a sign of the coexistence and/or co-opting of Inca imperial religion with local traditions. In this conception, Yschma was the name of the local deity who was later incorporated into the Inca pantheon with the name of Pachacamac. Makowski (this volume) challenges this idea; he proposes that Pachacamac was an Inca deity and not a local one and that the main temple was the Sun Temple.

The classic reading of Pachacamac's layout became the official narrative about the site (Ravines 1996), despite the fact that the actual research at the site was minimal and incomplete (Shimada et al. 2004). We believe the sanctuary's landscape was transformed by twentieth-century site managers to fit this story. For example, the formalization of a visitor's circuit developed principally by Arturo Jiménez Borja and his collaborators, beginning in the late 1960s, promoted this specific history of the site based heavily on ethnohistoric accounts (Bueno 1974). This interpretation of Pachacamac is the foundation for the "official version" explained to site visitors and the general public for the last 50 years. Significantly, the official version has proven to be monolithic and impermeable to incorporating any new knowledge derived from the continued archaeological research at the site.

In the last 25 years, this situation has been reversed dramatically. Pachacamac is now receiving an important amount of archaeological attention, either at the site or through the study of previously excavated collections now in Peruvian and U.S. museums. This new research has challenged the traditional chronological and functional interpretations of the site.

Pachacamac and the Central Coast in the Reconstruction of the Cultural Trajectories of the Andes

Based principally on stylistic analysis of ceramics, the cultural trajectory of pre-Hispanic Peru has been reconstructed using a chronological scheme divided into the Horizon and Intermediate periods. The Horizon Period comprises styles such as Chavín, Wari, or Inca, which are present throughout the Andean area. During the Intermediate periods, local cultures became stronger and more influential. Although it is not the only scheme, this is the most widely used proposal in Andean chronology. This scheme implicitly denies that pan-regional influences and local styles may be contemporary.

After several years of struggle, we realized that classification according to horizons of pan-Andean cultural diffusion favored the construction of models in which a nucleus radiates stylistic and cultural traits to the entire Andean cultural area (that is, Jennings 2006; Marcone 2019). Such constructs deny local agendas and interpret the evidence of political complexity as proof of the presence of pan-Andean societies.

Although we can critique this chronological scheme, we still use it because it allows us to contextualize Pachacamac temporally in a long-term Andean trajectory. Therefore, we favor the use of these periods as temporal boxes, while avoiding their use as categories of cultural or social complexity.

As reflected in several parts of the present volume, the impact of the El Niño phenomenon on the cultural trajectory of the region deserves special attention. This phenomenon, also known as the El Niño Southern Oscillation (ENSO), happens cyclically and has been used as a causal explanation for the rise and fall of several civilizations in the Andean area. The presence of ENSO as it relates to droughts and periods of intense rainfall on the Central Coast have been well documented (that is, Shimada et al. 1991; Rein et al. 2004). These periods, identified in the geological record, coincide with periods in which evidence suggests a depopulation of the area with a corresponding collapse of local cultural traditions, generating internal competition and a search for referents of legitimacy in distant societies (see, for example, Shimada et al. in this volume).

Table 1.1. Chronology of the Central Coast and Pachacamac

Dates	Periods	Culture Societies	Pachacamac
1535			Pilgrims' Plaza
	Late Horizon	Incas	Temple of the Sun
1470			
		Ishma	Pyramids with Ramp
	Late Intermediate		
1100			
			Painted Temple
	Middle Horizon	Pachacamac and other Wari-related styles	
			Mud-brick Compound
600			Old Temple
	Early Intermediate	Lima	
200			
		White-on-Red	
0	Early Horizon		

Source: Author.

Pachacamac: An Intellectual History of the Relationship between State, Heritage, and Population in Peru

Pachacamac is also a reflection of the intellectual history of archaeology and heritage management in Peru. Pachacamac's size, long history of archaeological research, and location so close to Lima, the highly populated capital of modern Peru, has made the site a point of reflection for Peruvian archaeological and heritage discourses. The site has played a particularly important role in the ways that archaeological remains are used in the social construction of national identities (Schaedel and Shimada 1982).

Travelers from the Eighteenth and Nineteenth Centuries

As early as the eighteenth and nineteenth centuries, Pachacamac was continuously visited by missionaries and travelers (Ravines 1996). These *viaje-*

ros began to promote a vision of the Peruvian past as splendid—therefore Peru and its people were worthy of being civilized (Riviale 2000)—based on the monumentality of sites such as Pachacamac. The agenda of these early studies fulfilled a growing demand from Western societies for exotic landscapes and remote cultures at the end of the nineteenth century. Travelers such as Charles Weiner, George Squier, Ernest Middendorf, and Thomas Hutchison are among those who visited the site during the eighteenth and nineteenth centuries.

These travelers were also the intellectual backbone of the European imperialist agenda and were used to build discourses of colonization, indigeneity, and modernity (Weems 2012). Although early foreign travelers recognized the indigenous manufacture of the great pre-Hispanic monuments, they also distanced the sites from contemporaneous indigenous populations, portraying local populations as survivors of former greatness, now careless about the past. Who then should inherit this greatness? Until the twentieth century the answer was simple: Europeans like them, people capable of truly appreciating the greatness of ancient ruins (Weems 2012). From the beginning, Pachacamac had a central role in these reconstructions and discourses about the past that were entangled in the formation of the idea of Peru, as we understand it today.

This colonial project was transformed with the creation of the republic in the early nineteenth century, but its imprint remains recognizable in the national project of the late nineteenth century and throughout the twentieth century (Gänger 2006, 2009; Méndez 1996). In this new modernist national project, the indigenous population was still excluded from the ownership of the past and portrayed as corrupt remnants of past societies. What changed was the answer to the question: Who are the rightful inheritors of this past? In the nationalist, postcolonial project, the rightful owners of the great pre-Columbian past were not seen as Western societies or an international audience, but the members of the *criollo* society (Peruvian-born descendants of Spaniards who controlled the new republic).

Twentieth Century at Pachacamac and the Building of the Peruvian Nation

After Uhle's (1903; Shimada 1991) pioneering work, archaeological projects at Pachacamac were intimately linked with the construction of the modern Peruvian nation, and they were directly sponsored by nationalist governments. For example, in 1939 on the occasion of the 37th International Congress of Americanists in Lima, a state-sponsored project was responsible for the cleaning of one of the principal temples at Pachacamac. The large-scale excavation of the "Painted Temple" was completed in order to present something impressive to the prestigious international visitors (Bueno 1974; Ravines 1996; Shimada 1991). The excavations uncovered the façade of the building and unveiled several mural paintings (Muelle and Well 1939). Today these paintings have almost completely disappeared (although important advances in the protection and record of these paintings have been done in recent years [Pozzi-Escot et al. 2013]). To this day, the Painted Temple is one of the only structures at Pachacamac at which a façade was completely exposed through archaeological operations. Hence, it is one of the principal attractions for the visitors to the site (Marcone 2003). Again, the relationship between archaeology and society left a permanent mark on the face of the sanctuary, as a footprint of our own intellectual trajectory.

Interventions in Pachacamac not only helped to build modern-day stories of national identity, they also actively transformed public perceptions of the past. The archaeologists responsible for these interventions are also the ones who construct the history of the site.

Julio C. Tello's Acllahuasi: Building a Peruvian Nation

In the 1940s Julio C. Tello began fieldwork at Pachacamac. This project was sponsored by the Peruvian state through the Junta Pro-Desocupados, a national program designed to help unemployed people (Bueno 1974; Ravines 1996; Shimada 1991; Villacorta 2004). Tello's project left an important mark on the history of Pachacamac. The restoration of the Inca Palace of the Mamacunas (Acllahuasi) was highly interpretive and appears to have reflected Tello's concern with transmitting a predetermined representation of the past rather than accurately reconstructing the edifice (Marcone 2010b). The building highlights stone cut in the Inca style as well as trapezoidal *hornacinas* (types of niches) and doorways in the building. These architectural features are most typically found at imperial Inca buildings in the Cuzco heartland.

The Acllahuasi can be said to have more Inca characteristics than any other Inca building on the Peruvian coast. Despite the consensus among archaeologists acknowledging the interpretative character of this building (Bueno 1974; Villacorta 2004), the Acllahuasi has become the image of the sanctuary in the popular imagination of both Peruvian and foreign visitors. People come to the sanctuary principally to visit this building. The heavy flow of visitors forces its constant maintenance, diverting funds that could otherwise be used for the preservation of other areas of the site that are less investigated or in greater danger of collapse.

Pachacamac and the National Agenda

The other class, adapting itself to the ideas, feelings, aspiration, manners, customs, etc of European civilization, makes an effort to shape nationality on the Spanish or Latin base, putting aside the bases left by the aboriginal civilization . . . our present Hispanic-Peruvian civilization cannot stand except on an indigenous pedestal. . . .

It cannot stand firm and last for a long time if does not completely adapt itself to its surroundings, if men do not try to use our own resources to discover secrets and wonders of our own nature, admire the labor or our ancestors, glorify the generations which lived on our own soil which holds their ashes and from which they took their sustenance, and which they defended and used many centuries.

The present generation is obligated to revive the past and retrieve everything that can be glorified. (Tello 2009 [1921]: 110–111)

It has been well established (for example, de la Cadena 2000; Molinié 2004) that the modernist project in Peru was a process in which several of the more prominent Peruvian intellectuals believed in the necessity of detaching indigenous people from the past in order to use the past in favor of their own national or regional agenda. Somewhat surprisingly within Peruvian archaeology, contrary to most other disciplines, this modernist and indigenist intellectual agenda has been systematically ignored. Research has focused on the pioneering contributions to the development of the discipline in Peru made by archaeologists who are considered the founding figures of Peruvian archaeology. These figures were used in the construction of a neoindigenist position (Kaulicke 2008) held by several Peruvian archaeologists. Again, the site of Pachacamac is a key component of the national perception of the past.

After several years of little archaeological work on the site, Arturo Jiménez Borja founded a small site museum in November of 1965. Jiménez Borja and his colleagues started several projects at the site and uncovered several buildings (Ravines 1996). They were responsible for the development of the minimal visitor infrastructure the site had until recently, they put together a public discourse about the history of the site and a visitor circuit, and they defined the attitude of the museum toward the local population for the future. They thought of the museum as responsible for the protection of the archaeological past against urban expansion or in other terms against the people's encroachment on the site. Despite its exclusionary attitude toward its neighbors, this effort has proved vital for the survival of the sanctuary:

> The negative aspect of Tello's work was the imaginative reconstruction of the "Mamacuna" and the installation of workers and their families in the archaeological site. This cancer had grown until 1963 and people unfamiliar with archaeological activities occupied a square kilometer of space atop buildings and a pre-Hispanic cemetery. That year, the Dirección General de Museos de Sitio had taken the site management in order to bring order and totally delineate the physical perimeter of the monuments. (Bueno 1974–75: 176, our translation, our emphasis)

In recent years (at least since 2003), a national-level project called Qhapaq Ñan, which is arguably the biggest heritage-based project in South America, carried out direct interventions at the site and even financed the building of a new site museum. Here we see again how, even today, the main cultural policies are linked with this important site.

About the Genesis of This Volume

In light of the importance of the site for archaeology and for the intellectual history of Peruvian archaeology and heritage, it was time to bring together the new research at Pachacamac and discuss it holistically. This is the objective of the present volume. The volume emerges from discussions held from November 30 to December 1, 2012, in Dumbarton Oaks Research and Library, Washington, D.C. This invitational event brought together an international group of scholars working at Pachacamac and its surroundings. The group of scholars—hailing from Peru, Europe, and the United States—were engaged in an intense and productive discussion that was truly international and represents most of the meaningful research conducted at the site and its surrounding valley in the last 25 years. This was the first time that the long historical trajectory of the site was discussed in detail and included expressly its relation to its hinterlands.

About the Book

After the productive discussions at Dumbarton Oaks and in light of the new data and the controversial nature of some proposals, all of the authors agreed that it was important to turn these conversations into a volume that addressed the disputed points, thus building the most comprehensive academic volume about Pachacamac since the pioneer work of Uhle.

The collection of essays is organized chronologically. Richard Burger and Lucy Salazar address the early evidence of occupation of the Lurín Valley and propose that, contrary to the official discourse, it is likely that Pachacamac was not important in this period, and the early occupation registered there should not be used as evidence of continuity in the site since the Initial Period.

Izumi Shimada and his collaborators explore the particular relation of the site with sources of water, explaining why Pachacamac was located where it is. This discussion is particularly relevant to understanding the rise and growth of the sanctuary during the Early Intermediate Period—Middle Horizon. They show us how the supposed continuity in the occupation of the site needs to be re-evaluated and how the Late Period site had a different layout and maybe different functions.

At this point in the discussion it is important to try to understand the cultural evolution of the site in relation to the Lurín Valley, to contextualize the site within a regional perspective. Here, I address the impact that the site had in the political organization of the Lurín Valley and how this relation can shed light on the functions of the sanctuary. Our own work discusses the Lima presence in the valley, particularly in the site of "Lote B" and at Pachacamac, proposing that is not until the Late Lima Period, concomitant with major political transformation in this society, that the sanctuary arose as a regional center linked to the expansion of the new Lima political system in the region. This proposal agrees with that of Izumi Shimada that a different site was founded during Lima times.

Continuing this contextualization of Pachacamac within its valley, López-Hurtado and Gonzales provide a good starting point for the discussion of the Late periods. They compare Panquilma (a community-sized settlement) in the Lurín Valley and its incorporation into the Inca Empire, to the process happening at Pachacamac at the same time. López-Hurtado and Gonzales argue that the relationship between Panquilma and Pachacamac was instrumental in Inca strategies for the valley.

The last part of the book focuses on understanding the last major occupation of the site. This occupation was usually defined on the basis of ethnohistoric data, which proved to be incomplete. The articles in this section give us plenty of new archaeological data to stimulate discussion about the nature and function of Pachacamac, without an overdependence on the written sources. In the discussion of these new data, two new hypotheses are arising. On one side, Krzysztof Makowski's essay challenges the idea that Pachacamac was an important sanctuary before the Incas; for him, the rise of the site and the association of the site with the Inca divinity of Pachacamac is something that happened in the Late Horizon. This idea, although provocative, needs to be discussed in depth, as it implies that Late Intermediate Period Lurín Valley society was less centralized than is usually assumed. According to Makowski, the site of Pachacamac was not the result of co-opting a pre-existing sanctuary, but the imposition of a new cult in the region. This is unusual compared to other Inca conquests. In contrast, Owens and Eeckhout, and Pozzi-Escot and Bernuy, support the idea of a strong, local, Late Intermediate Period polity that was only partially influenced by the Inca by the end of the sequence. Pozzi-Escot and Bernuy offer data to support the idea that the transformation of the site during Inca times was late and that there was a late local sequence prior to the Incas, confirming partially the idea of a strong, local-based site co-opted by Inca occupation. Eeckhout and Owens, in the context of a revision of the possible impact of the climate at the site, use data from more than 15 years working at the site to argue that the occupation of the site corresponds to a long trajectory of superposed temples, starting before the Inca occupation.

Final Remarks

This book is an update of the last 25 years of investigation at and around the site of Pachacamac. The research is truly international and collaborative, bringing together specialists with different approaches and different foci.

For the first time, the site is integrated into its hinterland and discussed in regional context. This perspective shows a site with regional influence shaping the outcomes of the cultural contacts in the region. The new data allow us to challenge the reactive dominant discourse about the Pachacamac Sanctuary. At the same time, it provides the basis to reevaluate not only Andean chronology, but also our understanding of Andean shrines.

Acknowledgments

This volume was inspired by discussions on the Pachacamac Sanctuary that took place in 2012 at Dumbarton Oaks. I would like to thank all of the Dumbarton Oaks staff who made these conversations possible, with special thanks to Joanne Pillsbury, who was director of the Pre-Columbian Studies Department at the time that I was a junior fellow. Her support and encouragement were vital to shaping the roundtable. I also would like to thank our late friend and colleague Colin McEwan, who was the director of the Pre-Columbian Studies Department at the time. He embraced the project enthusiastically and was the most graceful host to the visiting scholars.

I also want to thank the Institute of Andean Research, which provided valuable support for the editorial adventure in transforming the Dumbarton Oaks discussions into the present volume. A special thanks to Richard Burger, who always encouraged me to finish this volume, even during times when the project looked like it was falling between the cracks.

It is necessary to thank the patience of my colleagues who contributed to the book. This publication was a personal debt, and without the involvement and understanding from them it would had been impossible to finish.

I would like to thank especially Amy Mortensen and Gabriela García Benavente for their invaluable help preparing the manuscript at different stages, and to the staff at the University Press of Florida and the anonymous reviewers. Finally, a special thanks to Pachacamac, which "chose" me early in my career to run the site museum, changing my professional aspirations and trajectory. In that sense, this volume is also a personal debt to the site.

References Cited

Albornoz, Cristóbal
1967   Instrucción para descubrir todas las guacas del Pirú y sus camayos y haziendas. *Journal de la Société des Américanistes* 56(1): 7–39.

Benfer, Robert Alfred, Bernardino Ojeda, Neil A. Duncan, Larry R. Adkins, Hugo Ludeña, Miriam Vallejos, Víctor Rojas, Andrés Ocas, Omar Ventocilla, and Gloria Villarreal
2007   La tradición religioso-astronómica en Buena Vista. *Boletín de Arqueología PUCP* (11): 53–102.

Bueno, Alberto
1974   Cajamarquilla y Pachacamac: Dos Ciudades de la Costa Central del Perú. *Boletín Bibliográfico de Antropología Americana* 37 (46): 171–211.
1982   El Antiguo Valle de Pachacamac: Espacio, tiempo y Cultura. *Boletín de Lima* 24: 3–52.

Burger, Richard
2014   Centro de qué? Los sitios con arquitectura pública de la cultura Manchay en la costa central del Perú. In *El Centro Ceremonial Andino: Nuevas Perspectivas para los períodos Arcaico y Formativo*, edited by Yuji Seki, pp. 291–233. Senri Ethnological Studies 89, National Museum of Ethnography, Osaka.

de la Calancha, Antonio
1639   *Corónica moralizada del orden de San Agustín en el Perú*. Imprenta Pedro Lacavallería, Barcelona.

Canziani Amico, José
2007   Paisajes culturales y desarrollo territorial en los Andes. *Cuadernos de Arquitectura y Ciudad* 5: 1–120.

Castro, Cristóbal de, and Diego de Ortega Morejón
1974 [1558]   La Relación de Chincha (1558). *Historia y Cultura*, edited by Juan Carlos Crespo, pp. 91–104. Museo Nacional de Historia, Lima.

Coben, Lawrence A.
2006   Other Cuzcos: Replicated Theaters of Inka Power. In *Archaeology of Performance: Theaters of Power, Community, and Politics*, edited by T. Inomata and L. S. Coben, pp. 223–260. Altamira Press, Lanham, Maryland.

Cobo, Bernabé
1990 [1653]   Historia del nuevo mundo. Biblioteca de Autores Españoles, Madrid.

Córdova, Humberto A.
2003   La Cerámica Blanco sobre Rojo en el valle de Chancay y sus relaciones con el estilo Lima. *Bulletin de l'institut Français d'études andines* 32(1): 69–100.

Cornejo, Miguel
2000   Nación Ischma y la Provincia Inka de Pachacamac. *Arqueológicas* 7: 149–173.

de la Cadena, Marisol
2000   *Indigenous Mestizos: The Politics of Race and Culture in Cuzco, Peru, 1919–1991*. Duke University Press, Durham, North Carolina.

Eeckhout, Peter
2004   La sombra de Ychsma. Ensayo introductorio sobre la arqueología de la costa central del Perú en los periodos tardíos. *Bulletin de l'Institut français d'études andines* 33(3): 403–423.
2008   El Santuario de Oráculo de Pachacamac y los peregrinajes a larga escala. In *Adivinación*

y Orcáculos, edited by Marco Curatola and Mariuz Ziolkowski, pp. 161–180. Pontificia Universidad Católica del Perú, Instituto Francés de Estudios Andinos, Lima.

2010　Las pirámides con rampa de Pachacamac durante el horizonte tardío. In *Arqueología en el Perú: nuevos aportes para el estudio de las sociedades andinas prehispánicas*, edited by R. Romero Velarde and T. Pavel Sveden, pp. 415–434. Universidad Nacional Federico Villareal, Lima.

Gänger, Stefanie

2006　¿La mirada imperialista? Los alemanes y la arqueología peruana. *Histórica* 30 (2): 69–90.

2009　Estas Reliquias de mis antepasados: Saber y poder en la historia de la arqueología peruana en el siglo 19. Paper presented at the XXVIII International Congress of the Latin American Studies Association, Rio de Janeiro, Brazil.

Giersz, Milosz

2014　El hallazgo del mausoleo imperial. In *Castillo de Huarmey: el mausoleo imperial Wari*, edited by M. Giersz and C. Pardo, pp. 69–99.

Hyslop, John

1990　*Inka Settlement Planning*. University of Texas Press, Austin.

Jennings, Justin

2006　Understanding Middle Horizon Peru: Hermeneutic Spirals, Interpretative Traditions, and Wari Administrative Centers. *Latin American Antiquity*: 265–285.

Jiménez, Milagritos

2014　*En las puertas de Pachacamac: campamentos y talleres en la Pampa Norte*. Tesis de Licenciatura, Pontificia Universidad Católica del Perú, Lima.

Jiménez Borja, Arturo

1992　Las Huacas. Pachacamac. *Revista de Investigaciones del Museo Nacional del Perú* 1: 125–131.

Kaulicke, Peter

2000　La Sombra de Pachacamac: Huari en la Costa Central. *Huari y Tiwanaku: Modelos vs. Evidencias, Primera parte*, edited by P. Kauclicke and W. Isbell, pp. 313–217. Fondo Editorial de la Pontificia Universidad Catolica del Peru, Lima.

2008　Observaciones acerca de "¿La mirada imperialista? Los alemanes y la arqueología peruana" de Stefanie Gänger. *Histórica* 32 (2): 171–181.

Kaulicke, Peter, and Tom D. Dillehay

1999　Introducción: ¿por qué estudiar el Periodo Arcaico en el Perú? *Boletín de arqueología PUCP* 3: 9–17.

Marcone, Giancarlo

2003　Los Murales del Templo Pintado o Relación entre el Santuario de Pachacamac y la Iconografía Tardía de la Costa Central Peruana. *Anales del Museo de América* 11: 57–80.

2005　La rivalidad en la prehistoria de la Costa Central Peruana, vista a través de los templos de Pachacamac. ¿Existen los horizontes pan Andinos o la tiranía de las cronologías? In *War and Conflicts in Precolumbian Mesoamerica and the Andes: Selected Proceedings of the Conference Organized by the Société des Américanistes de Belgique with the Collaboration of Wayleb (European Association of Mayanists), November 16–17, 2002*, P. Eeckhout and G. Le Fort, pp. 99–109, Brussels.

2010a　El imperio de arriba, la política de abajo. La costa central peruana y su relación con los Imperios pan-Andinos. Comparative Perspectives on the Archaeology of Coastal South America. R. Cutright, L. E. López-Hurtado and A. Martin, pp. 127–146. Pittsburgh–Lima–Quito, *University of Pittsburgh Memoirs in Latin American Archaeology*. Pontificia Universidad Católica del Perú. Ministerio de Cultura del Ecuador, Lima.

2010b What Role did Wari Play in the Lima Political Economy? The Peruvian Central Coast at the Beginning of the Middle Horizon. *Beyond Wari Walls: Regional Perspectives on Middle Horizon Peru*. J. Jennings, pp. 136–154. University of New Mexico Press, Albuquerque.

2019 The Cultural Trajectory of the Central Peruvian Coast, The Territory and Its People in the Valleys of Pre-Hispanic Lima. In *A Companion to Early Modern Lima*, pp. 25–45. Brill, Leiden/Boston.

Méndez, Cecilia

1996 Incas si, indios no: Notes on Peruvian Creole Nationalism and Its Contemporary Crisis. *Journal of Latin American Studies* 1(28): 197–225.

Menzel, Dorothy

1964 Style and Time in the Middle Horizon. *Ñawpa Pacha* 2: 1–106.

Molinié, Antoinette

2004 The Resurrection of the Inca: The Role of Indian Representations in the Invention of the Peruvian Nation. *History and Anthropology* 15(3): 233–250.

Muelle, Jorge C., and Richard Well

1939 Las Pinturas del Templo de Pachacamac. *Revista del Museo Nacional* 8: 275–282.

Nair, Stella

2003 *Of Remenbering and Forgetting: The Architecture of Chinchero, Peru from Thupa'Inka to the Spanish Occupation.* Department of Architecture, University of California, Berkeley.

Patterson, Thomas C.

1985 Pachacamac: An Andean Oracle under Inca Rule. In *Papers from the Second Annual Northeast Conference on Andean Archaeology and Ethnohistory*, edited by S. Peter Kvietok and Daniel H. Sandweiss. Cornell University Press, Ithaca.

1966 *Pattern and Process in the Early Intermediate Period Pottery of the Central Coast of Peru.* University of California Press, Berkeley.

Pozzi-Escot, Denise, Carmen Rosa Uceda, and Gianella Pacheco

2013 Pachacamac: Templo Pintado, conservación e investigación. Ministerio de Cultura, Lima.

Quilter, Jeffrey

1989 The Origins and Development of the Andean State. *American Antiquity* 54(2): 431–433.

1991 Late Preceramic Peru. *Journal of World Prehistory* 5(4): 387–438.

Ravines, Rogger

1996 *Pachacamac: Santuario Universal.* Editorial Los pinos E.I.R.L., Lima.

Rein, Bert, Andreas Lückge, and Frank Sirocko

2004 A Major Holocene ENSO Anomaly during the Medieval Period. *Geophysical Research Letters*, 31(17).

Riviale, Pascal

2000 *Los Viajeros Franceses en busca del Perú Antiguo (1821–1914).* Instituto Francés de Estudios Andinos/ Pontificia Universidad Católica del Perú, Lima.

Rostworowski, María

1972 Breve ensayo sobre el señorío de Ychma o Ychima. *Boletín del Seminario de Arqueología PUC* 13: 37–51.

1973 Urpay Huachac y el "Símbolo del Mar." *Arqueología PUCP* 14: 13–22.

1999 *El señorío de Pachacamac: el informe de Rodrigo Cantos de Andrade de 1573.* Instituto de Estudios Peruanos IEP, Lima.

2002 *Pachacamac. Obras completas II.* Instituto de Estudios Peruanos, Lima.

Rowe, Jhon. H.

1960 [1959] Tiempo, estilo y proceso cultural en la arqueología peruana, 2nd edition, 16 pp. Instituto de Estudios Andinos, Berkeley.

1998 Max Uhle y la idea del tiempo en la arqueología americana. In *Max Uhle y el Perú antiguo*, edited by P. Kaulicke, pp. 5–24. Fondo Editorial de la Pontificia Universidad Católica, Lima.

Schaedel, Richard

1993 Congruence of Horizon with Polity: Huari and the Middle Horizon. *Latin American Horizons*: 225–261.

Schaedel, Richard, and Izumi Shimada

1982 Peruvian Archaeology, 1946–80. An Analytic Overview. *World Archaeology* 13(3): 359–371.

Shady, Ruth

1982 La cultura Nievería y la interacción social en el mundo andino en la época Huari. Arqueológicas 19: 5–18.

1988 Época Huari como interacción de las sociedades regionales. *Revista andina* 6(1): 67–99.

Shimada, Izumi

1991 [1903] Pachacamac Archaeology: Retrospect and Prospect. In *Pachacamac*, edited by Max Uhle, pp. 15–66. The University Museum of Archaeology and Anthropology, University of Pennsylvania, Philadelphia.

Shimada, Izumi, Crystal Barker, Lonnie G. Thompson, and Ellen Mosley-Thompson

1991 Cultural Impacts of Severe Droughts in the Prehistoric Andes: Application of a 1500-Year Ice Core Precipitation Record. *World Archaeology* 22(3): 247–270.

Shimada, Izumi, Rafael Segura Llanos, María Rostworowski De Diez Canseco, and Hirokatsu Watanabe

2004 Una nueva evaluación de la Plaza de los Peregrinos de Pachacamac: aportes de la primera campaña 2003 del Proyecto Arqueológico Pachacamac. *Bulletin de l'Institut français d'études andines* 33(3): 507–538.

Silva, Jorge

1996 *Prehistoric Settlement Patterns in the Chillón Valley, Peru.* Ph.D. dissertation. Department of Anthropology, University of Michigan, Ann Arbor.

Soriano, Valdemar

2014 La etnia Ishma (Ychsma, Ichma, Ichmay). *Investigaciones sociales* 18(32): 117–159.

Squier, Ephraim G.

1877 *Incidents of Travel and Exploration in the Land of the Incas.* Harper & Bros, New York.

Stumer, L. M.

1954 The Chillon Valley of Peru: Excavation and Reconnaissance, 1952–1953, Part 1. *Archaeology* 7(3): 171–178.

Tello, Julio C.

2009 [1921] Introducción a la Historia Antigua del Perú, Choque de dos civilizaciones. In *The Life and Writings of Julio C. Tello, America's First Indigenous Archaeologist*, edited by R. L. Burger. University of Iowa Press, Iowa City.

Uhle, Max

1903   *Pachacamac: Report of the William Pepper, M.D., LL.D., Peruvian Expedition of 1986.* Department of Archaeology, University of Pennsylvania, Philadelphia.

Villacorta, Luis Felipe

2004   Puruchuco, medio siglo después. In *Puruchuco y la sociedad de Lima: Un homenaje a Arturo Jiménez Borja*, edited by L. F. Villacorta O., L. Vetter, and C. Ausejo, pp. 69–96. Concytec, Lima.

Weems, Jason

2012   Wings over the Andes: Aerial Photography and the Dematerialization of Archaeology circa 1931. In *Past Presented: Archaeological Illustration and the Ancient Americas*, edited by J. Pillsbury. Dumbarton Oaks Research Library and Collection, Washington, D.C.

Willey, Gordon R., and John M. Corbett

1954   Early Ancón and Early Supe Culture: Chavín Horizon Sites of the Central Peruvian Coast (Vol. 3). Columbia University Press, New York.

2

The Lurín Valley before Pachacamac

RICHARD L. BURGER AND LUCY C. SALAZAR

Since the beginning of the practice of Peruvian archaeology, the Lurín Valley has attracted a disproportionate amount of attention from investigators. This is the result of the presence of the Late Horizon oracular center of Pachacamac along the northern banks of its lower valley. Of course, the Sanctuary of Pachacamac is not the only archaeological feature in the valley that has attracted interest. There are also early discussions of the Inca road system connecting Lurín with highland centers in Jauja and beyond, but the road's route through Lurín had less to do with the valley's qualities as a natural corridor for travel than to link the Inca road system with the religious center at Pachacamac so that pilgrims from throughout the Tahuantinsuyu might journey there. Another reason for the elevated scholarly interest in Lurín has been the repeated publication of the Colonial Era manuscript *Ritos y Tradiciones de Huarochirí*, much of which is set in the Lurín drainage. Nevertheless, Pachacamac plays a central role in the Huarochirí manuscript, both as a sacred place and as mythical protagonist.

Thus, it is not an exaggeration to state that the exceptional scholarly interest in the pre-Hispanic past of the Lurín Valley, a relatively small drainage along the Central Coast, has been inextricably tied to the existence of Pachacamac. This is not true only for archaeologists and historians. In fact, there is a simmering political conflict between the contemporary districts of Pachacamac and Lurín over the control of the famous archaeological site, and this has involved a campaign to refer to the drainage as the Valle de Pachacamac rather than the Valle de Lurín. As part of this modern political feud, some archaeologists have adopted this term (for example, Bueno 1982).

The purpose of this chapter is to explore the relationship of the site of Pachacamac and the occupation of the valley prior to the establishment of the monumental center. We will consider whether there is evidence among these earlier cultures for why Pachacamac was founded in the lower Lurín Valley and whether there is cultural and sociopolitical continuity between these initial populations and those responsible for the construction and transformation of Pachacamac that is the focus of the remainder of the volume. It will be argued here that there is little evidence of continuity between Pachacamac and the older cultures of the Lurín Valley, and that Pachacamac is not the logical or inevitable outcome of the cultural formations that preceded it.

History of Research on the Early Occupation of the Lurín Valley

The site of Pachacamac was not always the center of the Lurín Valley. Like all human creations, the archaeological site has a history that is limited by time as well as space. Based on the published literature, there is no archaeological evidence that would suggest its establishment prior to the Early Intermediate Period (AD 0–600). Patterson et al. (1983: 80) calculate its founding in Epoch 6 of the Early Intermediate Period, roughly AD 350–400, and the site may have become an oracular center at a still later date. Makowski, for example, estimates the founding date of Pachacamac's Old Temple at AD 600 (Makowski 2002: Table 4.1).

So what was the human occupation of the Lurín Valley like before Pachacamac was founded? A related question, especially relevant to this volume, is what, if anything, in the early occupation of the valley prior to the Early Intermediate Period might help to explain the creation of the famous sanctuary sometime during the first millennium AD? An attempt to answer these two questions must rely on the archaeological research that has focused on the early occupations of the drainage.

Thomas C. Patterson deserves credit for producing the first comprehensive vision of the history of the valley prior to the establishment of Pachacamac. During his 1963 survey of Lurín, Patterson successfully documented over 350 archaeological sites throughout the drainage (Patterson 1966; 1971; Patterson et al. 1983). Most of the sites recorded dated to the Early Intermediate Period and later periods, but some predated the founding of Pachacamac.

During the decades since Patterson's efforts, the Lurín Valley has been repeatedly resurveyed for archaeological sites, first by the archaeologist Luis

Watanabe and the architect Santiago Agurto in 1973 (Agurto and Watanabe 1974), and then by archaeologist Alberto Bueno Mendoza in the late 1970s, during the time he represented the National Institute of Culture in the valley (Bueno 1982). In 1978, Jane Feltham of the University of London also carried out a survey and small-scale excavations, although her work focused exclusively on the middle valley; the findings of this research served as the basis for her doctoral thesis (Feltham 1983, 2011). The architect Carlos Williams and archaeologist Francisco Merino carried out still another survey of sites in the valley, relying heavily on the aerial photographs provided by the Servicio Aerea Nacional (SAN) (Williams 1971). More recently, additional surface reconnaissance was conducted by the Pontificia Universidad Católica, Perú (PUCP) led by Krzysztof Makowski and by the Universidad Nacional Mayor de San Marcos (UNMSM), supervised by Jorge Silva Sifuentes.

Despite the proximity of the Lurín Valley to the urban core of Lima and the availability of survey data mentioned above, there have been few studies of sites dating before the establishment of Pachacamac. An early exception was Frederic Engel's pioneering excavation at the shoreline village of Curayacu in 1955 (Engel 1956). Edward Lanning participated in this and described the results in his unpublished doctoral dissertation (1960). The Initial Period/Early Horizon fishing village of Curayacu was later used as a field school in the 1970s for students from UNMSM, but these findings remain unpublished (Fung 1976).

Another landmark contribution to the early prehistory of Lurín prior to Pachacamac was made by members of the Universidad Católica (PUCP) at the vast cemetery covering at the sandy plateau known as Tablada de Lurín. Begun in 1958 under the direction of Josefina Ramos de Cox (1960), this work continued after Ramos de Cox's death under the supervision of Mercedes Cardénas (1999) and Krzysztof Makowski (2002). The cumulative scale of this research is unparalleled, and the number of intact graves recorded exceeds 1,500, many of which date to the end of the Early Horizon prior to the establishment of Pachacamac (Makowski 2002: 92).

As the modern urban population of Lima grew due to the migration of highland peoples following the Agrarian Reform, squatter settlements were established along the southern edge of the capital, and these gradually extended into the Lurín Valley drainage. Villa El Salvador, one of the largest of these settlements (*pueblos jovenes*), was established on top of a pre-Hispanic village site dating to end of the Early Horizon. Salvage archaeology by

Karen Stothert and Rogger Ravines produced valuable information, as did later work 5 km away on the roughly coeval remains of Lomo de Corvina by Mercedes Delgado and others (Paredes 1986; Jiménez 2009; Stothert 1980; Stothert and Ravines 1977).

In response to increasing urbanization of the valley, the Universidad Católica (PUCP) program has broadened its research interest in Lurín, and the excavations of Makowski and Jalh Dulanto at the Early Horizon site of Pampa Chica produced exciting contributions to our knowledge of the early occupation of the valley (Dulanto 2002, 2009).

Ducio Bonavia's pioneering research at Mina Perdida and five other lower valley sites for his 1965 bachelor's thesis at UNMSM should also be mentioned, although this study did not involve excavations.

In 1969, Harry Scheele mapped and test-pitted many of the early ceramic sites identified by Patterson's team in the 1963 valley survey. Scheele's doctoral thesis, *The Chavin Occupation of the Central Coast*, was presented to Harvard's Department of Anthropology in 1970, but the results were never published.

Sixteen years went by before the authors of this chapter, Richard Burger and Lucy Salazar, initiated research on the Initial Period centers of Lurín's lower valley. This research has involved multiple field seasons at the Initial Period sites of Cardal, Mina Perdida, and Manchay Bajo (Burger 1987; Burger and Makowski 2009; Burger and Salazar 1991, 1998, 2008, 2009, 2012, 2014, 2019; Salazar 2009). Christopher Milan's doctoral research focused on the middle valley section of the drainage (*chaupiyunga*); it involved excavations at the U-shaped center, Malpaso, and test-pitting and mapping at nearby Initial Period/Early Horizon hamlets (Milan 2014, 2019).

The Lurín Valley during the Preceramic

Given the history of research in the Lurín Valley, it might be assumed that a clear vision of the valley's history prior to Pachacamac would have been achieved by now. Unfortunately, this is far from true. In fact, the evidence for the early occupation of the valley is very limited. No published, well-documented sites are known for the Paleo-Indian Period, the Early Preceramic, the Middle Preceramic, or even the Late Preceramic (or Archaic). Patterson (1966) mentions lithic scatters near the *lomas* in the lower valley at Cerro Tortugas, Cerro Achona, and Cerro Conchitas, and assigns ages to these materials based on his work at Cerro Chivateros in the Chillón Valley. However, given the chronological problems with the latter research, it is difficult to feel confident about the dating or interpretation of the early Lurín materials mentioned by Patterson. Feltham (2009) suggests that the earliest remains referred to by Patterson may reflect seasonal movements of hunters and gatherers from the highlands into the coastal lomas during the winter months.

Patterson also refers briefly in passing to Middle Preceramic sites dating to the Gaviota Phase in the middle Lurín Valley, but these have never been dated, described or investigated. The absence of well-documented sites in Lurín from the Middle Preceramic is in sharp contrast with early village sites such as Paloma and Chilca 1 discovered by Federic Engel in the Chilca Valley (Donnan 1964; Engel 1980; Quilter 1989).

Even more astounding, considering the multiple valley-wide surveys, is the failure by archaeologists to discover sites dating to the Late Preceramic. During this time, numerous public centers with monumental architecture were constructed along the coast from as far north as Lambayeque to as far south as Chillón. In the north-central coast in valleys such as Supe and Pativilca, investigators have encountered multiple Late Preceramic sites, often featuring large-scale masonry platforms and sunken circular plazas (Haas and Creamer 2012; Shady and Leyva 2003). On the Central Coast, near Lurín in the nearby Chillón Valley, archaeologists have documented two major Late Preceramic centers, one in the lower valley and the other in the middle valley. The former is the famous site of El Paraiso, with its impressive terraced masonry constructions (Engel 1967; Quilter 1985). The latter, the site of Buena Vista, is known for its public buildings with freestanding clay sculpture and astronomical orientation (Benfer 2012).

Of course, we should not rule out the possibility that there was some occupation in the Lurín Valley during the Early, Middle, and Late Preceramic. It is possible that the evidence of these early populations is hidden beneath meters of alluvium along the valley bottom or buried under deposits of boulders and other rocky debris in the lateral ravines (*quebradas*) adjacent to the valley floor. Some Preceramic occupations could be buried beneath later sites such as Pachacamac. This scenario is illustrated by excavations by the PUCP in Tablada de Lurín that encountered traces of lomas camps dating to the Middle Preceramic below a Late Early Horizon cemetery (Makowski 2002: 96). On the other hand, Engel's assumption that the original occupation of some of the U-shaped centers such as Cardal dated to the Preceramic (Bernadino Ojeda, personal communication 2013) has not been confirmed by excavations at either these sites or at the site of Pachacamac.

In summary, given the extent of archaeological research in Lurín over the last five decades, it is difficult to demonstrate a significant occupation of the valley before the introduction of ceramics at the beginning of the second millennium BCE.

The "Formative" Occupation of the Lurín Valley

The first compelling evidence for the intensive exploitation of the Lurín Valley before Pachacamac was occupied occurs during the Initial Period (1800–800 BCE). Beginning with the introduction of pottery at the beginning of the second millennium BCE, populations began to settle along the shoreline and the lower and middle valley. Over the following centuries, the inland populations expanded in size until their settlements occupied most of the lower and middle portions of the drainage (Burger and Salazar 2012, 2014).

The basis of this demographic expansion was a subsistence system based on irrigation agriculture that produced reliable crops rich in calories such as manioc, sweet potato, achira, and potatoes, as well as a host of other domesticates including squash, beans, peanuts, and avocados (Tycott et al. 2006). There were also semi-domesticated fruits such as pacay, guava, and lucuma. Spice was provided in the diet by chili peppers and culinary variety was ensured by the collection of cactus fruit and other wild foods from the nearby lomas and valley edges (Burger 1987; Chevalier 2002; Umlauf 2009). While some hunting of birds and mammals occurred, most protein came from marine foods brought from fishing villages along the nearby Pacific shoreline (Meadors and Benfer 2009; Gorriti 2009). This mixed diet must have been reliable, since the valley seems to have experienced continuous demographic growth for at least 800 years.

At the beginning of the Initial Period, around 1700 cal BCE, Mina Perdida appears to have functioned alone in the lower valley, but by the end of the Initial Period around 850 cal BCE, there were some six other civic-ceremonial centers functioning in the lower valley: Parka, Huaca Candela, Manzano, Cardal, Manchay Bajo, and Pampa Cabrera. In the middle valley a large public center was established at Malpaso shortly after the founding of Mina Perdida (Milan 2014), and it remained in use into the Early Horizon. Each of these civic-ceremonial centers featured terraced platforms arrayed around three sides of an open central plaza area in a so-called U-shaped layout. Five of these eight U-shaped centers have been sampled by archaeologists, and while it is possible that one or two of the remaining complexes may prove to be dated incorrectly (Milan 2019), the pattern of growth in the number of major valley settlements is clear and the implication of corresponding population growth and intensive settlement in the valley during the Initial Period is difficult to avoid.

All of the Initial Period centers in Lurín that archaeologists have investigated in depth have shown some evidence of residential occupation behind or adjacent to the public architecture. At Mina Perdida, the oldest of the centers, there are no traces of such residential occupation during the first centuries of the center's use (1700–1200 BCE). During the following centuries, occupation seems seasonal rather than permanent, judging from the shallow refuse deposits and impermanent structures supported by wood poles (1300–1100 BCE). Only during the final two centuries of the Initial Period at Mina Perdida do we find more substantial residential structures with stone footings and subfloor burials that are suggestive at the sites of a permanent occupation by families (Burger 2009).

Traces of a similar pattern were encountered at Manchay Bajo (Burger 2003). Judging from the investigations at Cardal, where the residential remains are best preserved, the size of the resident population even during its apogee in the late Initial Period would seem to be only a fraction of the total population (Burger and Salazar 2012). But where did these other farmers live?

In the lower valley, the majority of this agricultural society probably lived in sites undetected thus far by archaeologists. It is likely that many of these were small hamlets distributed among the irrigated fields of the valley floor. In these areas, the Initial Period living surfaces are probably buried by meters of alluvium and are thus resistant to traditional archaeological survey methods emphasizing surface reconnaissance.

The problem can be illustrated by our work at Manchay Bajo where the surface of the central plaza was identified beneath more than 2 m of riverine deposits. The situation is different in Lurín's middle valley, where in addition to the U-shaped public center of Malpaso (also known as Piedra Liza), Patterson and others encountered a series of small villages such as Chillaco and Palma. These are located on the margins of rocky ravines that are partially protected from the alluvial deposits, but still vulnerable to landslides produced by earthquakes and El Niño (Milan 2019). The middle valley of Lurín is extremely narrow, less than 1 km across in most places.

Given the limited amount of bottomland suitable for farming, it is possible that some farmers chose to reside in the nearby rocky ravines rather than among the agricultural fields. Chris Milan has studied several of these middle valley sites and has confirmed the presence of small villages at Palma, Chillaco, Sisicaya, and Anchucaya in the lateral ravines during the Initial Period and the beginning Early Horizon (Milan 2014, 2019). At Milagrito, Jiménez likewise encountered "various domestic contexts from the Initial Period and Early Horizon covered by the Tablada de Lurín cemetery in the lomas zone" (Makowski 2002: 96).

As already noted, we have carried out multiple field seasons at three of Lurín's Initial Period centers and the investigations revealed that a principal purpose of the monumental architecture was to provide public and restricted environments for the religious rituals carried out on the summit of the terraced platforms that dominate the sites. A second goal of the public constructions was to produce formally defined open spaces or plazas where large groups of people could congregate for activities that transcended the scale of nuclear or extended households. Some of the central plazas cover 4 ha; this is 10 times the size of an American football field. These central plazas could have comfortably accommodated over a thousand people, including many of the members of the community and their visitors.

We have suggested that each civic-ceremonial center was associated with its own canal system and that the rituals held at the centers were designed to ensure the prosperity of the lands and the health of the community that farmed them (Burger 2009; Burger and Salazar 2012). It is also reasonable to speculate that matters related to management and coordination of the canal systems would have been resolved when the dispersed populations came together at the centers for their public gatherings. Thus, in our opinion, each public center served as a local axis of civic and ceremonial life, and the activities at these centers were crucial to the continuing success of the multiple small-scale social and economic systems in Lurín.

Each of the U-shaped centers studied in detail has a unique constellation of elements of architectural design, building techniques, and ceramic style. This diversity suggests that each center was autonomous, and that no single center was dominant, either politically or economically. As a result, no single cultural pattern was emulated or imposed by coercion. At the same time, the similarities between the layouts and religious iconography suggest that the different valley centers were linked together by a shared culture and religious ideology.

While the creation of new centers in the Lurín Valley during the Initial Period was probably the result of the fissioning or budding off of groups due to internal community disputes and population growth, they still shared a common history. Sourcing studies of the ceramics found at the centers of Cardal and Mina Perdida by Trisha Thorme (1999) and Christopher Milan (2014) confirm that there was contact between the different centers, and that it was reflected in a localized pattern of exchange of goods such as pottery and perhaps the exchange of spouses between these small-scale groups.

The creation of the large Initial Period civic-ceremonial centers in Lurín required considerable mobilization of labor. The monumental complexes served the public good by acquiring the cooperation of the gods by gifting them favored food and drink, or by singing their praises in poetry and song. Yet labor mobilization was likewise required for the creation and maintenance of the gravity canals without which these groups could not have survived. It seems reasonable therefore that the social mechanisms used to ensure reliable manpower for the upkeep of the irrigation system were also used to produce the work parties responsible for the maintenance and renovation of the U-shaped architecture.

One of the most interesting observations stemming from our excavations at the three centers in Lurín was that these seemingly colossal pyramid complexes were nothing more than the aggregation of an almost infinite number of small segmented building episodes, each of which would have required only a small group of men and women, and little specialized construction knowledge (Burger and Salazar 2014). The mobilization of community labor was not limited to gravity canals and public architecture; at Manchay Bajo public labor was also used to build and then renovate a massive wall or dike to protect the public center against the threat of floods and landslides produced by major El Niño events (Burger 2003).

The planning of these projects, nonetheless, would have required coordination and it is likely that particular families or lineages may have held special responsibility for organizing these annual building projects. Our excavations have produced anthropomorphic images that we interpret as ancestral leaders. These depictions of ancestral leaders in fired clay and carved bone appear to have been created to legitimize the authority of living leaders. The topknot hair styles of these figures presage the distinctive priestly hairstyles at later sites, such as Chavín de Huántar, while the depiction of their ribs suggests, as in the case of Pucara sculpture from the Altiplano, that the individuals shown are no longer among the living.

An elevated social status for those living at the centers is consistent with the presence of a relatively small residential population that represents only a fraction of the entire community. It is also consistent with the burial of one such group of leading families on Cardal's summit (Burger and Salazar 1991). Nonetheless, the artifacts and ecofacts associated with the residences and burials all suggest that, while this favored group may have enjoyed higher social status than other community members, their economic status remained unexceptional. The inability or lack of interest of this select group to amass wealth of any kind suggests the existence of powerful norms favoring community goals over individual interests. The failure to accumulate wealth also suggests a communal ideology that set limits on the development of inequality and coercive power.

In summary, the Initial Period in the Lurín Valley seems to be a time of rapid population growth and relative prosperity, with most interactions focused on nearby communities in the same valley but with religious and cultural values shared with neighboring valleys of the Central Coast.

The beach villages such as Curayacu and Chira-Villa and the hamlets in the middle valley such as Chillaco were integrated into this social, economic, and religious system. This is evident both in the products consumed at the shoreline and inland sites and in the presence of non-local pottery from the shoreline communities in the pottery assemblages recovered from the various U-shaped centers. There is also some evidence of contact with the upper valley, as reflected in the possible presence of starch grains of *chuño* in some of the cooking pots (Vasquez and Rosales Tham 2007). Finally, there are rare traces of contacts beyond the limits of the Lurín Valley, in the form of obsidian flakes or the occasional greenstone or spondylus bead.

Probably more significant are the strong architectural similarities that exist between the Initial Period centers of Lurín and coeval centers in the Rímac, Chillón, and Chancay valleys. This pattern, first identified by Carlos Williams (1980, 1985), has led us to suggest that the groups in the lower and midsections of these four valleys shared a common culture, which we have referred to as the Manchay culture (Burger and Salazar 2008: 86–92). How this cultural identity expressed itself in concrete activities is not completely understood. There must have been some patterned contact between the members of these valleys to have produced the observed similarities in architecture and iconography and for these to have been maintained for so many centuries.

Within the regional context of the Manchay culture, the Lurín Valley was not exceptional in either the number or size of its centers. On the contrary, valleys possessing more farmland than Lurín, most notably Rímac and Chancay, have both a larger number of centers and public architecture that includes terraced platforms and open plazas that are even grander in scale than those in Lurín (Patterson 1983, 1985). Perhaps the most distinctive feature of Initial Period occupation of Lurín is that it constitutes the southernmost expression of the Manchay culture. Contrary to Williams' assertations, no confirmed examples of U-shaped centers have been encountered in the Mala Valley (Williams 1980, 1985). The other valleys further to the south likewise lack monumental architecture of any kind dating to the Initial Period.

Collapse and Reorganization in Lurín during the Early Horizon

Beginning around 900 cal BCE, the U-shaped centers in the lower Lurín Valley began to be abandoned. From our excavations, this does not appear to have been a sudden response to a disaster or as a result of destruction by conquering forces. On the contrary, it seems to be the result of internal forces that undermined support for the centers. This stress was already evident before that at some centers where the final construction episodes are of lesser quality than the preceding ones and would have required less labor investment. Moreover, in the case of Cardal, there is a set of matching rectangular plazas that were initiated but never completed (Burger and Salazar 1992). This suggests that the leaders of the public centers were experiencing difficulty in mobilizing workers in support of their periodic renovation. This in turn suggests a crisis of legitimacy for the leadership and the religious ideology they represented.

Judging from the available evidence, Mina Perdida may have been the first center that ceased to function; its abandonment was followed by Cardal, probably less than a century later. Manchay Bajo, which is located directly across from Cardal, seems to have survived for another century or more before succumbing to the changing sociocultural environment. In the mid-valley, the U-shaped center of Malpaso likewise seems to have continued to function into the mid-Early Horizon (Milan 2014), even after most of the lower valley centers no longer functioned.

Burger (1981) observed that the decline of long-standing public centers occurred throughout the central and north coast at the end of the Initial Period, and that this trend transcended cultural and regional boundaries. This multivalley pattern suggests that there may have been some general environmental phenomenon that was causing the difficulties that these formerly stable coastal societies were experiencing. An apparent increase in the frequency and severity of El Niño events, for example, may have been one of the environmental factors that played a role in this destabilizing process (Sandweiss et al. 2001).

By 700 cal BCE, no large public centers were functioning in the lower Lurín drainage. The U-shaped centers were no longer renovated and they began to fall apart. It is difficult to imagine that the dispersed rural population that had supported these centers simply moved elsewhere, yet we cannot demonstrate their continued presence archaeologically. While a complete demographic collapse may not have occurred, there can be little doubt that the sociopolitical framework that had shaped daily life in the valley for a thousand years no longer existed.

It is within the context of sociopolitical collapse that a new type of public center emerges. Contrary to expectations, the new pattern does not appear to have been inspired by the pilgrimage center of Chavín de Huántar and the other centers in its sphere of interaction (Burger 1992). On the contrary, the pattern documented in Lurín shares some elements with societies in the lower valleys of Casma and the Norte Chico, where sites featuring multiple low platforms and courtyards were built for ancestor worship and feasting (Chicoine 2006; Chicoine and Ikehara 2010). On the north-central coast, these sites replace the pattern of massive terraced pyramids and large central plazas.

In Lurín, this pattern was first recognized at Pampa Chica, a small site in a dry *quebrada* just a few hundred meters to the north of Manchay Bajo. Featuring negative painted pottery, the Pampa Chica site appears to have functioned for only a few centuries, perhaps from 700 cal BCE to 400 cal BCE, and there is little evidence of a residential population associated with its modest ceremonial structures. Presumably the supporting population lived near their fields on the valley floor. There is ample evidence for feasting and the manipulation of the bodies of their ancestors (Dulanto 2002, 2009) and

Richard L. Burger and Lucy C. Salazar

these activities may have provided a sense of identity and social unity. Judging from its scale, it was no longer necessary to devote substantial amounts of communal labor toward this end. Whether or not it would have been possible to mobilize large amounts of the public under the changed circumstances remains unknown.

At Pampa Chica, a decision was made to consume ceramics that emulated the negative wares of the south coast, such as those of Cerrillos in Ica. This suggests that the farmers remaining in lower Lurín Valley had decided to opt out of the Chavín sphere of interaction, and in this respect, they were at odds with some nearby populations, such as the shoreline residents of Ancon near the mouth of the Chillón, or those at Karwa on the shoreline south of the Paracas peninsula (Burger 1992).

The diminished capacity to mobilize labor, and the apparent decline in demographic levels following the collapse of the long-standing Manchay culture occupation of the valley, provides the backdrop for the earliest occupation at Pachacamac. As K. Makowski (2002: 89) has written, "The collapse of the IP-EH traditions of ceremonial architecture and of complex religious iconography suggests a complete restructuring of the political order."

The latter process is not well documented. We remain uncertain of whether the first evidence of public activity at Pachacamac was coeval with the burials at Tablada de Lurín and the occupation of Villa El Salvador, or whether it followed on the heels of these developments and, as Patterson believed, dated to the Early Intermediate Period.

The transitional period at the end of the Early Horizon following the abandonment of Pampa Chica does seem to be a time of disruption and perhaps disorganization that lasted for several centuries. It provided a climate in which some important economic shifts occurred, and these changes had a lasting impact on daily life in the Lurín Valley in later times. Perhaps most notable among these was the emergence of maize as an important staple crop displacing the varied mixed diet that had characterized the U-shaped centers of Lurín during the Initial Period (Tykott et al. 2006). A second change relates to an increase in the consumption of domesticated camelid meat, complementing and, to some degree, displacing the traditional dependence on the ocean for protein. Both of these newly popular subsistence patterns may have their origin in the highlands and could have been promulgated by the presence or influence of highland groups in the valley. Makowski has noted the presence of highlanders in the Tablada de Lurín cemetery and argues that the ceramic style most similar to the Tablada de Lurín pottery style is the Higueras style from highland Huanuco. He also argues that there is a strong Recuay stylistic influence on the Tablada pottery, presumably coming from highland Ancash or the adjacent western slopes (Makowski 2002: 99–100). Still a third new component apparent at the Tablada de Lurín cemetery are elements, some of which are made of metal, that are linked with military activities and identity. The emergence of militarization as a central theme in late Early Horizon society appears to be present in the village site of Villa Salvador, where Stothert (1980) reports the recovery of mace heads and headless bodies. It is out of this time of trouble and reorganization that Pachacamac appears.

Conclusions

Has this brief overview of the Lurín Valley shed light on the emergence of Pachacamac? Perhaps it does not, but it does make clear that the creation of Pachacamac was not the result of a unilinear march toward sociopolitical complexity within the valley. Nor was Pachacamac's founding the product of an inexorable rise in population levels and agricultural intensification. The development of complex society in the Lurín Valley seems to have occurred later than in many of the valleys to the north. Even during the period of agricultural intensification and monument building during the Initial Period, the Lurín Valley does not display exceptionally large or complex centers when compared to the situation in Rímac or Chancay. One looks in vain for unique resources or geographical factors in the Lurín Valley that might explain why such an important center emerged within a valley so limited in land, water, and natural resources. And the pattern of having a monumental site that dominates part or all of the valley is likewise alien to the Lurín Valley prior to the emergence of Pachacamac. Even when there were large civic-ceremonial centers during the Initial Period in Lurín, these were arrayed throughout the valley as foci for small-scale independent societies.

In considering the varied and nonlinear history of Lurín, one may hypothesize Pachacamac's establishment as a response to the needs of a rural population that had been struggling for centuries to reorganize since the decline of the U-shape centers at the end of the Initial Period. Yet why did the pilgrimage center of Pachacamac appear in Lurín rather than in one of the larger and more prosperous valleys found to the north? Does its explanation lie in sacred geography and religious revelation rather than the sociopolitical processes and economic developments of the preceding millennia?

References Cited

Agurto, Santiago, and Luis Watanabe
1974 *Inventario, catastro y deliminitación del patrimonio arqueológico del Valle Bajo del Río Lurín.* Manuscript in the archives of the Center of Investigation and Restoration, Ministry of Culture, Lima.

Benfer Jr., Robert A.
2012 Monumental Architecture Arising from an Early Astronomical-Religious Complex in Peru, 2200–1750 BC. In *Early New World Monumentality,* edited by Richard L. Burger and Robert Rosenswig, pp. 313–363. University Press of Florida, Gainesville.

Bonavia, Duccio
1965 *Arqueología de Lurín (Seis sitios de ocupación en la parte inferior del valle).* La Universidad Nacional Mayor de San Marcos (UNMSM), Lima.

Bueno, Alberto
1982 El antiguo valle de Pachacamac. Espacio, tiempo y cultura. *Boletín de Lima* 4(24).

Burger, Richard L.
1981 The radiocarbon evidence for the temporal priority of Chavin de Huantar. *American Antiquity* 46(3): 592–602.
1987 The U-shaped Pyramid Complex, Cardal, Perú. *National Geographic Research* 3(3): 363–375.
1992 *Chavín and Origins of Andean Civilization.* Thames y Hudson, London.
1998 *Excavaciones en Chavín de Huantar.* Fondo Editorial Pontificia Universidad Católica del Perú, Lima.
2003 El Niño, Early Peruvian Civilization, and Human Agency: Some Thoughts from the Lurin Valley. In *El Niño in Peru: Biology and Culture over 10,000 Years* (Fieldana Botany New Series, No. 43), edited by Jonathan Haas and Michael O. Dillion, pp. 90–107. The Field Museum, Chicago.
2009 Los fundamentos sociales de la arquitectura monumental del Periodo Inicial en el valle de Lurín, Perú. In *Arqueología del Periodo Formativo en la cuenca baja de Lurín,* edited by R. Burger and K. Makowski, pp. 17–36. Fondo Editorial Pontificia Universidad Católica del Perú, Lima.

Burger, Richard L., and Krzysztof Makowski
2009 *Arqueología del Periodo Formativo en la Cuenca Baja de Lurín.* Fondo Editorial Pontificia Universidad Católica del Perú, Lima.

Burger, Richard L., and Lucy C. Salazar
1991 The Second Season of Investigations at the Initial Period Center of Cardal, Peru. *Journal of Field Archaeology* 18(3): 275–296.
1994 La organización dual en el ceremonial andino temprano: Un repaso comparativo. In *El mundo ceremonial andino,* edited by Luis Millones and Yoshio Onuki, pp. 97–116. Editorial Horizonte, Lima.
1998 A Sacred Effigy from Mina Perdida and the Unseen Ceremonies of the Peruvian Formative. *RES: Anthropology and Aesthetics* 33: 28–53.

2008   The Manchay Culture and the Coastal Inspiration for Highland Chavín Civilization. In *Chavín: Art, Architecture and Culture*, edited by W. Conklin and J. Quilter, pp. 85–105. Cotsen Institute, UCLA, Los Angeles.

2009   Investigaciones arqueológicas en Mina Perdida, valle de Lurín. In *Arqueología del Periodo Formativo en la cuenca baja de Lurín*, edited by Richard Burger and K. Makowski, pp. 37–58. Fondo Editorial Pontificia Universidad Católica del Perú, Lima.

2012   Monumental Public Complexes and Agricultural Expansion on Peru's Central Coast during the 2nd Millennium BC. In *Early New World Monumentality*, edited by Richard Burger and Robert Rosenswig, pp. 399–430. University Press of Florida, Gainesville.

2014   Centro de Que? Los sitios con arquitectura pública de la cultura Manchay en la costa central del Peru. In *El Centro Ceremonial Andino: Nuevas Perspectivas para los Períodos Arcaico y Formativo*, edited by Yuji Seki, pp. 291–313. Senri Ethnological Studies 89, National Museum of Ethnography, Osaka.

2019   New Insights into the Architecture and Organization of Cardal. In *Perspectives on Early Andean Civilization in Peru. Interaction, Authority, and Socioeconomic Organization during the First and Second Millennia BC*, edited by Richard Burger, Lucy C. Salazar, and Yui Seki, pp. 49–65. Yale University Publicatons in Anthropology Number 94, Yale University Press, New Haven, Conn.

Cárdenas, Mercedes

1999   *Tablada de Lurín: excavaciones 1958–1989, Patrones funerarios*, Vol I. Instituto Riva-Agüero, PUCP, Lima.

Chevalier, Alexandre

2002   L'exploitation des plantes sur la cote peruvienne en contexte formatif. Doctoral thesis, University of Geneva, Switzerland.

Chicoine, David

2006   Early Horizon Architecture at Huambacho, Nepeña Valley, Peru. *Journal of Field Archaeology* 31(1): 1–22.

Chicoine, David, and Hugo Ikehara

2010   Nuevas evidencias sobre el Periodo Formativo. Resultados preliminares de la primera temporada de investigaciones en Caylán. *Boletín de Arqueología PUCP* 12: 349–369.

Donnan, Christopher

1964   An Early House from Chilca, Peru. *American Antiquity* 30(2): 137–144.

Dulanto, Jalh

2002   The Archaeological Study of Ancestor Cult Practices: The Case of Pampa Chica: A Late Initial Period and Early Horizon Site in the Central Coast of Peru. In *The Space and Place of Death*, edited by Helaine Silverman and David Small, pp. 97–117. Archaeological Papers of the American Anthropological Association, Vol. 11. American Anthropological Association, Arlington, Virginia.

2009   Que sucedió en la costa central después del abandono de los templos en U? In *Arqueología del Periodo Formativo en la cuenca baja de Lurín*, edited by R. L. Burger and K. Makowski. pp. 377–399. Fondo Editorial Pontificia Universidad Católica del Perú, Lima.

Engel, Frederic

1956   Curayacu: A Chavinoid Site. *Archaeology* 9(2): 98–105.

1967   El Complejo El Paraiso en el Valle de Chillón Habitado Hace 3,500 Años; Nuevos aspectos de la Civilización de los Agricultores de Pallar. *Anales Científicas de la Universidad Agraria* 5: 241–280. Lima.

1980   Paloma Village 613. In *Prehistoric Andean Ecology*, edited by Frederic Engel, pp. 103–135. Humanities Press, New York.

Feltham, Jane

1983   The Lurin Valley: AD 1000–1532. Doctoral thesis, Institute of London, University of London.

2009   La arqueología de Sisicaya. In *La Revisita de Sisiscaya, 1588: Huarochirí vente años antes de Dioses y Hombres*, edited by Frank Salomon, Jane Feltham, and Sue Grosboll, pp. 57–101. Fondo Editorial de la Pontificia Universidad Católica del Perú, Lima.

Fung, Rosa

1976   Curayacu: un retorno arqueológico y la formación de una metodología. *Revista San Marcos* 17: 3–21.

Gorriti, Manuel

2009   Una primera aproximación al consume de moluscos en el sitio formativo de Mina Perdida. In *Arqueología del Periodo Formativo en la cuenca baja de Lurín*, edited by R. L. Burger and K. Makowski, Vol. I, pp. 111–118. Fondo Editorial de la Pontificia Universidad Católica del Perú, Lima.

Haas, Jonathan, and Winifred Creamer

2012   Why Do People Build Monuments? Late Archaic Platform Mounds in Norte Chico. In *Early New World Monumentality*, edited by Richard L. Burger and Robert Rosenswig, pp. 289–312. University Press of Florida, Gainesville.

Jiménez, Milagritos

2009   Ocupaciones tempranas de lomas en el valle de Lurín. In *Arqueología del Periodo Formativo en la cuenca baja de Lurín*, edited by R. L. Burger and K. Makowski, Vol. I, pp. 283–318. Fondo Editorial de la Pontificia Universidad Católica del Perú, Lima.

Lanning, Edward

1960   Chronological and Cultural Relationships of Early Pottery Styles in Ancient Peru. Ph.D. dissertation, Department of Anthropology, University of California, Berkeley.

Makowski, Krzysztof

2002   Power and Social Ranking at the end of the Formative Period: The Lower Lurin Valley Cemeteries. *Andean Archaeology I: Variations in Sociopolitical Organization*, edited by William H. Isbell and Helaine Silverman, pp. 89–120. Kluwer Academic/Plenum Publishers, New York.

2009   Tablada de Lurín: aspectos cronológicos de la ocpación de lomas costeros de Atacongo. In *Arqueología del Periodo Formativo en la cuenca baja de Lurín*, edited by R. L. Burger and K. Makowski, Vol. I, pp. 237–281. Fondo Editorial de la Pontificia Universidad Católica del Perú, Lima.

Meadors, Sara, and Robert Benfer

2009   Adaptaciones de la Dieta Humana a Nuevos Problemas y Oportunidades en la Costa Central del Perú (1800–800 aC). *Arqueología del periodo Formativo en la cuenca baja de Lurín*, 119–159.

Milan, Christopher

2014   The Initial Period (1800–800 BC) Occupation of the Middle Lurin Valley: A Discussion on the Interactions between Early Civic-Ceremonial Centers on the Central Coast of Peru and Nearby Hamlets. Ph.D. dissertation, Department of Anthropology, Yale University, New Haven, Conn.

2019   The Problem with Anchucaya: Site Formation Processes at Initial Period and Early Horizon Sites in the Central Andes. In *Perspectives on Early Andean Civilization in Peru*.

Interaction, Authority, and Socioeconomic Organization during the First and Second Millennia BC, edited by Richard Burger, Lucy C. Salazar, and Yui Seki, pp. 67–81. Yale University Publications in Anthropology Number 94, Yale University Press, New Haven.

Paredes, Ponciano

1986   El Panel-Pachacamac. Nuevo patron de enterramiento den la Tablada de Lurín. *Boletín de Lima* 44: 7–20.

Patterson, Thomas C.

1966   Early cultural remains on the central coast of Peru. *Ñawpa Pacha* 6: 115–134.

1971   Chavin: An Interpretation of its Spread and Influence. In *Dumbarton Oaks Conference on Chavin*, edited by Elizabeth Benson, pp. 29–48. Dumbarton Oaks Research Library and Collection, Washington, D.C.

1983   The Historical Development of a Coastal Andean Social Formation in Central Peru, 6000 to 500 B.C. In *Understanding the Andean Pas Papers from the First Annual Northeast Conference on Andean Archaeology and Ethnohistory*, edited by Daniel Sandweiss, pp. 21–38. Latin American Studies Program, Cornell University, Ithaca, New York.

1985   The Huaca La Florida, Rímac Valley, Peru. In *Early Ceremonial Architecture in the Andes*, edited by Christopher Donnan, pp. 59–70. Dumbarton Oaks, Washington, D.C.

Patterson, Thomas, J. P. McCarthy, and R. A. Dunn

1983   Polities in the Lurin Valley, Peru, during the Early Intermediate Period. *Ñawpa Pacha* 20: 61–82.

Quilter, Jeffrey

1985   Architecture and Chronology at El Paraiso, Peru. *Journal of Field Archaeology* 12(3): 279–297.

1989   *Life and Death: Society and Mortuary Practices at a Preceramic Peruvian Village*. University of Iowa, Iowa City.

Ramos de Cox, Josefina

1960   Necropolis de la Tablada de Lurín. In *Antiguo Peru: Espacio y Tiempo. Actas y Trabajos del II Congreso Nacional de Historia del Perú*. Época Prehispánica. Lima.

Ravines, Rogger, and William Isbell

1975   Garagay: sitio ceremonial temprano en el valle de Lima. *Revista del Museo Nacional* 41: 253–275.

Salazar, Lucy C.

2009   Escaleras al cielo: altares, rituales y ancestros en el sitio arqueológico de Cardal. In *Arqueología del Periodo Formativo en la cuenca baja de Lurín*, edited by R. L. Burger and K. Makowski, pp. 83–94. Fondo Editorial Pontificia Universidad Católica del Perú, Lima.

Sandweiss, Daniel H., Richard L. Burger, Kirk A. Maasch, James B. Richardson III, and Harold B. Rollins

2001   Variation in Holocene El Niño Frequencies: Climate Records and Cultural Consequences in Ancient Peru. *Geology* 29(7): 603–606.

Scheele, Harry

1970   The Chavin Occupation of the Central Coast of Peru. Ph.D. thesis, Department of Anthropology, Harvard University, Cambridge.

Shady, Ruth, and Carlos Leyva

2003   *La Ciudad Sagrada de Caral-Supe. Los origins de la civilización andina y la formación del primer estado pristine en el antiguo Perú*. Instituto Nacional de Cultura, Lima.

Silva, Jorge Elias

1998   Una aproximación al Periódo Formativo en el Valle del Chillón. *Boletín de Arqueología PUCP* 2: 251–268.

Stothert, Karen

1980   The Villa Salvador Site in the Beginning of the Early Intermediate Period in the Lurin Valley, Peru. *Journal of Field Archaeology* 7: 279–285.

Stothert, Karen, and Rogger Ravines

1977   Investigaciones arqueológicas en Villa El Salvador. *Revista del Museo Nacional* 43: 157–226.

Thorme, Trisha

1999   Trade Networks in the Lurin Valley Initial Period. Paper presented at the 64th Annual Meeting of the Society for American Archaeology, Chicago.

Tykott, Robert H., Richard L. Burger, and Nikolaas J. Van der Merwe

2006   The Importance of Maize in Initial Period and Early Horizon Peru. In *Histories of Maize: Multidisciplinary Approaches to the Prehistory, Linguistics, Biogeography, Domestication and Evolution of Maize*, edited by John Staller, Robert Tykot, and Bruce Benz, pp. 187–197. Elsevier, New York.

Umlauf, Marcelle

2009   Restos botánicos de Cardal durante el Periodo Inicial. In *Arqueología del Periodo Formativo en la cuenca baja de Lurín*, edited by R. L. Burger and K. Makowski, Vol. 1, pp. 95–110. Fondo Editorial Pontificia Universidad Católica del Perú, Lima.

Vásquez, Victor, and Teresa E. Rosales Tham

2007   Microscopic Analysis of Ancient Starch Grains on Fragments of Pottery from Cardal, Mina Perida and Manchay Bajo, Valley of Lurin. Manuscript on file, Yale University, New Haven, Connecticut.

Williams, Carlos

1971   Centros ceremoniales tempranos en el valle de Chillón, Rímac y Lurín. *Apuntes Arqueológicos* 1: 1–4.

1980   Complejos de pirámides con planta en U, patron arquitectónico de la costa central. *Revista del Museo Nacional* 44: 95–110.

1985   A Scheme for the Early Monumental Architecture of the Central Coast of Peru. In *Early Ceremonial Architecture in the Andes*, edited by Christopher Donnan, pp. 227–240. Dumbarton Oaks Research Library and Collection, Washington, D.C.

3

Pachacamac and Water

An Interdisciplinary Approach to the Origins, Significance,
and Resilience of Pachacamac

IZUMI SHIMADA, RAFAEL A. SEGURA,
AND BARBARA WINSBOROUGH

Pachacamac was the name the intrusive Incas imposed upon a pre-Inca divinity of the Central Coast associated with the creation, destruction, and renewal of the world known as Ychsma (Rostworowski 1992, 1999: 9), one of the most revered and powerful places, *huacas* (Mannheim and Salas 2015: 63), of the pre-Hispanic Andes. Pachacamac was a sacred place where different populations and natural forces continuously reconfigured the physical and social landscape and, presumably, associated cosmologies.

Why then is Pachacamac situated where it is? And how is Pachacamac's siting related to its origins, significance, and durability as a major pre-Hispanic religious center? This chapter addresses these two basic and persistent questions about Pachacamac. Our interdisciplinary fieldwork has revealed that this famed site resulted, on the one hand, largely from an intimate interplay between its unique environmental setting and processes, and, on the other hand, from large-scale architectural constructions and attendant landscape transformation over multiple occupational phases that together spanned more than 1,000 years. In other words, our work has illuminated how the site became revered and empowered.

One of the objectives of this chapter is to show that the siting of Pachacamac was underwritten by what we believe to be the unique convergence of natural features that were intimately tied to water—especially four major bodies of water that are permanent and both visually and physically easily accessible—and, by extension, to fertility and life. They consist of (1) four *pukios* (also called *puquios*—derived from a Quechua word, *pukyu*, that signifies spring or well; compare Rowe 1969; Schreiber and Lancho 2003) located within the site proper, (2) the Urpi Kocha Lagoon that is fed by an artesian well found at the bottom of the west bank of (3) the Lurín River that runs along the east edge of the site and (4) the Pacific Ocean.

Occupying the seaward end of an extensive promontory, the location also affords excellent visibility and viewshed to and from nearly all directions. Monumental temples from the Lima (Early Intermediate Period) to the Inca (Late Horizon) eras were built on high locations along the eastern periphery of the promontory, accentuating their sense of height, giving unobstructed views of the three largest bodies of water, what could be called an exceptional "watershed," and protecting them from severe surges and tsunamis that besieged the site and the surrounding coast during its pre-Hispanic occupation. Lastly, the nearby presence of the Islas de Pachacamac (the Pachacamac Islands; see below) further distinguishes the Pachacamac location. The connection between life-giving water and cosmological conceptions of its circulation appears to have persisted into Inca occupation of the site, during which a new sacred landscape was created with white sand at the base of their Sun Temple that we infer to symbolize a great body of water.

In this chapter, Pachacamac is conceived as a dynamic entity shaped by a continuous interplay of cultural and natural features and forces within and outside the site proper. Although this conception applies to all settlements to varying degrees, Pachacamac distinguishes itself for the intimacy and the extent of culture-nature interaction it expresses. The synergism of interaction seems to have imbued Pachacamac with identity and agency.

To address the above two questions, we have adopted a historical, interdisciplinary perspective that in essence parallels that of historical ecology (for example, Balée 1998, 2006; Crumley 1994; Erickson 2010) which seeks to elucidate how humans adapt and shape the environment and, in the process, create the landscape.

More specifically, our inquiry focuses on archaeological and environmental data (both modern and ancient) collected by the Pachacamac Archaeological Project, both at the site and from its immediate surroundings, supplemented by historical data. We discuss the physical and symbolic association between Pachacamac and on- and off-site bodies of water, as well as the occurrences of geophysical and hydrological phenomena that we believe to have structured how Pachacamac occupants perceived their world and influenced the worldviews of successive occupants and pilgrims to Pachacamac from near and far. In essence, we argue that there is a critical linkage between the durable and notable ideological significance of the site, on one hand, and the natural features of its landscape and location, on the other. In essence, Pachacamac is an exemplary case of the transformation of a unique environment into an extraordinary, millenarian, revered, and powerful landscape.

The Lima Occupation and Origins of Pachacamac

There is emerging agreement that construction on the first monumental temples at Pachacamac began by the middle phase of the Lima culture, circa AD 400 (for example, Shimada et al. 2004; also see Bueno 1982; Eeckhout 1995). There is a possibility, however, that there was an earlier Lima (that is, Early Lima, circa AD 200) occupation in the western periphery of the site as suggested by the discovery of an Early Lima textile near the Urpi Kocha Lagoon (see below; also, Franco and Paredes 2016). Nearby densely occupied cemeteries dating to the beginning of the Early Intermediate Period (400 BCE–AD 550; for example, El Panel [Paredes 1984, 1986], and Villa El Salvador [Stothert 1980, Stothert and Ravines 1977, Pechenkina and Delgado 2006]), as well as white-on-red sherds found beneath the Inca Temple of the Sun (Strong and Corbett 1943; Patterson 1966), indicate that the lower reaches of the Lurín Valley already had an extensive occupation and major funerary/ceremonial significance during the first centuries of our era. In this sense, it seems the origins of the sanctity and power of Pachacamac are best approached from the cosmological ideas of the Lima culture, rather than extrapolating Inca or even Ychsma or Wari beliefs backward in time as has often been done (for example, Dulanto 2001; Rostworowski 2001). Thus, we first focus our attention on basic characteristics of the Lima occupation at Pachacamac.

There are three known multilevel Lima platform mounds built with small hand-made adobe bricks known as *adobitos* (Bueno 1974/75, 82). The first is the Urpi (Urpay) Wachak Temple on the westernmost promontory of the site, located about 230 m southeast of the Urpi Kocha Lagoon (Ccosi 2007a). Our 2003 ground-penetrating radar (GPR) survey of the mound and an accompanying 5 × 5 m test excavation at its northeastern sector (Shimada et al. 2004} not only confirmed Tello's 1941 findings that the squarish temple occupies the apex of a conical mound, but also revealed that the mound has at least five superimposed and sealed sand-filled levels whose edges are cardinally oriented with the west side facing the lagoon. Each level is capped by

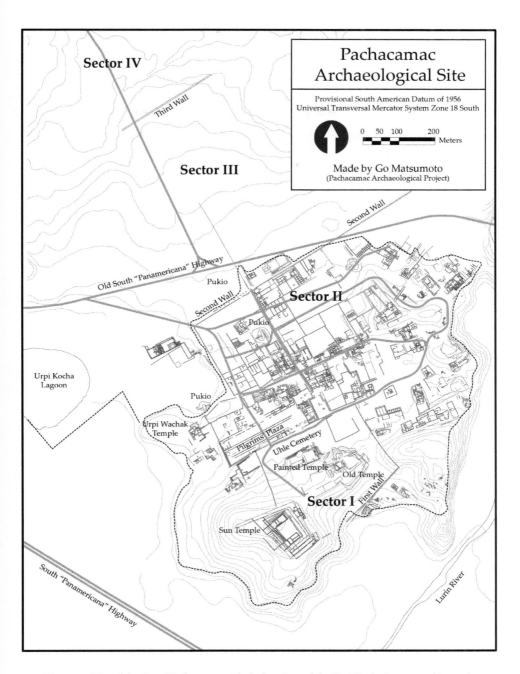

Figure 3.1. Map of the site of Pachacamac with the locations of the Urpi Kocha Lagoon, *pukios*, and major architecture, including temples that are discussed in the text. Map by Go Matsumoto.

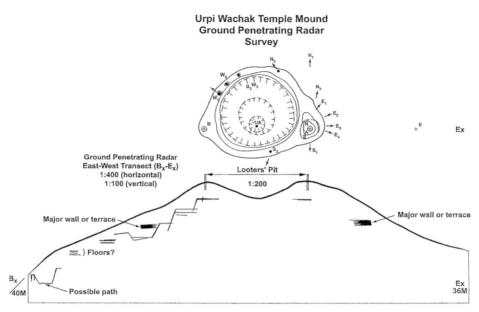

Figure 3.2. Schematic east-west cross-sectional view of the sand-covered Temple of Urpi Wachak showing the floors and walls detected by our 2003 ground-penetrating radar survey. Scale: 1:200. Illustration by Izumi Shimada.

adobito flooring and retaining walls (see figure 122 in Ccosi 2007a: 100; Shimada 2007: 16). The second platform mound is an unnamed building on the southernmost promontory, probably a temple judging by the massive human sacrifice with which it was associated (Strong and Corbett 1943). This excavation was prematurely terminated, although it seems certain that the building underlies the Inca Temple of the Sun (Fig. 3.3). Last is the Lima Temple (also known as Old Temple of Pachacamac), 160 m east of the preceding and located just southeast of the Painted Temple (Franco 1993; Franco and Paredes 2000). The Lima temple is discussed later in this chapter.

Less massive but still formalized contemporaneous *adobito* architecture covered much of the area between these three temples and the northwest end of the site as detailed below. Evidence of Lima occupation on the east side of the site, on the other hand, is negligible (for example, Eeckhout 1995, 1999; Paredes and Franco 1987). Associated ceramics and radiocarbon dates together suggest abandonment of these three temples at roughly the same time, or closely follow the mega–El Niño event at the end of the sixth century

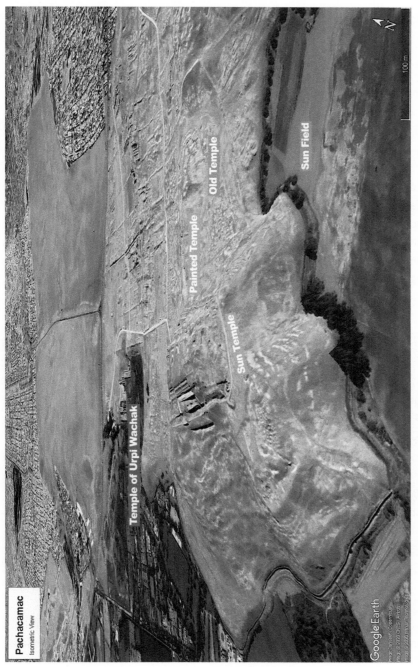

Figure 3.3. Oblique aerial view of the south edge of the Tablazo de Lurín showing the steep cliff formed by the exposed sedimentary bedrock of the Pamplona Geological Formation. The area with modern cultivation corresponds to a portion of the "Sun Field." Prepared by Kayeleigh Sharp based on Google Earth 2020.

(see below; compare Bourget 2001; Franco 1993; Franco and Paredes 2000; Mauricio 2018; Shimada et al. 1991; Winsborough et al. 2012)

Local Geology, Hydrology, and Water Bodies

We believe local geology, hydrology, and water bodies have not received adequate attention in earlier studies. Geologically, Pachacamac lies on the south edge of the gently sloping Tablazo de Lurín, an extensive, sandy plain formed by thick Quaternary aeolian deposits overlying sedimentary bedrock corresponding to the Pamplona Geological Formation (INGEMMET Mapa Geológico Cuadrángulo Lurín, Hoja 25-J; Allende 2003). The south end of the plain has been uplifted and eroded by ocean waves to present a steep cliff face. The south base of the Inca Sun Temple is some 20 to 30 m above the flat plain below, giving the temple (as well as the underlying, unnamed Lima period temple) a particularly lofty character, while, at the same time, protecting it from destructive surfs and tsunamis. E. G. Squier (1877: 68), describing

Figure 3.4. Oblique angle, 3-D projection of the site of Pachacamac seen from the southwest. Map by Izumi Shimada based on Digital Globe/Google Earth 2013.

Izumi Shimada, Rafael A. Segura, and Barbara Winsborough

the placement of the Incaic Sun Temple at the seaward edge of Tablazo de Lurín, offers a dramatic description of its viewshed and watershed, stating the temple gives the impression that "it reaches close to the shore, so that the ocean may be said to break at its feet." Uhle (1903) called the flat plain the Sun Field, suspecting that it was cultivated during the Inca occupation of the site. The evidence described below suggests that the generally flat area surrounding the Urpi Kocha Lagoon and extending to the Sun Field was artificially modified and cultivated (see below; Shimada et al. 2010; Winsborough et al. 2012) since the earlier Lima occupation.

The east edge of the Tablazo de Lurín plain is defined by the entrenched and artificially canalized course of the Lurín River. The natural topography not only provides a rather dramatic architectural setting, it also presents the hydrological conditions essential for understanding the landscape at Pachacamac.

While some scholars have correctly observed that the Pacific Ocean and the Lurín River were not just economically important to Pachacamac residents but also symbolically important (for example, Glowacki and Malpass 2003), little has been said about how water bodies were associated with Pachacamac and what were their management and significance. We now turn our attention to them.

The Urpi Kocha Lagoon

The Urpi Kocha Lagoon situated at the northwestern corner of Pachacamac, less than 1 km inland from the Pacific, is fed by a natural spring (artesian well) resulting from the aquifer created by the uplifted Pamplona Geological Formation underlying the Pachacamac site. This formation runs parallel to the coast and underlies an aquifer that is fed from the bottom of the Lurín River. The formation also blocks the flow of the aquifer, forcing groundwater to a low-lying area on the surface.

The Urpi Kocha Lagoon was an important body of water during the entire pre-Hispanic occupation of Pachacamac. Considering the location of the old embankment that still surrounds the lagoon, it could have had a pre-Hispanic maximum extent of about 9 to 10 ha (about 330 m [NW-SE] × 300 m [NE-SW]). Its greatest modern extent, in the mid-twentieth century, encompassed about 2.2 ha of open water. Today, the lagoon is no more than an estuarine wetland undergoing an accelerated process of desiccation. It is severely en-

Figure 3.5. The November 1941 photo of the Urpi Kocha Lagoon taken by J. Robert Wells. Photo courtesy of the Archivo Julio C. Tello del Museo de Arqueología y Antropología de la Universidad Nacional Mayor de San Marcos (Archive Code No. X/B19/P11/F17/549).

Figure 3.6. The Urpi Kocha Lagoon in 2003 overgrown by vegetation and with almost no surface water. Photo by Izumi Shimada.

croached upon by modern constructions. Modern exploitation (pumping) of this aquifer by the ever-expanding local (inland) human population, and the significant reduction of dense *loma* vegetation on coastal mountain slopes that once captured moisture from thick winter fog to replenish the aquifer (Brack 1977; Mujica 1991; Rostworowski 1981), are responsible for the drying of the lagoon (Winsborough et al. 2012).

Local mythology dealing with "Urpay Huachac" (also known as the Urpi Wachak Temple) shows the long-standing importance of the lagoon, at least from the Late Pre-Hispanic Era as documented by María Rostworowski (1973, 1983, 1992) and independently supported by archaeological data. Test excavations conducted by Julio C. Tello and his team in the 1940s (Espejo 2007; Huapaya 2007a) revealed a corridor defined by two parallel masonry walls running along the south and west sides of the lagoon. A stairway near the west end of the south corridor appears to have provided the only access to the *walled-in* lagoon. The walls were associated with two inferred sacrificial offerings, each consisting of partially articulated human bones, camelid bones, and what appear to be intentionally smashed Ychsma ceramic vessels. In addition, a well-preserved "Early Lima" textile with interlocking designs was recovered. As noted earlier, Tello's 1941 excavation, as well as our 2003

Figure 3.7. Photo of the south corridor and the associated stairway exposed by J. Tello and his crew in November 1940. Adapted from Espejo 2007. (Museo de Arqueología y Antropología, Universidad Nacional Mayor de San Marcos Archive Code No. X/B19/P11/F12/408).

excavations, unequivocally establish the Urpi Wachak Temple as a Lima construction (Huapaya 2007b; Shimada 2007).

Our 2003 and 2004 GPR surveys along the western to northwestern border of the lagoon indicate various deeply buried structures. We infer these structures to pertain to Lima occupation, situated between the Adobito Complex next to the modern site museum and the Urpi Wachak Temple (Shimada et al. 2004; also see Lavallée 1966; Marcone 2000). Recent excavations close to the Inca Mamacona Convent ("Templo de la Luna") have provided archaeological remains that also provide positive support of our survey data (Marcelo Saco, personal communication 2007). These Lima constructions, including the temple, form a rough semicircle as if to physically and symbolically *embrace the lagoon.*

The lagoon also provided a wide variety of fish and birds (including migratory ducks after which the lagoon is named) to the site residents. The fish and birds were used for food and/or ritual use (Shimada et al. 2010). The lagoon also provided *junco* grass (*Scirpus limensis*) and *totora* reeds (*Typha domingensis*) which were used to make baskets, mats, roof mats, and for the

Figure 3.8. Mats that under- and overlay the mummy bundles excavated, as well as roofing and other contents of Tomb 1/2 that we excavated in 2005 from Trench 7 in front of the Painted Temple. These items were likely to have been made of totora reeds (*Typha domingensis*), which still grow in abundance at the Urpi Kocha Lagoon. Photo by Izumi Shimada.

preparation of mummy bundles (Shimada et al. 2010). The lagoon also would have been a way to monitor seasonal changes because it was sensitive to environmental conditions; for example, migratory birds that settle seasonally in coastal wetlands (*pantanos* or *albuferas*) are extremely sensitive to climatic changes, as has been observed recently in the extensive marsh land of Pantanos de Villa, 9.5 km northwest of Pachacamac (Guillén and Barrio 1994; Pautrat and Riveros 1998). Pollens identified in sediment cores that we extracted from the lagoon reveal that there were a limited range of plants cultivated in the immediate vicinity of the lagoon (for example, in the flat area at the south base of the Urpi Wachak and Sun temples), including ritually important maize and tobacco (a tentative identification made by the project archaeobotanist, Lee Newsom; Winsborough et al. 2012). These activities occurred perhaps as early as during Lima occupation, further reinforcing our vision of the sanctity of the lagoon.

The ecology of the lagoon, in a broad sense, significantly contributed to its symbolic meaning and consequent veneration by Pachacamac residents. Taken together, it is evident that the lagoon was a key nexus of the evolving anthropogenic and sacred landscape from the time of Lima occupation.

Pukios

Pukios, or springs, are yet another important body of water at Pachacamac. As with the Urpi Kocha Lagoon, they are fed by the Pamplona Formation aquifer. In fact, there is a permanent spring at *Pukio* 1 at the northeast edge of the site. This spring is located just north of the present-day Lurín Bridge (Puente de Lurín). This spring remains viable, providing plenty of potable water for modern local residents. Like the aforementioned lagoon, these *pukios* are modified and managed sources of water, not mere bodies of water, as explained below.

Within the site proper, *Pukio* 4 (Fig. 3.9), located about 140 m northeast and downslope from the Urpi Wachak Temple, is still readily recognizable as a roughly circular depression (about 27 m in diameter and over 5 m in depth) overgrown with *junco* grass, *totora* reeds, and small trees. As a part of their 1941 investigation of the temple, Tello and his team excavated an E-W trench on its west slope (see figs. 189, 190 in Ccosi 2007b: 131–132). It is not clear whether they recognized its significance as a *pukio*. Apparently, nothing was found in the trench, although our GPR survey in 2003 detected two terraces

Figure 3.9. (*above*) 2004 sediment coring at *Pukio* 4 at the north base of the Urpi Wachak Temple. Photo by Izumi Shimada.

Figure 3.10. (*right*) 2003 ground-penetrating-radar survey at *Pukio* 2. Note how this feature dips toward the scale on the right side. The darkness of the soil derives from ash and refuse deposited. Photo by Izumi Shimada.

on the north slope of the conical depression that probably facilitated access to water. Two other *pukios*, numbered 2 and 3, that had been largely obliterated by pre-Hispanic (during the Inca occupation) and modern anthropogenic actions, respectively, were detected in the same GPR survey. *Pukio* 2 (Fig. 3.10), located close to the north end of the North-South Street, is by far the largest of all known *pukios* at the site, still measuring over 30 × 50 m and 6 m in depth. Our 2003 test excavation in the deepest area reached about 7.5 m below the modern surface before we stopped, due to the difficulty of excavating in the sandy soil that filled this feature. The *pukio* is largely filled in with dark gray sandy soil containing Incaic refuse that included ash and charcoal bits, suggesting that it may have been dried out by the Late Horizon or at some point during the Late Horizon. The radar detected three levels of artificial terraces on the western side of this crevicelike depression.

Although *Pukio* 3 was largely filled in several decades ago to provide a visitor parking area just north of the Pyramid with Ramp No. 1 (Late Intermediate construction; Eeckhout 2000; Jiménez 1985), it was not only readily visible (an exposed area of about 2 m north-south and 1 cm east-west), but still preserved by stone retaining walls on the east and west sides, containing a good deal of water at least until 2005. We suspect that these *pukios* provided a more stable source of fresh water than the Lurín River, which largely dries up during its low-flow period of May to October. We have not yet tested, however, the drinkability of water from these on-site *pukios*. At the same time, all on-site *pukios* are clearly artificially shaped, with terraces for easy access and integrated into built spaces prior to Inca domination of Pachacamac, which began in the second half of the fifteenth century. Whether all *pukios* were accessible to both long-term and transitory residents remains unresolved. Pilgrims' privilege to ingress into the interior of the site where these *pukios* were situated was tightly controlled; many pilgrims from far and wide had to fast and wait (up to a year) before being allowed to reach the inner sacred zones, according to various early Colonial Spanish writers (for example, Calancha 1976[1638], Cieza 1932[1554], Estete 1985[1534]). *Pukios* 1 and 3, being close to the Urpi Wachak Temple and Pyramid with Ramp No. 1, respectively, may have had access restricted to those closely affiliated with the maintenance of these structures.

Imperial sites throughout the Inca Empire commonly featured elaborately built features that displayed water bodies and/or carefully designed movement of water such as stone-lined baths, pools, canals, and waterfalls (for example, Curatola 2020; Nair and Protzen 2015; Wright et al. 2006). Clearly, the Incas took advantage of the hydrology of Pachacamac; the stone-lined pool inside the largely reconstructed *acllawasi* (also known as "Temple of the Moon") would have depended on water from the aforementioned aquifer as well as the nearby Urpi Kocha Lagoon and *Pukio* 4. On the other hand, the relatively small (estimated 3 m²) "bath," built of fine ashlar masonry near the northeast corner of the "Pilgrims' Plaza," would have required a canal to feed and drain it. Exposed segments of stone-lined canals suggest that they covered a large portion of Sector II of the site and carried relatively small volumes of water (cross-sectional dimensions of about 20–25 × 20 cm high). The extent of canals as well as their location may well have been conditioned by a surge in the resident population during Ychsma occupation of the site (circa 1100–1533 CE). Determination of the history of these intra-site canals, as well as the spatial extent and use of the water they carried, is a topic for further research in our understanding of the role of water in the operation and significance of post-Lima Pachacamac.

Social Life and Water-Oriented Cosmology

The cosmological importance of water at Pachacamac is also recognizable in the *placement* of three Lima temples atop the west and south hills of the site, which provided unimpeded visual access to the Urpi Kocha Lagoon, the Pacific Ocean, and the mouth of the Lurín River, respectively. On the basis of this spatial relationship, one would expect to find additional lines of evidence in each temple pointing to a strong connection with water. Indeed, excavations at the Lima Temple by Régulo Franco and Ponciano Paredes (2000) documented elaborate offerings composed largely of *Spondylus crassisquama* (*Sp. princeps* is an outdated and incorrect identification) and small ceramic vessels representing a remarkable array of fishes, mollusks, and crustaceans. Further, a map of the site of Pachacamac made in 1793 by Joséf Juan (see figure 3 in Kosok 1965: 40; also photo 7 in Jiménez Borja 1985: 54; unnumbered figure in Rostworowski 1992: 82) shows a highly unusual, star-shaped construction with eight regularly spaced triangular projections (that is, a circular building with a sawtooth perimeter) where the Lima Temple is situated. We believe this depiction is in reality a schematized version of the Lima Temple. Shimada's field inspection of the relatively well-preserved and exposed northeastern exterior of this tem-

Figure 3.11. Spatial relationship between the three temple mounds, on the one hand, and the three nearby bodies of water, on the other. Map by Rafael Segura based on Google Earth 5.1 (2010).

ple identified two acute (about 80°) angled projections built of *adobitos*. They project outward at least 2 m in length, although their full extent cannot be determined due to erosion and overburden. We suggest the shape of this temple represented a stylized *Spondylus crassisquama* and readily recognizable, symbolic linkage with water and the Pacific (Shimada 2007). Certainly, in the Sicán and Chimú iconographies, *Spondylus crassisquama* shells are represented as semicircles with serrated edges (see examples on various artistic media illustrated in Cordy-Collins 1990), much like the preserved northeastern exterior of the Lima Temple.

The physical orientation of the Lima burials at Pachacamac may further reflect the symbolic importance of water. It is well known that the Lima populations of the Rímac and Chillón valleys placed their dead in extended positions oriented to the south. In contrast, our excavations in 2005 at the north border of the Uhle cemetery in front of the Painted Temple documented five Lima burials. These burials were mostly disturbed by late Middle Horizon and Ychsma burials, but they contained individuals who were clearly in seated flexed position and consistently faced west or southwest toward the Pacific Ocean. It is worth noting that contemporaneous burials at nearby

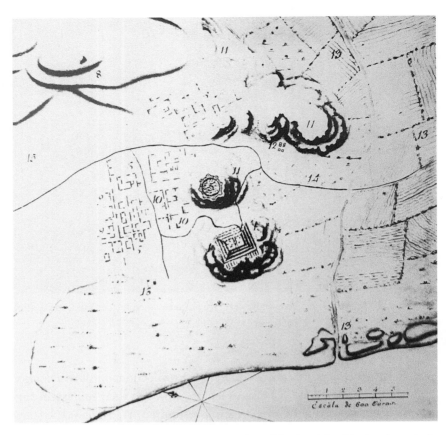

Figure 3.12. The star-shaped construction adjacent to the multilevel Temple of the Sun shown in the 1793 map of Pachacamac by Joséf Juan in the British Library. Taken from Kosok 1965: 40, fig. 3.

sites in the lower Lurín Valley share the same burial position and orientation (Paredes 1984, 1986; Stothert 1980; Stothert and Ravines 1977).

While settlement organization and mortuary practices of succeeding periods completely diverged from those of the Lima, the post-Lima cosmology of Pachacamac residents continued to emphasize concepts, creatures, and resources associated with bodies of water. This is evident in the documented polychrome murals that decorated the façade of the Pachacamac or Painted Temple (Bonavia 1974; Marcone 2003; Muelle and Wells 1939; Uhle 1991 [1903]). It is worth noting that when Pedro Pizarro visited the Pachacamac Temple, the central atrium had a simple door covered with a cloth with *Spondylus crassisquama* sewn on at its top. This cover is most likely the same

Izumi Shimada, Rafael A. Segura, and Barbara Winsborough

Figure 3.13. Lima burial excavated in Uhle's Cemetery 1 in front of the Painted Temple. Photo by César Samillán.

one that was found by Alberto A. Giesecke in 1938 (Lindo and Gerbert 2019; Dulanto 2001: 161, his fig. 49) together with the well-known carved wooden idol atop the temple.

The Turbulent Pacific and Pachacamac as a Stable and Safe Sanctuary

As stated earlier, we view Pachacamac as the evolving synergistic development of a unique set of natural and cultural factors. Accordingly, one of the two basic aims of the Pachacamac Archaeological Project has been the clarification of paleoenvironmental conditions and processes that shaped the Pachacamac landscape and cultural developments. To this end, our project extracted four 3-m-deep sediment cores from the Urpi Kocha Lagoon. Interdisciplinary analysis revealed over 2,300 years of complex environmental history characterized by alternating periods of severe drought and catastrophic floods (Winsborough et al. 2012). The lagoon was brackish early in the core sequence until a catastrophic flood sometime during the Late Lima era isolated it from the Pacific with a corresponding gradual reduction in salinity. Sedimentological and associated diatom and macrophytic records established four mega–El Niño-ENSO events over a 2,300+-year span. The two most severe events have been AMS-dated to between AD 436 and 651 (Beta-185162, 1540±40 BP) and 1000 and 1100 AD (Beta-185161, 1010 ±40 BP; Beta-240415, 1030±40 BP; all AD dates are 2 sigma corrected using the SHCal04 [McCormack et al. 2004]). This corresponds roughly to the Late Lima and Pachacamac-Ychsma transition. The former appears to have *permanently* isolated the lagoon from the Pacific and transformed the water quality and lacustrine ecology (Winsborough et al. 2012). We believe it is the same event that left behind a thick layer of mud atop the Lima Temple that Franco and Paredes (Franco 1993: 60; Franco and Paredes 2000: 613) date to circa AD 600 near the end of Lima occupation at the site. This mega–El Niño may have perhaps occurred during a severe and prolonged drought, or closely followed one as recorded in the 1,500-year-long annual precipitation records from the Quelccaya Ice Cap (Shimada et al. 1991; Thompson et

Table 3.1. Significant flood events documented in the Pachacamac sediment cores

Event #	Depth cm	AMS Date (Yrs BP)	Corrected Date BC–AD	Depth (cm) of Dated Sample	Historical Association	Inferred Event Type
1	126–135	1010	AD 995–1008	126	Naymlap Flood	El Niño + Tsunami
2	160–194	1540	AD 436–651	195	6th-century Flood	El Niño + Tsunami
3	240–250	2018	436 BC–AD 93	240		River flood + El Niño
4	270–285	2293	398 BC–177 BC	260		Tsunami

Source: Authors.

Figure 3.14. Sliced sediment core extracted from the Urpi Kocha Lagoon; this reveals a long sequence of deposits in segments of different color and texture that represent different environmental conditions and events. Photo by Izumi Shimada.

al. 1984, 1985). This is an example of what Moseley (1997) calls "convergent catastrophes" with major and lasting environmental impacts.

These two mega–El Niño events also seem to coincide with the so-called late Moche and Naymlap floods documented at various sites on the north coast (Craig and Shimada 1986; Donnan 1987, 1990; Nials et al. 1979; Shimada 1990, 1994; Shimada et al. 2018). The nature as well as the extent and intensity of occupation during the time span between these two events, corresponding to much of the Middle Horizon, remain elusive at both site and regional levels (Segura and Shimada 2010; Shimada et al. 2004, 2010). Pachacamac retained some significance during this time span as it served occasionally as a burial ground, but performance of ritual offerings largely ceased (Shimada et al., 2004, 2010). A similar occupation and construction hiatus for this period was documented at the major urban settlement of Cajamarquilla at the neck of the Rímac Valley (Segura and Shimada 2010). Population dispersal and attendant difficulty in major labor and material mobilization may well account for this elusiveness (Segura and Shimada 2010: 131). We are well aware that site abandonment and population dispersal are typically multifactorial in nature with multilayered short- and long-term factors working together (for example, Cowgill 1988; McAnany and Yoffee 2010; Middleton 2017). In this sense, it is likely that we have illuminated only a few such layers and factors. Available evidence now indicates, however, that within as short as a few generations after the second mega–El Niño, around 1000–1100 CE, Pachacamac saw a major resurgence in occupation, construction, and ritual offerings by the Ychsma population (Eeckhout 2003, 2004; Shimada et al. 2010; also see Faulseit 2016; Schwartz and Nichols 2010). Overall, the two mega–El Niño events appear to bracket in time the ebb and flow of cultural activities at Pachacamac.

Tsunamis

A major finding of our sediment core analysis that is directly pertinent to the primary objectives of this chapter is the documentation of the three major tsunamis over the past 2,300+ years that also contributed to shaping the local landscape (Shimada and Winsborough 2012; Winsborough et al. 2012).

As a part of the Circum-Pacific "Ring of Fire" and being close to the subduction zone of the Nasca Plate in the Peru-Chile Trench, the Central Coast of Peru faces the constant threat of strong earthquakes and associated tsunamis. This point is dramatically illustrated by the historical documentation of the October 28, 1746, earthquake—what is believed to be the largest to strike central Peru in recorded history (the epicenter was located some 90 km north-northwest of Lima) and accompanying tsunamis. The magnitude of this earthquake is estimated to have been around 8.6 to 8.8 on the Richter scale (Chlieh et al. 2011; Dorbath et al. 1990). The first of the two tsunami waves that hit the port and the city of Callao some 30 minutes after the shock is said to have had a 24-m runup (incoming waves) and 5-km inundation, destroying much of the city and killing most of the estimated 5,000–6,000 inhabitants (Walker 2008: 7). The tsunami resulting from the 8.5 magnitude earthquake in 1868 centered near the Peru-Chile border region farther south is estimated to have had a 27-m-high runup (Berninghausen 1962; Dorbath et al. 1990; Lockridge 1985).

Of particular importance to our identification of ancient tsunamis in the cores is the composition of diatoms, microscopic unicellular algae that are highly sensitive indicators of water quality and salinity. The sudden appearance of a chaotic mixture of freshwater, brackish, and especially marine diatoms points to a tsunami with brief but catastrophic saltwater inundation into a freshwater environment. We found three segments of cores that reflect an abrupt and major change in the ecosystem (see Table 3.1).

Although ten AMS dates were obtained for the cores, we can only estimate approximate timings of inferred tsunamis. The earliest of the three inferred tsunamis has a 2-sigma calibrated date of circa 398–177 BCE (AA65266, 2293±52 BP). At the beachfront site of Huaca Prieta just north of the mouth of the Chicama River on the north coast, J. Bird (Bird and Hyslop 1985: 17; also R. Bird 1987) documented an even earlier tsunami with runups estimated at over 12 m in height, undoubtedly quite destructive in force, but considerably less than the two aforementioned events of 1746 and 1868.

Two later tsunamis identified in our sediment core analysis may well have been powerful surges caused by strong landward winds during two mega–El Niño events much like what happened in New York City and the surrounding region along the Atlantic coast of the United States during "Superstorm Sandy" in 2012, the second costliest hurricane in U.S. history (Bennington et al. 2014). Within the site proper of Pachacamac, we have not found any thick or extensive chaotic deposits that are readily visible as would be expected from major floods and tsunamis. The locations of all temples along the seaward edges of the plateau-like pediment of the Pamploma Formation appear to have protected Pachacamac from the direct impact of powerful tsunamis and surges. The most seaward point, where the Inca temple was erected above an unnamed Lima temple, has a steep cliff face that lies about 50 masl. The masonry base of the earlier Urpi Wachak temple that was built farther inland in a more protected, covelike setting stands about 20 masl.

It is worth noting that Max Uhle observed traces of a massive dam between the seashore and the Urpi Kocha Lagoon that had been broken by the sea. He speculated this dam was the remains of a massive wall (Uhle 1991 [1903]: 63). It is likely that this wall or dam was a post-Lima construction, judging from the correlations that Uhle made between it and other walls of the "Outer City." It was likely intended to protect the lagoon and surrounding constructions/occupations in the low-lying area at the site. It also attests to the fact that the people occupying Pachacamac recognized the repeated risk and destructive power of tsunamis and storm surges of the Pacific. At the same time, the plateau atop the Pamploma Formation appears to have offered a stable and safe natural sanctuary for the four monumental temples of varied periods.

Discussion

From its founding sometime early in the fifth century C.E. or earlier by a Lima population, the site of Pachacamac has been both physically and symbolically inseparable from water and, by extension, fertility and life. The physical setting of Pachacamac is unique along the entire Peruvian coast in various important regards, which, we argue, underwrote its millennial religious significance:

1. Most importantly, Pachacamac *occupies a node of four major, perennial bodies of water* that were both physically and visually accessible: the Pacific, the Lurín River, the Urpi Kocha Lagoon, and multiple *pukios*. An underlying aquifer supported at least three on-site *pukios* (that we have documented) and another along the Lurín River at the northeast edge of the site, and contributed to a high water-table area at the base of the site, the area Uhle [1903] called the Sun Field;

2. Pachacamac is a *nexus between land and sea*, with the seaward base of the plateau where the site and the mouth of the Lurín River are separated only about 850 m from the Pacific;

3. Being located atop and at the southwest corner of the plateau with cliff-like perimeters that stand 20 to 30 m above the flat land below, it can be recognized from afar and has a commanding view of the surrounding landscape, including the Pacific Ocean, the Lurín River, and the Islas de Pachacamac. *The site overall distinguishes itself not only for having excellent visibility and surrounding viewshed, but also for its unique watershed*;

4. The same topographic features afford the site safety from powerful tsunamis and surges from the Pacific; and, lastly,

5. The nearby presence of the Islas de Pachacamac may have added an extra dimension of meaning to the location of Pachacamac for several reasons as inferential data suggest: (A) the main island is only about 2,750 m from the mouth of the Lurín River; (B) it was clearly pre-Hispanically utilized, as Inca, pre- and non-Inca ceramics have been found there (regrettably they remain unanalyzed and unpublished); and (C) other offshore islands farther north and south such as the Chincha, Macabí, Guañape, and Islas Lobos de Afuera, served as ritual offering sites and were deemed the resting places of the dead (for example, Cieza [1554]1932; Garcilaso [1609]1960; Hutchinson 1873; Kubler 1948; Netherly 1977). Future explorations of the Islas de Pachacamac may well yield evidence in support of this inference.

Our examination of aerial photos and satellite images as well as ground surveys of selected areas of the Peruvian coast have revealed that the aforementioned features, especially the convergence of four major bodies of water at Pachacamac and the site's excellent view- and watershed are indeed unparalleled even in light of the significant modifications to the shoreline-coastal landscape and ecology (including the reduction of swamps, or *pantanos*) that have occurred since the colonial era (for example, Rostworowski 1981).

Figure 3.15. The Pachacamac Islands seen from the west base of the site of Pachacamac. Photo by Izumi Shimada.

What our examination has also shown is that there are a handful of major coastal sites that *share some* of the above features. On the south coast, La Centinela, the capital of the Kingdom of Chincha in the lower Chincha Valley (Morris and von Hagan 1993; von Hagen and Morris 1998: 157–158, figs. 105, 106), with monumental ceremonial mounds and extensive residential zones, is one such site. It is situated over 1 km north of the San Juan River (the nearest river), about 1.7 km east of the Pacific, and about 30 km to the southwest of the closest of the Chincha Islands. In contrast, it has neither any known on-site lagoons or springs, nor a viewshed comparable to that of Pachacamac.

On the north coast, there are a number of important coastal religious centers that occupy the junction of rivers and the Pacific Ocean, for example, Chornancap, a Middle Sicán (circa 1000–1100 CE) religious site on the north bank of the Lambayeque River. The site otherwise does not share any of the other major features that distinguish Pachacamac.

Perhaps the most notable comparative case among all coastal religious sites for the reasons explained below is Pacatnamú (for example, Donnan and Cock 1986, 1997; Hecker and Hecker 1985; Kosok 1965; Ubbelohde-Doering 1967). It occupies the flat top of the very southwest tip of the elevated desert pediment (on the north bank) that not only overlooks the mouth of the Jequetepeque River, but also offers excellent visibility and has an expansive viewshed. In addition, the site has multiple occupations spanning the Early Intermediate (Gallinazo and Moche) to the Late Intermediate Period (Sicán, Chimú, and limited Inca and Colonial—a total span of about 1,300 years; see Donnan 1997: 10–14), boasts numerous burials and offerings and multiple, major platform mounds, and also has access controlled by means of two major concentric enclosing walls just as at Pachacamac (see Shimada 1990; Uhle 1903). These natural and cultural features perhaps merit our consideration of Pacatnamú as a north coast branch Pachacamac (compare Menzel 1977 and Netherly 1977 for the site of Huacas de Moche representing a branch Pachacamac). Close contact between Pacatnamú and Pachacamac is intimated by the presence of fine Pachacamac-style textiles at the former (Keatinge 1978).

A close examination, however, reveals that Pacatnamú does not have the extraordinary convergence of major, perennial water bodies or readily visually or physically accessible islands nearby. Overall, none of the coastal religious sites we have examined has a comparable multiplicity and diversity of water bodies to those documented at Pachacamac, that together would have impressed visitors with the extraordinary quality of the location, particularly its contrasting, barren, sand-covered plateau and surrounding hills. While the discharge volume of the perennial Lurín River fluctuates seasonally, the *pukios* and the lagoon fed by the underlying aquifer would have offered a more stable water supply for ritual, agricultural, and drinking use. We also argue that the nearby presence of the Islas de Pachacamac added a greater symbolic and ritual importance to the site. Further, the cliff-top placement of temples at Pachacamac afforded not only an unimpeded view of the afore-mentioned bodies of water and islands, but also protection from the destructive forces of tsunamis and other flooding—a veritable sanctuary.

The physical forms of the architecture and their placement emphasizing connection to bodies of water clearly indicate that one of the major motivations for the initial Lima occupation of Pachacamac was symbolic-religious in nature, and that this factor may have been the single major impetus facilitating its longevity.

We argue that each of the three Lima temples was dedicated to a specific body of water. We further posit that the star-shaped Lima Temple emulated the shape of *Spondylus crassisquama* and thus symbolized water, fertility, and life. This symbolism and its primordial significance would have transfigured Pachacamac into a highly powerful entity, *huaca* (Mannheim and Salas 2015). This shape is not found in any other Lima mound construction and thus requires a distinct explanation, as we have presented here.

The landscape of Pachacamac was dynamic and ever changing, as documented by the sediment cores we extracted from Urpi Kocha, as well as the excavations and remote sensing surveys we conducted at the site. Water in various forms shaped and sustained Pachacamac's sacred landscape much more than previously recognized. Major El Niño–ENSO-related floods, tsunamis, flash floods from highland rains, and droughts contributed as much as the anthropogenic modifications to this landscape that continues to evolve (for example, modern pilgrims and tourists, construction of the new national museum). Even the large-scale modification of the sacred landscape undertaken by the Incas at the site, we hypothesize, was underlain by the concept of *cocha* (*kocha*), or the sacred body of water. They used a massive quantity of white sand to bury pre-Inca Lima and Ychsma remains in order to create the extensive Pilgrims' Plaza at the base of the Sun Temple (Shimada et al. 2004). This landscape transformation of unprecedented scale, with the white sand, replicated the creation of the main plaza of Cusco that served as a material symbol of the sacred Pacific (Cummins 2015:173; McEwan and Bray 2015).

Figure 3.16. Sand that buried the pre-Inca constructions and other features in the Pilgrims' Plaza (Trench 9–2005), looking toward the north base of the Incaic Sun Temple. Many small offerings, ranging from maize kernels and peanuts to precious metal lumps and textile pieces, were deposited in the sand layer. Photo by Izumi Shimada.

Although the origins of the practice of creating sacred *cocha* remain to be defined, it is tempting to consider the long pre-Incaic veneration of the nurturing and destructive power of water that evolved out of Pachacamac, as having contributed to the importance of the site within the Inca Empire.

Conclusions

Overall, our interdisciplinary and historical ecological perspectives suggest that the unique physiography and hydrology of Pachacamac mitigated the adverse effects of natural hazards, thereby contributing to the resilience and longevity of the site as a religious center. It is likely that these processes and conditions also contributed to the ideological evolution of the patron deity of Pachacamac, which possesses both the nurturing and destructive power of water. While respecting the sanctity and importance of this pre-Inca ideology, deity, and landscape (that is, the Painted Temple), the intrusive Incas imposed their own cosmological vision of sacred landscapes by building their Sun Temple atop an earlier Lima temple with an unimpeded view of the Pacific, and by burying earlier structures with white sand to create a symbolic representation of the ocean (that is, Pilgrims' Plaza). Thus, water was represented by the extraordinary confluence of four major perennial bodies of water: the Pacific Ocean, the Urpi Kocha Lagoon, the Lurín River, and at least four *pukios*, from which the site of Pachacamac remained inseparable throughout its long pre-Hispanic occupation.

Lastly, we argue that understanding of the cosmology and long-term and cross-cultural significance of Pachacamac must begin with a careful assessment of factors relevant to the establishment of the site and the water-centered ideology of the Lima culture, rather than the common practice of extrapolating backward in time from complex Inca and Ychsma cosmologies documented by the Spaniards in the sixteenth century. Discussions of Pachacamac ideology are typically based on analysis of the iconography carved on the famed wooden idol found atop the Painted Temple. We suggest, however, that, when we peel back the political and religious dogmas introduced by groups such as the Wari and Sicán, we find the substratum of an earlier Lima ideology based on water, life, and fertility. In essence, our study illustrates how the challenging task of illuminating Pachacamac ideology and its significance can be productively pursued by integrating interdisciplinary and historical ecology perspectives within nested contexts, in a manner that first focuses on local and regional conditions and developments before external perspectives and models are brought to bear.

Acknowledgments

We are grateful for the generous support of the National Science Foundation (grant nos. BCS-0313964, 0411625), National Geographic Society (grant nos. 7472-03, 7668-04, 7724-04) and John Heinz III Foundation. Similarly, we are thankful for the collaboration of members of the Pachacamac Archaeological Projects. The successive fieldwork seasons of the Pachacamac Archaeological Project (2003–2005) were authorized by Resoluciones Directoriales Nos. 166–2003, 622–2004, and 919–2005 of the Instituto Nacional de Cultura of Peru. We are grateful to Kayeleigh Sharp for her helpful editorial comments and to Upesh Nepali for preparing Figure 3.4.

References Cited

Allende C., Teófilo

2003   Cuenca del Río Lurín: Visión Geológico-Ambiental. *Revista del Instituto de Investigación de la Facultad de Geología, Minas, Metalurgia y Ciencias Geográficas, UNMSM* 6(12): 44–58.

Balée, William

1998   *Advances in Historical Ecology.* Columbia University Press, New York.

2006   The Research Program of Historical Ecology. *Annual Review of Anthropology* 35(5): 15–24.

Bennington, J. Bret, and E. Christa Farmer (eds.)

2014   *Learning from the Impacts of Superstorm Sandy.* Academic Press, New York.

Berninghausen, William H.

1962   Tsunamis Reported from the West Coast of South America 1562–1960. *Bulletin of the Seismological Society of America* 52(4): 915–921.

Bird, Junius B., and John Hyslop

1985   The Preceramic Excavation at the Huaca Prieta, Chicama Valley, Peru. *Anthropological Papers of the American Museum of Natural History* 62.1(1985): 8–294.

Bird, Robert McK.

1987   A Postulated Tsunami and Its Effects on Cultural Development in the Peruvian Early Horizon. *American Antiquity* 52(2): 285–303.

Bonavia, Duccio

1974   *Ricchata Quellcani: Pinturas Murales Prehispánicas.* Banco Industrial del Perú, Lima.

Bourget, Steve

2001   Rituals of Sacrifice: Its Practice at Huaca de la Luna and Its Representation in Moche Iconography. In *Moche Art and Archaeology in Ancient Peru*, edited by Joanne Pillsbury, pp. 177–205. National Gallery of Art, Studies in History of Art 63, Washington, D.C.

Brack, Antonio J.

1977   *El Ambiente En Que Vivimos.* Lima: Editorial Salesiana.

Bueno, Alberto

1974/1975   Cajamarquilla y Pachacamac: Dos Ciudades de la Costa Central del Perú. *Boletín Bibliográfico de Antropología Americana* 36: 171–201. Instituto Panamericano de Geografía e Historia, Mexico City.

1982   El Antiguo Valle de Pachacamac: Espacio, Tiempo y Cultura, Primera Parte. *Boletín de Lima* Año 4, 24: 10–29.

Calancha, Antonio de la

1976 [1638]   Corónica Moralizada del Orden de San Agustín en el Perú con Sucesos Egemplares Vistos en Esta Monarquía. P. Lacavallería, Barcelona.

Ccosi S., Luis

2007a   Pachacamac. Notas Diarias de los Trabajos Arqueológicos. In *Cuadernos de Investigación del Archivo Tello N° 5. Arqueología de Pachacámac: Excavaciones en Urpi Kocha y Urpi Wachac,* edited by Rafael Vega-Centeno, pp. 93–108. Museo de Arqueología y Antropología, Universidad Nacional Mayor de San Marcos, Lima.

2007b   Apuntes de los Trabajos Arqueológicos en Pachacamac. In *Cuadernos de Investigación del Archivo Tello N° 5. Arqueología de Pachacámac: Excavaciones en Urpi Kocha y Urpi Wachac,* edited by Rafael Vega-Centeno, pp. 109–179. Museo de Arqueología y Antropología, Universidad Nacional Mayor de San Marcos, Lima.

Chlieh, Mohamed, Hugo Perfettini, Hernando Tavera, Jean-Philippe Avouac, Dominique Remy, Jean-Mathieu Nocquet, Frédérique Rolandone, Francis Bondoux, Germinal Gabalda, and Sylvain Bonvalot

2011   Interseismic Coupling and Seismic Potential Along the Central Andes Subduction Zone. *Journal of Geophysical Research* 116(B12).

Cieza de León, Pedro

1932 [1554]   *La Crónica del Perú.* Espasa-Calpe, S.A., Madrid.

Cordy-Collins, Alana

1990   Fonga Sigde, Shell Purveyor to the Chimu Kings. In *The Northern Dynasties: Kingships and Statecraft in Chimor,* edited by Michael E. Moseley and Alana Cordy Collins, pp. 393–417. Dumbarton Oaks, Washington, D.C.

Cowgill, George L.

1988   Onward and Upward with Collapse. In *The Collapse of Ancient States and Civilizations,* edited by Norman Yoffee and George Cowgill, pp. 244–276. University of Arizona Press, Madrid.

Craig, Alan K., and Izumi Shimada

1986   El Niño Flood Deposits at Batán Grande, Northern Peru. *Geoarchaeology* 1(1): 29–38.

Crumley, Carole L. (ed.)

1994   *Historical Ecology: Cultural Knowledge and Changing Landscapes.* School of American Research Press, Santa Fe, New Mexico.

Cummins, Thomas B. F.

2012   Inka Art. In *The Inka Empire: A Multidisciplinary Approach,* edited by Izumi Shimada, pp. 165–196. University of Texas Press, Austin.

Curatola, Marco

2020   Inca Shrines: Deities in Stone and Water. In *Sacred Waters: A Cross-Cultural Compendium of Hallowed Springs and Holy Wells,* edited by Celeste Ray, pp. 110–120. Routledge, New York.

Donnan, Christopher B.

1987   Introduction to *The Pacatnamu Papers,* Vol. 1, edited by Christopher B. Donnan and

Guillermo A. Cock, pp. 19–26. Museum of Cultural History, University of California, Los Angeles.

1990   An Assessment of the Validity of the Naymlap Dynasty. In *The Northern Dynasties. Kingship and Statecraft in Chimor*, edited by Michael E. Moseley and Alana Cordy-Collins, pp. 243–274. Dumbarton Oaks Research Library and Collection, Washington, D.C.

1997   Introduction to *The Pacatnamu Papers*, Vol. 2, edited by Christopher B. Donnan and Guillermo A. Cock, pp. 9–16. Museum of Cultural History, University of California, Los Angeles.

Dorbath, Louis, A. Cisternas, and Catherine Dorbath

1990   Assessment of the Size of Large and Great Historical Earthquakes of Peru. *Bulletin of the Seismological Society of America* 80(3): 551–576.

Dulanto, Jahl

2001   Dios de Pachacamac: El ídolo y el templo. In *Los dioses del antiguo Perú, Tomo 2*, edited by Krzysztof Makowski, pp. 158–181. Collección Arte y Tesoros del Perú. Banco de Crédito del Perú, Lima.

Eeckhout, Peter

1995   Pirámide con Rampa No. 3, Pachacamac: Resultados Preliminares de la Primera Temporada de Excavaciones (Zonas 1 & 2). *Bulletin de l'Institut Français d'Etudes Andines* 24(2), 102–156.

1999   Pirámide con Rampa No. III, Pachacamac. Nuevos Datos, Nuevas Perspectivas. *Bulletin de l'Institut Français d'Etudes Andines* 28(2), 169–214.

2000   The Palaces of the Lords of Ychsma: An Archaeological Reappraisal of the Function of Pyramids with Ramps at Pachacamac. *Revista de Arqueología Americana* 17–19: 217–254. D.F. México.

2003   Ancient Monuments and Patterns of Power at Pachacamac, Central Coast of Peru. *Beiträge zur Allgemeinen und Vergleichenden Archäologie* 23: 139–182.

2004   Pachacamac y el Proyecto Ychsma (1999–2003). In *Arqueología de la Costa Central del Perú en los Periodos Tardíos*, edited by Peter Eeckhout. Boletín del Instituto Francés de Estudios Andinos 33(3): 425–448.

Erickson, Clark

2010   The Transformation of Environment into Landscape: The Historical Ecology of Monumental Earthwork Construction in the Bolivian Amazon. *Diversity* 2: 618–652.

Espejo N., Julio

2007   Trabajos en la Laguna de los Patos o Urpi Kocha. In *Cuadernos de Investigación del Archivo Tello N° 5. Arqueología de Pachacámac: Excavaciones en Urpi Kocha y Urpi Wachac*, edited by Rafael Vega-Centeno, pp. 19–38. Museo de Arqueología y Antropología, Universidad Nacional Mayor de San Marcos, Lima.

Estete, Miguel de

1985 [1534]   Relación del Viaje que Hizo el Señor Capitán Hernando Pizarro por Mandado de su Hermano desde el Pueblo de Caxamarca a Parcama y de Allí a Xauxa. In *Verdadera Relacíon de la Conquista del Perú y Provincia del Cuzco Llamada Nueva Castilla* by Francisco de Xérez. C. Bravo, Madrid.

Faulseit, Ronald K. (ed.)

2016   *Beyond Collapse: Archaeological Perspectives on Resilience, Revitalization, and Transformation in Complex Societies*. SIU Press, Carbondale, Illinois.

Franco J., Régulo

1993   El Centro Ceremonial de Pachacamac: Nuevas Evidencias en el Templo Viejo. *Boletín de Lima* 86: 45–62.

Franco, Régulo G., and Ponciano F. Paredes

2000   El Templo Viejo de Pachacamac: nuevos aportes al estudio del Horizonte Medio. In *Huari y Tiwanaku: Modelos y Evidencias. Primera Parte*, edited by Peter Kaulicke and William H. Isbell, pp. 607–630. Boletín de Arqueología PUCP No. 4. Fondo Editorial de la Pontificia Universidad Católica del Perú, Lima.

2016   *Templo Viejo de Pachacamac: Dioses, Arquitectura, Sacrificios y Ofrendas.* Fundación Augusto N. Wiese, Lima.

Garcilaso de la Vega, El Inca

1960 [1609]   *Los comentarios reales, primera parte.* Biblioteca de Autores Españoles, No. 133. Editorial Atlas, Madrid.

Glowacki, Mary, and Michael Malpass

2003   Water, Huacas, and Ancestor Worship: Traces of a Sacred Wari Landscape. *Latin American Antiquity* 14(4): 431–448.

Guillén, Carlos, and Javier Barrio

1994   Los Pantanos de Villa y sus Aves. *Boletín de Lima* 16(91–96): 53–58.

Hecker, Giesela, and Wolfgang Hecker

1985   *Pacatnamú y sus construcciones, centro religioso prehispánico en la costa norte peruano.* Verlag Klaus Dieter Vervuert, Frankfurt.

Huapaya M., Cirilo

2007a Trabajos en Pachacamac [en la Laguna de Urpi Kocha]. In *Cuadernos de Investigación del Archivo Tello N° 5. Arqueología de Pachacámac: Excavaciones en Urpi Kocha y Urpi Wachac*, edited by Rafael Vega-Centeno, pp. 39–71. Museo de Arqueología y Antropología, Universidad Nacional Mayor de San Marcos, Lima.

2007b Diario de los Trabajos que se Realizan en las Ruinas de Pachacamac bajo la Dirección del Dr. Julio C. Tello. In *Cuadernos de Investigación del Archivo Tello N° 5. Arqueología de Pachacámac: Excavaciones en Urpi Kocha y Urpi Wachac*, edited by Rafael Vega-Centeno, pp. 73–83. Museo de Arqueología y Antropología, Universidad Nacional Mayor de San Marcos, Lima.

Hutchinson, Thomas

1873   *Two Years in Peru with Exploration of Its Antiquities.* Sampson Low, Marston, Low and Searle, London.

Jennings, Justin, and Edward R. Swenson (eds.)

2018   *Powerful Places in the Ancient Andes.* University of New Mexico Press, Albuquerque.

Jiménez Borja, Arturo

1985   Pachacamac. *Boletín de Lima* 7(38): 40–54.

Keatinge, Richard W.

1978   The Pacatnamu Textiles. *Archaeology* 31: 30–41.

Kosok, Paul

1965   *Life, Land and Water in Ancient Peru.* Long Island University Press, New York.

Kubler, George

1948   Towards Absolute Time: Guano Archaeology. In *Reappraisal of Peruvian Archaeology*, assembled by Wendell C. Bennett, pp. 29–50. Memoir of the Society for American Archaeology 4.

Lavallée, Danièle

1966 Una Colección de Cerámica de Pachacamac. *Revista del Museo Nacional* 34: 220–246.

Lindo, Asencios, and Rodolfo Gerbert

2019 Albert A. Giesecke Parthymüeller and the Preservation of the Painted Temple: Unpublished Documents Regarding Preservation in Pachacamac in 1938. *Intervención* 10(19): pp. 36–50. Mexico City.

Lockridge, Patricia A.

1985 *Tsunamis in Peru-Chile.* World Data Center for Solid Earth Geophysics, Report SE-39. Boulder, Colorado.

Mannheim, Bruce, and Guillermo Salas Carreño

2015 Wak'as: Entifications of the Andean Sacred. In *The Archaeology of Wak'as: Explorations of the Sacred in the Pre-Columbian Andes*, edited by Tamara Bray, pp. 47–76. University of Colorado Press, Boulder.

Marcone, Giancarlo

2000 El Complejo de los Adobitos y la Cultura Lima en el Santuario de Pachacamac. In *Huari y Tiwanaku: Modelos y Evidencias. Primera Parte*, edited by Peter Kaulicke and William H. Isbell, pp. 597–605. Boletín de Arqueología PUCP No. 4. Fondo Editorial de la Pontificia Universidad Católica del Perú.

2003 Los Murales del Templo Pintado o Relación entre el Santuario de Pachacamac y la Iconografía Tardía de la Costa Central Peruana. *Anales del Museo de América* 11: 57–80.

Mauricio, Ana C.

2018 Reassessing the Impact of El Niño at the End of the Early Intermediate Period from the Perspective of the Lima Culture. *Ñawpa Pacha; Journal of Andean Archaeology* 38(2): 203–231.

McAnany, Patricia A., and Norman Yoffee (eds.)

2010 *Questioning Collapse: Human Resilience, Ecological Vulnerability, and the Aftermath of Empire.* Cambridge University Press, Cambridge.

McCormack, F. Gerry, A. G. Hogg, P. G. Blackwell, C. E. Buck, T. F. G. Higham, and P. J. Reimer

2004 SHCal04 Southern Hemisphere Calibration 0–11.0 cal kyr BP. *Radiocarbon* 46: 1087–1092.

McEwan, Colin, and Tamara L. Bray

2015 Ordering the Sacred and Recreating Cuzco. *The Archaeology of Wak'as: Explorations of the Sacred in the Pre-Columbian Andes*, edited by Tamara Bray, pp. 265–292. University of Colorado, Boulder.

Menzel, Dorothy

1977 *The Archaeology of Ancient Peru and the Work of Max Uhle.* Robert H. Lowie Museum of Anthropology, University of California, Berkeley.

Middleton, Guy D.

2017 *Understanding Collapse: Ancient History and Modern Myths.* Cambridge University Press, Cambridge.

Morris, Craig, and Adriana Von Hagen

1993 *The Inka Empire and Its Andean Origins.* Abbeville Press, New York.

Muelle, Jorge C., and Robert Wells

1939 Las Pinturas del Templo de Pachacamac. *Revista del Museo Nacional* 8: 275–282.

Mujica, Elias

1991   Las lomas de Malanche: sociedades complejas en un medioambiente frágil. *L'imaginaire* 1(3): 61–70. Lima.

Nair, Stella, and Jean-Pierre Protzen

2015   The Inka Built Environment. In *The Inka Empire: A Multidisciplinary Approach,* edited by I. Shimada, pp. 215–231. University of Texas Press, Austin.

Netherly, Patricia

1977   Local Level Lords on the North Coast of Peru. University Microfilms International, Ann Arbor, Michigan.

Nials, Fred L., Eric E. Deeds, Michael E. Moseley, Shelia G. Pozorski, Thomas G. Pozorski, and Robert A. Feldman

1979   El Niño: The Catastrophic Flooding of Coastal Peru. *Field Museum of Natural History Bulletin* 50(7): 4–14 (part 1), 50(8): 4–10 (part 2).

Paredes B., Ponciano

1984   El Panel (Pachacamac): Nuevo tipo de Enterramiento. *Gaceta Arqueológica Andina* (10): 8–9.

1986   El Panel—Pachacamac. Nuevo Patrón de Enterramiento en la Tablada de Lurín. *Boletín de Lima* 44: 7–20.

Paredes, Ponciano, and Régulo Franco

1987   Pachacamac: Las Pirámides con Rampa, Cronología y Función. *Gaceta Arqueológica Andina* 4(13): 5–7.

Patterson, Thomas C.

1966   *Pattern and Process in the Early Intermediate Period Pottery of the Central Coast of Peru.* University of California Publications in Anthropology 3, Berkeley.

Pautrat, Lucila, and J. C. Riveros

1998   Evaluación de la Avifauna de los Pantanos de Villa, Lima. Los Pantanos de Villa, Biología y Conservación. *Museo de Historia Natural, UNMSM. Serie de Divulgación* (11): 85–95.

Pechenkina, Ekaterina, and Mercedes Delgado

2006   Dimensions of Health and Social Structure in the Early Intermediate Period Cemetery at Villa El Salvador, Peru. *American Journal of Physical Anthropology* 131: 218–235.

Rostworowski, María

1973   Urpay Huachac y el Símbolo del Mar. *Arqueología PUC* 13: 37–51.

1981   *Recursos naturales renovables y Pesca, Siglos XVI y XVII.* Instituto de Estudios Peruanos, Lima.

1983   *Estructuras Andinas del Poder: Ideología Religiosa y Política.* Instituto de Estudios Peruanos, Lima.

1992   *Pachacamac y el Señor de los Milagros: Una Trayectoria milenaria.* Instituto de Estudios Peruanos, Lima.

1999   *El Señorío de Pachacamac: El Informe de Rodrigo Cantos de Andrade de 1573.* Instituto de Estudios Peruanos, Lima.

2001   La religiosidad andina. In *Los dioses del antiguo Perú, Tomo 2,* edited by Krzysztof Makowski, pp. 185–221. Collección Arte y Tesoros del Perú. Banco de Crédito del Perú, Lima.

Rowe, John H.

1969   The Sunken Gardens of the Peruvian Coast. *American Antiquity* 34: 320–325.

Schreiber, Katharina J., and Josué Lancho

2003   *Irrigation and Society in the Peruvian Desert: The Puquios of Nasca.* Lexington Books, Lanham, Maryland.

Schwartz, Glenn M., and John J. Nichols (eds.)

2010   *After Collapse: The Regeneration of Complex Societies.* University of Arizona Press, Tucson.

Segura, Rafael A., and Izumi Shimada

2010   The Footprint of Wari on the Central Coast: A View from Cajamarquilla and Pachacamac. In *Beyond Wari Walls: Regional Perspectives on Middle Horizon Peru*, edited by Justin Jennings, pp. 113–135. University of New Mexico Press, Albuquerque.

Shimada, Izumi

1990   Cultural Continuities and Discontinuities on the Northern North Coast of Peru, Middle-Late Horizons. In *The Northern Dynasties. Kingship and Statecraft in Chimor*, edited by Michael E. Moseley and Alana Cordy-Collins, pp. 297–392. Dumbarton Oaks Research Library and Collection, Washington, D.C.

1994   *Pampa Grande and the Mochica Culture.* University of Texas Press, Austin.

2007   Las Prospecciones e Excavaciones en Urpi Kocha y Urpi Wachaq: Estudio Preliminar. In *Cuadernos de Investigación del Archivo Tello N° 5. Arqueología de Pachacámac: Excavaciones en Urpi Kocha y Urpi Wachac*, edited by Rafael Vega-Centeno, pp. 13–18. Museo de Arqueología y Antropología, Universidad Nacional Mayor de San Marcos, Lima.

Shimada, Izumi, John F. Merkel, Amy Szumilewicz, and Edinson Napa

2018   Ampliando nuestra comprensión holística de la metalurgia Sicán: excavación de un taller de oro en Huaca Loro, Perú. *Actas del II Congreso Nacional de Arqueología*, Vol. I, pp. 42–51. Ministerio de Cultura del Perú, Lima.

Shimada, Izumi, Crystal Schaaf, Lonnie Thompson, and Ellen Moseley-Thompson

1991   Cultural Impacts of Severe Droughts in the Prehistoric Andes: Application of a 1500-Year Ice Core Precipitation Record. *World Archaeology* 22(3): 247–270.

Shimada Izumi, Rafael Segura Llanos, María Rostworowski de Diez Canseco, and Hirokatsu Watanabe

2004   Una Nueva Evaluación de la Plaza de los Peregrinos de Pachacamac: Aportes de la Primera Campaña 2003 del Proyecto Arqueológico Pachacamac. In *Arqueología de la Costa Central del Perú en los Periodos Tardíos*, edited by Peter Eeckhout. Boletín del Instituto Francés de Estudios Andinos 33(3): 507–538.

Shimada Izumi, Rafael Segura Llanos, David J. Goldstein, Kelly J. Knudson, Melody J. Shimada, Ken-ichi Shinoda, Mai Takigami, and Ursel Wagner.

2010   Un Siglo después de Uhle: Reflexiones sobre la Arqueología de Pachacamac y Perú. In *Max Uhle: Evaluaciones de sus Investigaciones y Obras*, edited by Peter Kaulicke and Manuela Fischer, pp. 109–150. Fondo Editorial de la Pontificia Universidad Católica, Lima.

Shimada, Izumi, Rafael A. Segura, and Barbara Winsborough

2012   Pachacamac and Water: An Empirical Approach to the Origins, Significance, and Resilience of Pachacamac. Paper presented at the Pachacamac Sanctuary: Roundtable Workshop, November 30–December 1, 2012. Dumbarton Oaks, Washington, D.C.

Squier, E. George

1877   *Peru, Incidents of Travel and Exploration in the Land of the Incas.* Harper and Brothers, New York.

Stothert, Karen

1980　The Villa El Salvador Site and the Beginning of the Early Intermediate Period in the Lurín Valley, Peru. *Journal of Field Archaeology* 7: 279–295.

Stothert, Karen E., and Rogger Ravines

1977　Investigaciones Arqueológicas en Villa el Salvador. *Revista del Museo Nacional* 43: 157–226.

Strong, William D., and John M. Corbett

1943　A Ceramic Sequence at Pachacamac. In *Archaeological Studies in Peru, 1941–1942*, by William D. Strong, Gordon R. Willey, and John M. Corbett, pp. 27–122. Columbia University Studies in Archaeology and Ethnology, Vol. 1, No. 2. Columbia University Press, New York.

Thompson, L. G., E. Mosley-Thompson, J. F. Bolzan, and B. R. Koci

1985　A 1500-Year Record of Tropical Precipitation in Ice Cores from the Quelccaya Ice Cap, Peru. *Science* 229: 971–973.

Thompson, L. G., E. Mosley-Thompson, P. M. Grootes, M. Pourchet, and S. Hastenrath

1984　Tropical Glaciers: Potential for Ice Core Paleoclimatic Reconstructions. *Journal of Geophysical Research* 89(D3): 4638–4646.

Ubbelohde-Doering, Heinrich

1967　*On the Royal Highways of the Inca: Civilizations of Ancient Peru.* Praeger, New York.

Uhle, Max

1991 [1903]　*Pachacamac: A Reprint of the 1903 Edition by Max Uhle.* University Museum Monograph 62. University Museum of Archaeology and Anthropology, University of Pennsylvania Philadelphia.

Von Hagen, Adriana, and Craig Morris

1998　*The Cities of the Ancient Andes.* Thames and Hudson, London.

Walker, Charles F.

2008　*Shaky Colonialism: The 1746 Earthquake-Tsunami in Lima, Peru, and Its Long Aftermath.* Duke University Press, Durham, North Carolina.

Weismantel, Mary

2018　Cuni Raya Superhero: Ontologies of Water on Peru's North Coast. In *Powerful Places in the Ancient Andes*, edited by Tamara Bray, pp. 175–208. University of Colorado Press, Boulder.

Winsborough, Barbara, Izumi Shimada, Lee A. Newsom, John Jones, and Rafael A. Segura

2012　Paleoenvironmental Catastrophies on the Peruvian Coast Revealed in Lagoon Sediment Cores from Pachacamac. *Journal of Archaeological Science* 39(3): 602–614.

Wright, Kenneth R., Gordon F. McEwan, and Ruth Wright

2006　*Tipón: Water Engineering Masterpiece of the Inca Empire.* American Society of Civil Engineers, Reston, Virginia.

4

In the Pit of the Bi-Headed Serpent

Lurín and Pachacamac under the Lima Culture

GIANCARLO MARCONE

There are two influential articles (Eeckhout 2004; Kaulicke 2000) that use the idea of the Central Coast being "under" the shadow of Pachacamac during pre-Hispanic times. However, this simile does not just refer to the idea that the site could have had a central role in pre-Hispanic social development, it also refers to how we tend to understand the sociopolitical development of the region based on what we can reconstruct with the limited evidence at Pachacamac (a monumental site).

Despite how partial the data is, the interpretations of the political development of the Central Coast had the Pachacamac site as a starter point. So, not surprisingly, they ended up pointing to the site as one of the principal centers of the region with an active role in the development of the Central Coast, especially the Lurín Valley.

This idea used the particularities of Pachacamac to generalize a process of social transformation in the Lurín Valley that is far from the reality of the valley, which in fact looks small and unimpressive. The understanding of the Lima presence in the Lurín Valley was such a case. We have limited knowledge of the development outside the site, which make us biased to its monumentality as the capital of the Lima presence in the region, although recently the discussion of the Lurín Valley sociopolitical processes during the Early Intermediate and Middle Horizon is rising (Makowski and Vallenas 2015; Marcone 2015; Marcone and López-Hurtado 2015).

In recent years, scholars studying political power in ancient societies have been calling increasingly for the need to take a relational perspective concerning how power is constructed and negotiated in societies (Halperin and Foias 2010; McGuire 2008; Tilley 2001). This relational perspective conceives political power as the result of the practice of social relations between individuals and collectivities. In this framework, the understanding of social relations is the key component in reconstructing power configurations in ancient societies. But these social relations only have meaning if they are understood in relation to the wider context of the society as a whole. Therefore, it is necessary to understand how these relations cut across social scales and groups.

We think that both the monumental elite site of Pachacamac and the small rural sites of the Lurín Valley, as well as the comparison with neighboring valleys, together tell us a better story, one where elite context and evidence of daily life are integrated.

The present chapter explores the nature of the Lima culture presence in the Lurín Valley and its relation with the Pachacamac Sanctuary. Specifically, this chapter asks how the presence of Lima social and culture organizations were at the same time cause and effect of the growth of the Pachacamac site in the region, and at what level the history of the Lima culture is related to the history and functions of the site. Whatever we can infer from this relationship will help us to understand Andean sanctuaries in general and also to characterize the understudied Lima culture.

Based on the results of my excavation in both Pachacamac's Adobitos compound and the site of Lote B in the lower Lurín Valley, only 10 km away from Pachacamac, this chapter seeks to reconstruct a regional scenario of the Lima culture and its presence in Lurín at the Early Intermediate and the start of the Middle Horizon that successfully integrated the valley and the site. Both of these interventions revealed evidence of a process of political centralization on the go by the start of the Middle Horizon. This process, linked with the increased presence of the Lima culture's political formation in the valley, brought new levels of sociopolitical organization to the region.

What possible roles did Pachacamac play in the sociopolitical developments of the Lurín Valley and the Central Coast during the Early Intermediate and the start of the Middle Horizon? What was the scale of influence of Pachacamac before and after these processes of centralization? Our initial data showed that although the sanctuary was likely used as a door to the Lurín Valley for the Lima, their role was more likely of a ceremonial center irradiating prestige and cultural values, than a centralized capital or center of the valley (Burger and Salazar, this volume). This chapter seeks to show that this situation changed by the start of the Middle Horizon where Lima presence showed signs of increasing centralization in the valley and the site grew in importance not only locally, but also regionally.

In this way, this chapter seeks to depart from traditional approaches to the Lurín Valley that tend to reconstruct the history of the valley from the Pachacamac reconstructions. On a deeper level, the chapter seeks to develop an example of a contextual reconstruction of a period that allows understanding political and economic relationships between segments of society.

The "Lima Culture" on the Peruvian Central Coast

What is known as the "Lima culture" is a long ceramic tradition that lasts at least six centuries (circa AD 50–800, between the Early Intermediate and Middle Horizon periods of Andean chronology). This ceramic tradition, which is dominated by a particular design identified as interlocking (a bi-headed serpent), is spread over the Peruvian Central Coast. The extent to which a political entity corresponds to this ceramic tradition is still a matter

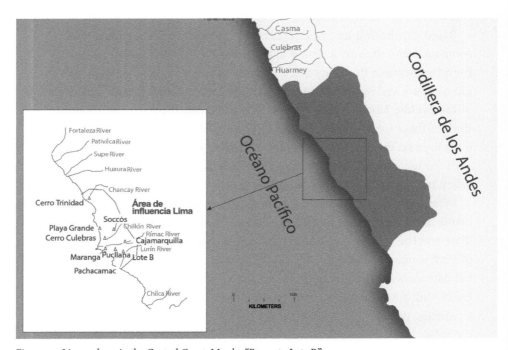

Figure 4.1. Lima culture in the Central Coast. Map by "Proyecto Lote B."

of debate, but the known settlement hierarchies—with monumental sites like Playa Grande, Maranga, and Cajamarquilla that cover several hectares composed of public buildings and domestic structures, sites of medium size with monumental architecture like Huaca Pucllana, and several small domestic sites dispersed through the valleys (Marcone 2015) sharing this ceramic tradition—indicate that the Lima culture roughly corresponds to a state-level political formation. How was this society organized? And how did this social arrangement transform over time? These questions have been poorly answered since the focus on stylistic discussion that characterized the Lima culture studies remains until today.

Pachacamac, the Lima Culture, and the Beginning of Archaeology in Peru

In 1886, Max Uhle (1903) started a large-scale project in the Pachacamac Sanctuary on the Peruvian Central Coast. This research is believed by many to be the first scientific excavation in Andean archaeology and a landmark in the formation of archaeology as a scholarly discipline in the Andean region (Rowe 1998; Schaedel 1993; Shimada 1991). Based on materials recovered in Pachacamac, Uhle posited the existence of a society that he called "proto-Lima" as an antecedent of the greater civilization of Tiahuanaco in the "Lima" region. From that moment, and for the decades that followed, the study of the Lima culture had a central role in Andean archaeology. Several pioneer figures of Andean archaeology worked on the Central Coast studying the Lima culture: Alfred Kroeber (1926a, 1954), William D. Strong (1925; Strong and Corbett 1943), Gordon R. Willey (1943), Julio C. Tello (Marcone 2010b), Luis Villar Cordova (1935), and Louis M. Stumer (1953, 1954a, 1954b, 1956).

However, by the mid-1950s interest in the study of the Lima culture waned, and other areas (like Moche or Nazca) gained more popularity with archaeologists and the general public. Despite the fine ceramics associated with the Lima culture and the impressive monumentality of their buildings, the society came to be progressively undervalued in the reconstruction of the regional scenario of the ancient Andes. This progressive disinterest came in part as a consequence of the aggressive growth of the present-day city of Lima. The advancement, in turn, made it necessary to redirect resources to protect the more "valuable" monuments (elite centers). As a consequence, the reconstructions were biased toward a particular segment of society, preventing a clear picture of Lima's social organization in its entirety.

After the 1950s, the most important work in the area was carried out by Patterson in 1966. In recent years the study of the Lima culture has been revamped intellectually (that is, Flores 2005; Mauricio et al. 2014; Mauricio and Prieto 2015; Mogrovejo 1999; Mogrovejo and Segura 2000; Rios and Ccencho 2009; Segura 2001, 2004), but this increase in research does not mean an increased interest in reconstructing social organization. We are still focused on proving the limitations of the stylistic, chronological sequences (especially Patterson 1966) and challenging its temporal reconstruction (Escobedo and Goldhausen 1999; Falcon 2003; Kaulicke 2000; Segura 2004).

Chronology

Initially, archaeologists working in the area recognized in the ceramic style of this cultural development two stylistic phases, which they equate with two major chronological periods in the Lima sequence (that is, Kroeber 1926a; Kroeber 1954; Strong and Corbett 1943; Stumer 1953; Willey 1943). They identified these periods with different names like Playa Grande, Interlocking, Proto Lima, and Maranga (Flores 1981; Kaulicke 2000; Patterson 1966). Despite this apparent confusion, in 1953 within the framework of the "Terminology Round Table of Peruvian Archaeology," researchers working in the area agreed to use the terms Playa Grande and Maranga as the valid names for the Early and Late phases of the Lima culture ceramic style (Escobedo and Goldhausen 1999).

As discussed above, Thomas Patterson (1966) redefined these two period divisions of the Lima style. He subdivides the Lima style into nine consecutive phases and relates them with John Rowe's master sequence for the whole Andean region (Earle 1972: Table 1; Patterson 1966).

Although current agreement that Patterson seriation represents an overdivision of a ceramic style that is rather homogenous and continuous (Escobedo and Goldhausen 1999; Segura 2004), authors still use it as a general framework, regrouping Patterson's phases into Early, Middle, and Late Lima periods (Escobedo and Goldhausen 1999; Falcon 2003; Goldhausen 2001; Segura 2004).

Lima Culture Social Organization

It had been proposed that the Central Coast experienced a process of population growth during the Early Intermediate period (Earle 1972; Silva 1992).

This growth was concomitant with the increase of the agricultural frontier to levels that resemble present-day capacities (Silva 1992, 1996; Stumer 1954b). It was during this time that the first manifestations of the Lima culture in the region appeared. Sites associated with Lima culture materials were initially centered in the northern valleys (Chancay and Chillón rivers) of the Central Coast, progressively moving south, and by the end of the Lima sequences, centered in the Rímac Valley (Kaulicke 2000; Stumer 1954a).

Social differences within the organization of this culture are recognizable, at least from the middle phase of its development. These social differences are reflected in a settlement pattern with at least three tiers of sites (Silva 1996; Patterson et al. 1982). The first tier of sites, located principally in the plain valley floors of the lower Chillón and Rímac valleys, are composed of a compound of structures with a mud-brick public building at the center. The second tier of sites corresponds to slightly smaller sites in close proximity to the first-tier sites, and also presents a clumping of residential structures, but they lack any monumental architecture. The third-tier sites correspond to a clearly different settlement pattern. A pattern of dispersed sites composed of a few residential structures scattered over the slopes flanking the narrow valley floor of the *chaupiyunga* (the buffer zone between the coastal lower valley and the middle valley, with more highland-like cultural and ecological characteristics) of the Chillón and Rímac valleys and the Lurín Valley.

The monumental buildings are impressive structures of several meters high, built with mud-bricks, and generally painted in yellow and/or with decorative mud-friezes in Lima culture style over their walls. It is not clear if these monumental buildings had secular or religious functions (likely both) or if one of these sites held the position of overall center or capital.

Among the dispersed settlements of the third tier, not all are the same. There are sites that present more quantities of highly decorated ceramics in Lima style, a privileged location (usually at the highest part of the hill), and preferred building materials. Based on this evidence, it has been proposed that they belong to rural elites, with influence in the surrounding dispersed settlements (Dillehay 1979; Earle 1972; Marcone 2010b). By the end of the Lima culture temporal sequence, some of these hilltop sites present new rectangular structures of Lima filiations (that is, Dillehay 1979; Earle 1972; Guerrero and Palacios 1994), evidence of a process of increased centralization that ends with the political incorporation of these dispersed settlements in a multivalley polity (Stumer 1954a: 144).

Other evidence that speaks to a deep social-political transformation during the last century of this cultural development is: the increase in the number and monumentality of the sites; an important stylistic change in ceramics decoration—from figurative designs of "serpent" heads to more stylized representations of the same motif (I will refer to these styles as Middle and Late Lima from this point forward [Playa Grande to Maranga or Middle Lima to Late Lima]); changes in burial practices; and the appearance of a foreign (Wari)–influenced ceramic style present in relation to elite burials and sites with monumental architecture. For some archaeologists these transformations are indications of the emergence of a state-level society on the Peruvian Central Coast around this time (that is, Dillehay 1979; Earle 1972; Kaulicke 2000; Patterson et al. 1982; Stumer 1954a).

Lima in Lurín

The moment and nature of the Lima expansion to the Lurín Valley remain poorly understood. According to one hypothesis (Makowski 2002), the population in Lurín was organized regionally into a system of kin-based chiefdoms. These chiefdoms were incorporated into Lima's cultural sphere of influence during the Early to Middle phases of this culture. This hypothesis is built principally upon evidence recovered in the monumental site of Pachacamac and a handful of burials (Makowski 2002).

An alternative hypothesis sees Lima's cultural presence in the valley as a relatively late phenomenon, more or less corresponding with the emergence of the peristate society discussed above, and bringing unification to the Lurín population, which was previously dispersed and lacked centralized political organization. This hypothesis was constructed mainly using data from surveys and superficial ceramics (Earle 1972; Patterson et al. 1982).

The main difference in the reconstruction between these two sets of hypotheses is the thought that the Lima culture presence in the Lurín Valley was earlier and had some degree of centralization from the beginning. The first hypothesis shows a complete integrated Lurín population into the Lima culture milieu by Middle Lima times. The second hypothesis shows more independent groups having indirect ties with the Lima elites from the Rímac-Chillón valleys, until late in the Lima sequence where the presence of Lima was in the form of a state.

The first hypothesis put too much weight on ceramics-stylistics evidence and stylistic sequences, sometimes equating the presence of one or the other style as a direct indication of political manifestations and social developments. In this way the scattered presence of Middle Lima ceramics in the Lurín Valley is proof enough of the political presence of this society in it. Following Makowski's (2002) ideas—despite the lack of major evidence of centralization in Middle Lima times in the Lurín Valley—there was a cohesive Lima-culture political system during this period. There is not enough evidence to support the noncentralization/centralization proposed by Makowski, even if we try to discuss these political formations and their changes in terms of a "power system," "religious ceremonial centers," or "kinship lineages," as proposed by him. These lines of evidence are too speculative and we do not have enough reliable evidence for those in the archaeological record. The presence of these Middle Lima ceramics is an indication of contact between the regions, but any other relation need not be assumed, rather it needs to be confirmed by other archaeological data. Usually the risk of comparing the presence of a style with the presence of a political formation in the Lurín Valley is the result of the idea that because a Pachacamac building presented Middle Lima ceramics, the site necessarily had importance and a central role in Lima presence (see Makowski and Vallenas 2015 for support of this idea).

The only article dealing with the settlement pattern in the valley for the Early Intermediate Period is the one by Patterson et al. 1982). This is an example of the pioneering use of computers to organize and synthesize archaeological data, kind of an early GIS attempt (Patterson et al. 1982). In view of this goal, the article had clear shortcomings in the presentation of the archaeological materials. The low resolution of the article's maps makes it impossible to identify site locations and it relies too much on a rigid chronology of nine phases, which has recently been rejected, at least partially, by researchers working in the Central Coast region (with the exception of Makowski 2015, who still defends the functionality of the sequence). Nevertheless, if we complement this article with the review of Patterson's survey field notes (Patterson [1966]), we can see that Patterson did not find monumental architecture of Middle Lima times in the Lurín Valley, with the exception of Pachacamac. We can also see that there were several small sites without decorated pottery around the agriculture frontier. Patterson, in his article of 1982, made identification of the sites conform to his own proposal of a chronological scheme by comparing ceramic shapes between decorated and nondecorated fragments. Patterson, in his article of 1982, made the identification of the sites conform to his own chronological scheme by comparing ceramic shapes between decorated and nondecorated fragments. In line with this evidence, we think that the Middle Lima occupation in the Lurín Valley is not as strong as is the Late Lima period. By contrast we can see in it an increase in monumental architecture and the presence of more Lima-decorated ceramics. This process is similar to the process reported for the Chillón and Chancay valleys and the middle part of the Rímac and Chillón valleys.

Lima in Pachacamac

The oracle function of Pachacamac is best known from ethnohistoric sources. The nature, role, and character that the sanctuary had in Late pre-Hispanic times have been projected into earlier times. So, for example, it has been argued that Pachacamac was an Early Intermediate sanctuary co-opted by the Wari Empire, from which the empire based its expansion throughout the Central Coast (Glowacki and Malpass 2003; Menzel 1964). This idea almost mimics the situation of the sanctuary in Inca times as described by the written sources. Examination shows that there is actually little that we can really say about the Lima Period at Pachacamac.

The evidence of Lima Period occupation at the site can be divided into three types: (1) burials, most of which were uncovered by early archaeologists or looters, and for which, good contextual information is mostly absent; (2) monumental architecture in the central area of the sanctuary, including the "old temple of Pachacamac," the "Urpiwachac" temple, and other structures; and (3) the dearth of monumental structures located in the western part of the site, the best known of these being the Complex of the Adobitos. These less monumental structures have been proposed to have served as secondary temples, or as administrative structures oriented to more secular activities than those performed at the larger central temples. The "little mudbrick compound" was initially explored in 1968 by Jiménez Borja and Alberto Bueno (Bueno 1982), and I excavated there in 2000 (Marcone 2000, 2010b).

The "Old Temple of Pachacamac" is traditionally viewed as the main building at the site during the Lima occupation. Archaeologists have identified three phases of construction, falling in the later part of the Early Intermediate Period, before the temple was abandoned in favor of new temples during the Middle Horizon (Franco Jordan and Paredes 2000; Shimada 1991).

The Old Temple was connected by a platform to another Lima Period mound buried underneath the Inca-constructed Temple of the Sun. The first to report this earlier mound was Uhle, and the observation was confirmed years later by Strong and Corbett (1943; Shimada 1991). According to the analysis of Patterson, this mound under the Temple of the Sun would belong to Phase 7 of his stylistic sequence (Patterson 1966), roughly corresponding to the Late Lima phase. Another building traditionally assigned to the Lima culture in the sanctuary is the Temple of Urpiwachac. This building bordered the pre-Hispanic Lagoon of Urpiwachac, along the west side of the site. Ponciano Paredes (1991) has also chronologically placed this temple in the Late Lima phase.

Despite the presence of small amounts of Early/Middle Lima–phase ceramics at Pachacamac, especially in the lower levels of the Old Temple, it is not until the Late Lima phase that the site begins to take on monumental dimensions. The secondary structures like the "little mud-brick compound" will have been constructed during this Late Lima time and represent an expansion of Lima occupation at the site.

The "Little Mud-Brick Compound"

As said above, to the northwest of the sanctuary, there were several nondomestic structures that include the "little mud-brick compound." Today these structures are covered by sand and it is difficult to appreciate them from the surface. In 2000, as part of Pachacamac site museum activities, a portion of this complex was excavated (Marcone 2000a). The goal of the project was to gain exposition areas for the visitors to the sanctuary and complement the excavation of Bueno in the 1960s (Bueno 1982). After the first layers it was possible to distinguish a structure built of *adobitos* (little mud-bricks) walls and earthen tamped floors.

Excavation showed at least three moments of reoccupation of the building. After the initial occupation, the walls were dismantled and the floor covered with a wide layer of sand. Over this filling a new floor was built and new *adobitos* walls were built, but without transforming significantly the layout of the building. The ceramics recovered in these three constructive moments were similar and identified as Late Lima (Marcone 2000a, 2010b). The ceramic assemblages initially excavated in the 1960s by Jiménez Borja and Bueno had been studied by Lavallée (1966), who determined that the ceramics closely resembled those found in the Rímac Valley. The ceramic fragments that Lavallée (1966) published are possible to identify also as Late Lima. The ceramics recovered in direct association with the compound, both by me and by Borja and Bueno, do not show any nonlocal or highland styles (Lavallée 1966; Marcone 2000a). This assemblage has a high component of bottles, *cantimploras* (canteens), and jars. There are also a large number of decorated dishes.

Based on the ceramic associations, reuse of building materials, and the relative continuity in architectural layout, I believe that the little mud-brick compound at Pachacamac was constructed and remodeled in a relatively short span of time (Marcone 2000a, 2010a). These characteristics suggest intensified activity at the site in the Late Lima phase, which I link to the incorporation of the site (and the Lurín Valley as a whole) into an overarching Lima system (Marcone 2000a, 2010a). I have proposed elsewhere that the activities carried out in the *adobitos* complex were feasting activities, with ritualized distribution of food acting to create social debts, and oriented toward obtaining labor and support from commoners (Marcone 2010a, 2010b, 2015).

The building explosion in Pachacamac is more or less contemporaneous with the last occupational phase (Late Lima) at Lote B and with the construction of the majority of the extant public structures known for the sanctuary (Marcone 2010b).

Lote B in the Lurín Lower Valley

Lote B, also known as Cerro Manchay, is located in the lower Lurín Valley, on the summit of a hill overlooking the Manchay "quebrada" pass connecting the Lurín and Rímac valleys. It was first recorded as a site (#PV48–145) in the Patterson survey (Patterson et al. 1982). The site can be divided on the basis of topography and surface architecture into four sectors. Sectors 1 and 2 represent a compound of domestic architecture. Sector 3 contains a rectangular, nondomestic architectural unit that combines small rooms with large patio areas. Sector 4 contains another nondomestic architectural complex, likely for storage, with smaller rooms and a restricted access.

The excavations in 2009 identified at least two occupations. The first occupation was identified in the summit of Cerro Manchay (Sectors 1 and 2) and corresponds to a residential compound of a group of a relatively high social position in the valley. By the time of the second occupation, the layout of the site was transformed where the buildings of Sectors 3 and 4 were built. These buildings, public in nature, were contemporaneous with the last occupation

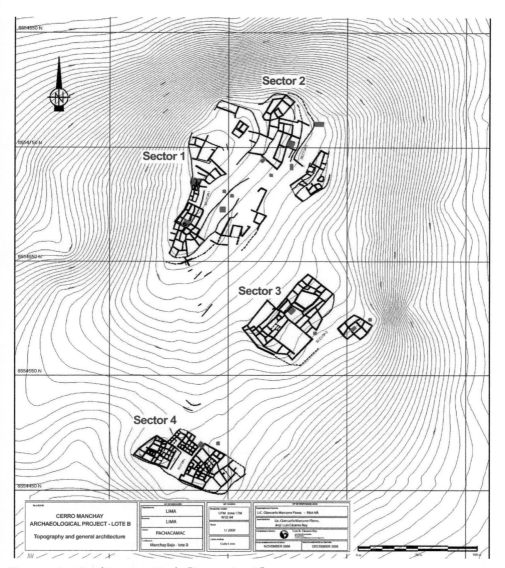

Figure 4.2. Lote B and its sectors. Map by "Proyecto Lote B."

of the summit. The addition of the public buildings came not with the abandonment of the residential compound, it actually came with an increase in activities.

The presence of these storage areas, public buildings, and highly decorated ceramics in domestic spaces suggests that Lote B was a settlement of a relatively prestigious and powerful group in the valley. The commoners' settlements that would have been associated with Lote B would likely have been scattered, in a relatively dispersed way, at the base of the hill, overlooking the river plain. Patterson's survey in the 1960s around the foot of the hill recorded thin artifact scatters, lacking stone architecture, including his sites #149, 151, 152, 154, and 155 (Patterson et al. 1982). The small size of these sites, the presence of grinding stones, and a few decorated sherds caused Patterson's team to identify them as domestic structures (Patterson [1966]). Patterson and his colleagues thought that this distribution of sites was a change in the settlement pattern of the valley over time where the population progressively moved uphill as the agricultural frontier expanded (Earle 1972; Patterson et al. 1982).

The long sequence found at the summit challenges the idea that these different locations over the hill correspond to temporal differences. Following the brief description in Patterson's field notes about these sites, we propose that the differences in the quantities of decorated ceramics reported and their position on the lower slopes could correspond to differences in social and/or economic status. Sadly, their lower position had made these structures more affected by the present-day presence of populations and a modern road that connects the lower and middle valley.

As a working hypothesis, we propose that the domestic compound corresponds to the location of a small elite group with limited power or leverage over several dispersed small domestic settlements placed over the lower slopes of the hill, through the management of the feasting activities. By the time of the last occupation—associated with Late Lima ceramics—the increase of the feasting activities, storage facilities, and the improvement of building materials could imply that the inhabitants of this compound fortified a leadership position by the end of the Early Intermediate. Paradoxically, with this apparent improvement of the architecture of the domestic compound, there is evidence in Sectors 3 and 4 that suggests this group lost some of the prestige associated with their leadership during Late Lima times. The construction by outsiders of two buildings with public functions just a few meters under the summit compound implies a challenge to the authority and independence of this group. Sector 3 building, for example, was built with stone and mud mortar and covered with a mud plaster painted in bright yellow. Similar painted buildings have been reported for other Lima sites (Flores 2005; Franco 1993; Franco & Paredes 2000). For example, in the Huaca Pucllana in the Rímac Valley (Flores 2005), it has been determined that the last

Lima occupation of the main building was characterized by its being painted a similar yellow color. This paint and the layout of the Lote B, Sector 3, building suggest a strong Lima pattern in the construction of this building and allow us to infer an increased centralization and direct control of a Lima polity. The exclusive Late Lima ceramics association of this sector and the yellow paint in the building similar to the edifications in the Rímac Valley suggest that those responsible for the construction of these buildings came from outside the community of Lote B.

The rectangular building of Sector 4 is composed of two compounds of small rooms separated by a plaza. Each of these rooms also presents several subdivisions. Our excavation proves that these subdivisions were small storage rooms. It is likely that the entire building was dedicated to storage activities. This building was constructed over an area that was used as burial grounds. The burials predate the new building and we believe they correspond to the period of transition between Middle Lima (at the end of the Early Intermediate) and the Late Lima (early Middle Horizon) political organization of the state. The buildings will represent the advent of the state to the local setting. These burials were both made in traditional Lima extended style, and we thought they showed a survival of local traditions expressed in traditional Lima style of extended burials (Marsteller and Marcone 2012).

These burials present two distinctive styles, although the individuals were of similar ages (less than two years of age). In the first burial style, the body is in an extended, prone, or supine position with a cane litter or *estera* above and/or below the body; this type of burial is characteristic of classic Lima-style burials excavated throughout the Central Coast region (for example, Jijón y Caamaño 1949: 95; Sestieri 1971: 102; Stumer 1953: 46; Stumer 1954b: 221).

The second burial style at Lote B occurs as a flexed bundle. In these burials, the body is in a seated and flexed position, wrapped into a bundle with simple cotton textiles secured with small vegetal fiber ropes. This is a traditional style in the Lurín Valley dating to at least the Late Formative Period (Makowski 2002; Pechenkina and Delgado 2006; Stothert and Ravines 1977) that reappears again in the Middle Horizon throughout the Central Coast (DeLeonardis and Lau 2004; Menzel 1964). Excavations at Lote B have so far failed to recover a single Wari- or Nievería-style sherd to suggest the choice of traditional bundle-style burial resulted from Wari influence (Marsteller and Marcone 2012).

Comparison of Ceramics Sites

As noted, Lote B contains relatively high quantities of decorated sherds, especially for a site with a significant domestic component. Despite this difference in size and social scale, the decoration on pottery from Lote B assemblages differs little from assemblages published for Lima monumental sites such as: Pachacamac (Marcone 2000b, 2010b; Patterson 1966; Strong and Corbett 1943), Maranga (Jijon y Caamaño 1949; Kroeber 1954; Olivera 2009), and Cajamarquilla (Gayton 1926; Segura 2001) in the Rímac Valley; and Cerro Trinidad and other Lima sites in the Chancay Valley (Kroeber 1926b, Willey 1943). The Lima-style material we recovered from the lower and middle levels in our excavations at Lote B is sufficiently similar to that from the monumental sites that there is no reason to believe that the Lote B material was not produced in the same context or that it was an imitation, although the circuit of production and distribution of Lima ceramics is still a pending task.

The abundant decorated ceramics at this mid-level site, and the stylistic congruence to pottery from monumental sites in the core area of the Lima culture's political development, suggest that the circulation, use, and iconography of these ceramics played a role in the integration of this society, and/or were important items of social affiliation and distinction.

The biggest difference between the ceramic assemblages from the main monumental Lima site and Lote B in terms of the decoration is the lack of Nievería-style ceramics. This Nievería style, once thought of as post-Lima, in fact has been shown to co-occur with Late Lima–style ceramics at several monumental sites. Yet this style is completely absent from Lote B and from the little mud-brick compound of Pachacamac. One possibility is that Lote B was outside the circulation pattern of this pottery or that the activities for which this pottery was used at the major center of the Rímac Valley were not replicated at Lote B or Pachacamac. In this case, we think it is safe to propose that the distribution of Nievería ceramics was secondary to the distribution of Lima-style ceramics in the progressive centralization of the Lurín Valley. This is consistent with the pattern of inclusionary feasting described for Lote B and the little mud-brick.

A more comprehensive and quantitative comparison of the Lote B ceramic assemblages with those from other Lima sites (including the centers) is very difficult, based on what has been published. Most of these publications present only limited information on the frequency or proportion of the formal ceramic categories recognized within the assemblages. In addition, the definition of these categories is not always clear, nor comparable among sites and researchers.

Nevertheless, we still made this comparison with the limitations of sample size, context, and analyses between the different assemblages (see Table 4.1, hosted by the University of Florida Digital Collections: http://ufdc.ufl.edu/AA00087976/00001). This information is a starting point for a more systematic future analysis, but it does hint at some general tendencies. First, bottles make up low proportions of the assemblages at every site but are more abundant in cemetery contexts. The definitive design elements for the Lima style have largely been drawn from goblets and bottles, perhaps because these are more likely to be recovered complete from tombs. Burial excavations also represented the initial research focus in Lima culture archaeology. In sum, most of the canon of Lima decorative style has been based on two pottery forms that make up a small proportion of the Lima pottery assemblage.

Second, Lote B displays a relatively high proportion of plates. This difference could be because the Lote B excavations included more "domestic" components, and plates, which are an easily recognized form, are often without decoration. Therefore, the bias toward decorated pottery in the investigation at the other Lima sites might account for the relative under-representation of plates at these sites. Relatively higher proportions of plates also occur at the Adobitos Compound, and in the lateral structures of Huaca 20 (Mac Kay and Santa Cruz 2000; Mauricio 2015). As discussed previously, these buildings likely served a secondary or complementary function to the main mounds at the respective centers and are consistent with an exclusionary feasting pattern. The mounds themselves, at Cajamarquilla or Maranga, yielded substantially lower proportions of plates, but higher proportions of jars and pots with necks. The latter vessels are more likely to have been used in connection with liquid contents, while plates and shallow bowls are more suitable for solid foods.

I have proposed elsewhere (Marcone 2010b) that at least two distinct feasting patterns coexisted in Lima society. In one pattern, associated with the main mounds and adjacent plazas, jars and pots were used to serve chicha, followed by the intentional, ceremonial breaking of these vessels. This pattern, and its diacritical feasting character (Dietler and Hayden 2010 sensus), have been clearly described for Cajamarquilla by Segura (2001), and reported for other sites like Maranga and Pucllana (Rios 2015) in the Rímac Valley. The second feasting pattern was spatially associated with secondary structures at monumental sites. In these contexts, where plates (and by extension, food serving) are more heavily represented, we are proposing this assemblage to represent more inclusive feasting practices.

If these initial conclusions hold after a more comprehensive analysis of the proportions of forms among different sites, we can propose that the activities held at the secondary buildings of monumental sites—like the little mud-brick compound—resemble those activities, even mimic or replicate, those conducted at secondary sites, such as Lote B. This would be significant in upholding important sociopolitical changes even with the emergence of a Lima State in the Central Coast. The rituals carried out in Pachacamac were emulated at the local settlement, as at Lote B, and became a link between the regional political economy of the Lima state and the local.

The "Chaupiyungas" and the Continuous Increase of Lima Presence

Similar processes of increased centralization have been reported for other valleys. In the chaupiyungas (buffer zone between the low and middle course of the valley) of the Rímac and Chillón valleys, researchers have recognized evidence of an expansion of Lima polities to the upper parts that is concomitant with the process of centralization detailed above.

In these chaupiyunga areas, the process of centralization is linked with Late Lima ceramics and the construction of new public buildings of rectangular shape, in areas that before were exclusively built for domestic structures. For example, Guerrero and Palacios (1994) briefly studied several village sites in the chaupiyunga of the Rímac Valley. They excavated at El Vallecito and Huampani. They refer to social differences inside the El Vallecito settlement, based on the presence in Sector C of a rectangular building with more elaborate architecture (plastered walls) and larger internal rooms (Guerrero and Palacios 1994: 280). The authors believe this rectangular building could have served public functions, and the surrounding dwellings would likely have been the higher status inhabitants of the site (Guerrero and Palacios 1994: 306–308).

In the Chillón Valley's chaupiyunga, Tom Dillehay notes a transformation in a settlement call Huancayo Alto late in the Early Intermediate Period, with the construction of a "coastal style adobe multiroom secular building" (associated with Lima ceramics in Maranga style or Late Lima style, together with "elaborate coastal-style textiles"), at the same time as the building of a set of circular dwellings (lacking associated Lima-style pottery) representing highland colonists (Dillehay 1979: 27). Dillehay proposes that the building had secular administrative functions (Dillehay 1979). Dillehay further proposes social differences between the new highland inhabitants of Huancayo Alto, and the coastal-affiliated population already living there. Dillehay proposes that the coastal population corresponded to coastal administrators with a high social status (Dillehay 1979: 29). For Dillehay, the coexistence of two adobe administrative buildings associated with such different ceramic assemblages, together with the expansion of storage facilities at the site, indicates a "social and political dual structure functioning at the site" (Dillehay 1979: 28).

A few kilometers away from Huancayo Alto is Soccos, a site with another rectangular, nondomestic building associated with domestic terraces and structures. Based on ceramics and textile fragments recovered from the surface and from the rectangular building, and from what they viewed as the orthogonal layout of the structure with interior storage rooms, Isla and Guerrero (1987) argue that the site represents the incorporation of the area into the Wari polity (Jennings and Craig 2001; Schreiber 2001). However, Silva (1992) has pointed out correctly that the material found on the surface has at best a weak association with the domestic structures and the rectangular building. The Middle Horizon materials are rare and likely come from burial contexts. Also, the Middle Horizon materials correspond to the Middle Horizon 3 and 4, a time after the imperial expansion of Wari. In addition, the published surface assemblages include fragments from different periods, such as Lima, Late Middle Horizon, and Late Intermediate Period. In comparison with these other sites, we suggest that Soccos is part of the Lima centralization, which includes the construction of buildings like those in Huancayo Alto or el Vallecito. The construction of the new buildings and the change of the layout of the site is contemporaneous with the transformation identified in Lote B, and we think they are related to the same process of political centralization.

Scenarios of Possible Relation between Pachacamac and the Lurín Valley at Lima Times

Lote B, as we propose here, shows clear evidence of the existence of a process of political centralization in the Lurín Valley, concomitant with a process of political change in the whole region corresponding to the late part of the Lima cultural sequence, starting with the Middle Horizon. So, our main question arises: What role did the site of Pachacamac play in this social-political reorganization of the valley and the region?

One possible answer is that the site of Pachacamac had a central role in this process of political centralization. The site will become a regional center, one of the important centers or capital of the Lima culture development, as important as other major sites in the Rímac Valley, like Maranga or Cajamarquilla. If so, it would imply that independently of the level of political complexity, the valley was part of the Lima culture core area. Pachacamac would be an important part of a regional arena. Pachacamac would act first as a center of the Lima tradition in the valley and control its population directly. Expect a direct correspondence or similarity between the material culture of both sites, Pachacamac and Lote B. Therefore, in order to have highly decorated ceramics, like the ones in Lote B, they should come from or through the networks with Pachacamac at the center.

A second possible answer is that the site of Pachacamac became part of the Lima mileu only late in the sequence, acting as a point of the lance of the Lima expansion in the valley. In this scenario, the site had not been part of the Lima tradition since the Early Intermediate phase. The Middle Lima ceramics present at the site were part of a foreign exchange and not a foreign imposition. In this scenario, Pachacamac would gain importance at the Late Lima sequence while fulfilling administrative functions as a link between the valley of Lurín and the central area of Lima culture (Rímac Valley). If so, Lima culture materials in Pachacamac could be simpler than ceramics recovered from other monumental Lima sites, although Lote B activities would be related to activities (therefore their assemblages) happening at Pachacamac. In summary, in this scenario, Pachacamac would be a local center transformed into a provincial center. This would explain the increase in the number of secondary structures on the site.

A third possibility is that the site of Pachacamac did not fulfill any role in the Lima culture's political expansion. In this scenario the site would continue to have local significance with no major changes in the nature of the site, no matter the growing presence of Lima ceramics in the valley. In this case, we would see continuation in Lima occupation of the site. Also, there would be little relation between the material cultures of Pachacamac and Lote B.

Finally, it is possible to think of a fourth scenario where Pachacamac has an international pan-Andean reputation, but little relevance to the local environment. In this model, the site was completely oriented to the international arena, independently of what was happening in the local or regional arena. This is the idea proposed by ethnohistoric sources, where Pachacamac had an importance and a role that transcended the border of the Central Coast. This scenario would be more along the lines of classical interpretations and should be restricted to small groups of elites, with a large presence of foreign material activities.

Conclusions

The evidence is still inconclusive, but the presence of Lima ceramics and the clear intensification of the occupation suggest that Lima culture was in the valley at least from the middle part of the sequence, which corresponds—more likely—to the second scenario described above. Although the fine ceramics are reported either for the valley or for the Lote B site, there is no evidence that those ceramics were distributed directly by the Lima people from the northern valley, or that they implied a control and centralization. It is not until Late Lima when other lines of evidence point to a progressive assimilation of the Lima into a regional formation.

The role that Pachacamac played at the beginning of the Lima occupation would be purveyor of the Lima tradition in the Lurín area, later becoming the head of the Lima state in the Lurín Valley during the Late Lima Period. We think that it was not until this moment that the site became important, and we suspect that the importance and influence were more than limited, even at the level of the Lurín Valley before that. Pachacamac was the place where different activities took place, like marcaya, in the Nazca region (Vaughn 2006).

For us the presence of Middle Lima ceramics in Lurín could represent cultural relations that did not necessarily imply direct/hierarchical political relations with the Rímac Valley. The evidence, based on the changing layout of the Lote B site, proves, to our eyes, that there was a political change in the Late Lima Period and this came with a growing political and economic centralization. The evidence at the Pachacamac site suggests that although the presence of Lima exists from early times, the late part of the sequence shows an explosion—the second scenario, but not completely.

The evidence is inconclusive; however, the fact that during this late stage of the Lima culture and concomitant with the process described for Lote B, the site of Pachacamac shows an explosion in size and monumentality. This explosion is related to the emergence of nonceremonial structures where activities, which have been interpreted as banquets, suggest the site served as a beachhead of Lima expansion in the Lurín Valley. Similarly, this suggests that its importance was limited during the Early Intermediate, just having a presence first in the valley and then in the region. There is no evidence that tells us the pan-Andean character that this came to be. One may interpret it as a secondary center, although its role seems to be marked with rituals and religious activities. Or perhaps we should not forget that it was only when it acquired administrative functions that the sanctuary acquired a regional importance.

References Cited

Barraza Lescano, S.
2000   Las excavaciones de Louis Stumer en Playa Grande (1952): una aproximación a las prácticas funerarias lima. *Boletín del Instituto Riva-Agüero* No. 27.

Bueno, Alberto
1982   El Antiguo Valle de Pachacamac: Espacio, tiempo y Cultura. *Separata del Boletín de Lima* 24: 3–52.

DeLeonardis, Lisa, and George Lau
2004   Life, Death, and Ancestors. In *Andean Archaeology,* edited by H. Silverman, pp. 77–115. Blackwell, Malden, Massachusetts.

Dietler, Michael, and Brian Hayden
2010   *Feasts: Archaeological and Ethnographic Perspectives on Food, Politics, and Power.* University of Alabama Press, Tuscaloosa.

Dillehay, Tom D.
1979   Pre-Hispanic Resource Sharing in the Central Andes. *Science, New Series* 204(4388): 24–31.

Earle, Timothy
1972   Lurin Valley, Peru: Early Intermediate Period Settlement Development. *American Antiquity* 37: 467–477.

Eeckhout, Peter
2004   La sombra de Ychsma. Ensayo introductorio sobre la arqueológía de la costa central del Perú en los periodos tardíos. *Bulletin de l'Institut français d'études andines* 33(3): 403–423.

Escobedo, Manuel, and Marco Goldhausen
1999   Algunas Consideraciones acerca de la Iconografía Lima. *Baessler Archiv, Neue Folge* 47: 5–37.

Falcon Huayta, Victor
2003   El Motivo Interlocking a Traves del Idolo de Playa Garnde. *Arqueologicas* 26: 163–178.

Flores, Isabel
1981   Investigaciones arqueológicas en la Huaca Juliana, Miraflores–Lima. *Boletín de Lima* 13: 65–70.

2005   *Pucllana: Esplendor de la cultura Lima.* Instituto Nacional de Cultura del Peru, Lima.

Franco, Régulo

1993   *Excavaciones en la Pirámide con rampa n°2, Pachacamac.* Tesis de Licenciatura, Universidad Nacional Mayor de San Marcos, Lima.

Franco, Régulo, and Ponciano Paredes

2000   El Templo Viejo de Pachacamac: nuevos aportes al estudio del Horizonte Medio. *Huari y Tiwanaku: Modelos vs. Evidencias, Primera parte* edited by P. Kauclicke and W. Isbell, pp. 607–630. Fondo Editorial de la Pontificia Universidad Católica del Peru, Lima.

Gayton, Anna H.

1926   *The Uhle Pottery Collection from Nieveria.* University of California Publications in American Archaeology and Ethnology, Berkeley.

Glowacki, Mary, and Michael Malpass

2003   Water, Huacas, and Ancestor Worship: Traces of a Sacred Wari Landscape. *Latin American Antiquity* 14(4): 431–448.

Goldhausen, Marco

2001   Avances en el Estudio de la Iconografia Lima. *Arqueológicas* 25: 223–263.

Guerrero, Daniel, and Jonathan Palacios

1994   El surgimiento del estilo Nieveria en el valle del Rímac. *Boletín de Lima* 16: 91–96: 275–311.

Halperin, Christina T., and Antonia E. Foias

2010   Pottery Politics: Late Classic Maya Palace Production at Motul de San José, Petén, Guatemala. *Journal of Anthropological Archaeology* 29(3): 392–411.

Isla, Elizabeth, and Daniel Guerrero

1987   Socos: Un Sitio Wari en el Valle de Chillon. *Gaceta Arqueológica Andina* 4(41): 23–28.

Jenning, Justin, and Nathan Craig

2001   Politywide Analysis and Imperial Political Economy: The Relationship between Valley Political Complexity and Administrative Centers in the Wari Empire of the Central Andes. *Journal of Anthropological Archaeology* 20(4): 479–502.

Jijon y Caamaño, Jacinto

1949   *Maranga: Contribucion al conocimiento de los aborigenes del valle del Rímac, Peru.* La Prensa Católica, Quito.

Kaulicke, Peter

2000   La Sombra de Pachacamac: Huari en la Costa Central. In *Huari y Tiwanaku: Modelos vs. Evidencias, Primera parte,* edited by P. Kauclicke and W. Isbell, pp. 313–317. Fondo Editorial de la Pontificia Universidad Católica del Peru, Lima.

Kroeber, Alfred

1926a   Culture Stratification in Peru. *American Anthropologist, New Series* 28(2): 331–351.

1926b   *The Uhle Pottery Collections from Chancay.* University of California Publications in American Archaeology and Ethnology, Berkeley.

1954   Proto-Lima: A Middle Period Culture of Peru. *Fieldiana Anthropology* 44(1): 157.

Lavallée, Daniele

1966   Una Colección Cerámica de Pachacamac. *Revista del Museo Nacional* 34: 220–246.

Mac Kay, M.

2012   Cerámica Lima en las cuencas altas de los valles de la Costa Central. *Arqueología y Sociedad* 24: 269–282.

Mac Kay, M.

2007   Contextos funerarios de la Huaca 20: Reconstrucción del ritual funerario y la vida cotidiana del Valle del Rímac en los Inicios del Horizonte Medio. *Letras y Ciencias Humanas, Pontificia Universidad Católica del Perú.*

Mac Kay, Martin, and Raphael Santa Cruz

2000   Las excavaciones del Proyecto Arqueológico Huaca 20 (1999 y 2001). *Boletín de arqueológía PUCP* 4: 583–595.

Makowski, Krzysztof

2002   Power and Social Ranking at the End of the Formative Period: The Lower Lurin Valley Cemeteries. In *Andean Archaeology I: Variation in Sociopolitical Organization,* edited by W. H. Isbell and H. Silverman, pp. 89–121. Kluwer Academic/Plenum, New York.

Makowski, Krzysztof, and Alain Vallenas

2015   La ocupación lima en el valle de Lurin: en los orígenes de Pachacamac monumental. Avances en la Arqueológía de la Cultura Lima. *Boletín de Arqueológía PUCP* 19: 97–145.

Marcone, Giancarlo

2000a El Complejo de los Adobitos y la cultura Lima en el Santuario de Pachacamac. In *Huari y Tiwanaku: Modelos vs. Evidencias, Primera parte,* edited by P. Kauclicke and W. Isbell, pp. 604–665. Fondo Editorial de la Pontificia Universidad Católica del Peru, Lima.

2000b La Cultura Lima en el Santuario de Pachacamac. *Boletín del Instituto Riva-Aguero* 27: 289–307.

2010a El imperio de arriba, la política de abajo. La costa central peruana y su relación con los Imperios pan-Andinos. In *Comparative Perpectives on the Archaeology of Coastal South America,* edited by R. Cutright, L. E. López-Hurtado and A. Martin, pp. 127–146. University of Pittsburgh Memoirs in Latin American Archaeology. Pontificia Universidad Católica del Peru. Ministerio de Cultura del Ecuador, Pittsburgh, Lima, Quito.

2010b What Role Did Wari Play in the Lima Political Economy? The Peruvian Central Coast at the Beginning of the Middle Horizon. *Beyond Wari Walls: Regional Perspectives on Middle Horizon Peru,* edited by J. Jennings. Albuquerque, University of New Mexico Press: 136–154.

2015   Proceso Político y reorganización social Lima desde la perspectiva de los grupos intermedios: El ejemplo de Lote B. *Boletín de Arqueológía* PUCP 19: 171–190.

Marcone, Giancarlo, and Enrique López-Hurtado

2015   Dual Strategies of the Rural Elites: Exploring the Intersection of Regional and Local Transformations in the Lurín Valley, Peru. *Latin American Antiquity.* 25(3): 401–420.

Marsteller, S., and Giancarlo Marcone

2012   Entierros de niños en el sitio Lote B y su significancia sociopolítica para el valle bajo de Río Lurín a finales del Periodo intermedio temprano. *Arqueológía y Sociedad* 22: 249–268.

Mauricio, Ana C.

2015   La cerámica Lima de Huaca 20. In *Huaca 20: un sitio Lima en el antiguo Complejo Maranga,* edited by A. C. Mauricio, L. M. Ynonan, and C. O. Astete, pp. 40–63. Fondo Editorial de la Pontificia Universidad Católica del Perú, Lima.

Mauricio, Ana C., and Gabriel Prieto

2015   Nota Introducctoria. *Boletín de Arqueológía PUCP* 19: 5–6.

Mauricio, Ana C., Gabriel Prieto, and Cecilia Pardo

2014   Avances en la arqueológía de la cultura Lima. *Boletín de Arqueológía PUCP* 18: 5–14.

Mcguire, Randall

2008   *Archaeology as Political Action.* Berkeley: University of California Press.

Menzel, Dorothy

1964   Style and Time in the Middle Horizon. *Ñawpa Pacha* 2: 1–106.

Mogrovejo, Juan

1999   Cajamarquilla y el fin de la Cultura Lima. *Boletín del Instituto Riva-Aguero* 26: 227–245.

Mogrovejo, Juan, and Rafael Segura

2000   El Horizonte Medio en el Conjunto arquitectónico Julio C. Tello de Cajamarquilla. In *Huari y Tiwanaku: Modelos vs. Evidencias, Primera parte,* edited by P. Kauclicke and W. Isbell, pp. 565–582. Fondo Editorial de la Pontificia Universidad Católica del Peru, Lima.

Olivera, Carlos E.

2009   *Análisis de la arquitectura Lima en asentamientos no monumentales: Una visión desde la arquitectura de la zona este del sitio arqueológico Huaca 20.* Licenciatura Thesis. Facultad de Humanidades, Pontificia Universidad Católica del Perú, Lima.

Paredes, Ponciano

1991   Pachacamac. In *Los Incas y el antiguo Perú, 3000 años de historia,* edited by S. Purin, pp. 364–383. Sociedad Estatal Quinto Centenario, Barcelona Madrid: Centro Cultural de la Villa de Madrid, Barcelona, Madrid.

Patterson, Thomas

[1966] Field Notes: Lurín Valley Project 1966: Unpublished notes on file at Museo de sitio de Pachacamac.

1966   *Pattern and Process in the Early Intermediate Period Pottery of the Central Coast of Peru.* University of California, Berkeley.

Patterson, Thomas, John P. Mc Carthy, and Robert A. Dunn

1982   Polities in the Lurin Valley, Peru, during the Early Intermediate Period. *Ñawpa Pacha* 20: 61–82.

Pechenkina, Ekaterina A., and Mercedes Delgado

2006   Dimension of Health and Social Structure in the Early Intermediate Period Cemetary at Villa El Salvador, Peru. *American Journal of Physical Anthropology* 131: 218–235.

Rios, Nilton

2015   Evidencia de rituales de clausura y renovación arquitectónica en una plaza de Huaca Pucllana. *Boletín de Arqueológía PUCP* 19: 7–32.

Rios, Nilton, and José E. Ccencho

2009   Cambios en la sociedad Lima reflejados en el centro ceremonial de Pucllana durante las primeras epocas del Horizonte Medio: Las Evidencias de la Plataforma IV. *Arqueología y Sociedad* 20: 91–118.

Rowe, John H.

1998   Max Uhle y la idea del tiempo en la arqueológía americana. *Max Uhle y el Peru antiguo,* edited by P. Kauclicke, pp. 5–24. Fondo Editorial de la Pontificia Universidad Católica, Lima.

Schaedel, Richard P.

1993   Congruence of Horizon with Polity: Huari and Middle Horizon. In *Latin American Horizons,* edited by D. S. Rice, pp. 225–261. Dumbarton Oaks, Washington, D.C.

Schreiber, Katharina

2001 The Wari Empire of Middle Horizon Peru: The Epistemological Challenge of Documenting an Empire without Documentary Evidence. In *Empires: Perpectives from Archaeology and History*, edited by S. Alcock, T. D'altroy, K. Morrison, and C. Sinopoli, pp. 70. Cambridge University Press, New York.

Segura, Rafael

2001 *Rito y Economía en Cajamarquilla. Investigaciones Arqueologicas en el Conjunto Arquitectónico Julio C. Tello*. Pontificia Universidad Católica del Peru, Lima.

2004 La cerámica Lima en los albores del Horizonte Medio y algunas notas para el debate. In *Puruchuco y la sociedad de Lima: Un homenaje a Arturo Jiménez Borja*, edited by L. F. Villacorta O., L. Vetter, and C. Ausejo Lima, pp. 97–118. Concytec, Lima.

Sestieri, Pellegrino

1971 Cajamarquilla, Peru: The Necropolos on the Hauca Tello. *Archaeology* 24(2).

Shimada, Izumi

1991 *Pachacamac Archaeology: Retrospect and Prospect. Pachacamac, a Reprint of the 1903 edition by Max Uhle*, edited by I. Shimada. The University Museum of Archaeology and Anthropology, University of Pennsylvania, Philadelphia.

Silva, Jorge

1992 *Patrones de asentamiento en el Valle del Chillon. Estudios de arqueológía peruana*. D. Bonavia. Fomciencias, Lima

1996 Prehistoric Settlement Patterns in the Chillon Valley, Peru. Department of Anthropology. Ph.D diss., University of Michigan, Ann Arbor.

Stothert, Karen E., and Rogger Ravines

1977 Investigaciones arqueologicas en villa El Salvador. *Revista del Museo Nacional Lima* 43: 157–225.

Strong, William D.

1925 *The Uhle Pottery Collection from Ancon*. University of California Publications in American Archaeology and Ethnology, Berkeley.

Strong, William D., and John M. Corbett

1943 A Ceramic Sequence at Pachacamac. In *Archaeological Studies in Peru*, edited by W. D. Strong, G. R. Willey, and J. M. Corbett, Vol. 1, No. 3. Columbia University Press, New York.

Stumer, Louis M.

1953 Playa Grande: Primitive Elegance in Pre-Tiahuanaco Peru. *Archaeology* 6(1): 42–48.

1954a The Chillon Valley of Peru: Excavation and Reconnaissance, 1952–1953, Part 1. *Archaeology* 7(3): 171–178.

1954b Population Centers of the Rímac Valley Peru. *American Antiquity* 20(2): 130–148.

1956 Development of Peruvian Coastal Tiahuanacoid Styles. *American Antiquity* 22(1): 59–69.

Tilley, C.

2001 Relational Origins of Inequality. *Anthropological Theory* 1: 355–372.

Uhle, Max

1903 *Pachacamac: Report of the William Pepper, M.D., LL.D., Peruvian Expedition of 1986*. Department of Archaeology, University of Pennsylvania, Philadelphia.

Vaughn, Kevin J.

2006 Craft Production, Exchange, and Political Power in the Pre-Incaic Andes. *Journal of Archaeological Research* 14: 313–344.

Villar Cordova, Pedro E.

1935   *Las Culturas Prehispánicas de Lima. Homenaje al IV Centenario de la fundación de Lima o antigua Ciudad de los Reyes.* Talleres Gráficos de la escuela de la guardia civil y policía, Lima.

Willey, Gordon R.

1943   *Excavations in the Chancay Valley. Archaeological Studies in Peru,* edited by W. D. Strong, G. R. Willey, and J. M. Corbett. New York. 1(3): 123–195.

5

Panquilma

A Rural Community under the "Shadow of Pachacamac"

ENRIQUE LÓPEZ-HURTADO AND ANDREA GONZALES LOMBARDI

One of the most frequent topics in the archaeology of ancient complex societies is the relationship between the emergence and institutionalization of power relations and the role that religion played within that process. In the Peruvian Central Coast, the Lurín Valley has been a particularly fruitful scenario for this discussion, as it is the location of Pachacamac, one of the most renowned pre-Hispanic religious centers, occupied for more than a thousand years before the Spanish arrival. The site's long historical process produced a vast, monumental, and multicomponent settlement with an abundant material record. These archaeological features, along with a great amount of ethnohistorical information about the site and its hinterland, generated the expectation that the deeper and wider archaeologists dug into Pachacamac, the better its hierarchy within the Lurín Valley and the Central Coast would be understood.

Consequently, it is not unexpected that the first years of archaeological research in the Lurín Valley were focused on the characterization of Pachacamac—from its architectural features, occupational sequence, and chronology, to the study of funerary remains (for example, Bueno 1982; Strong 1943; Uhle 1897). This first group of findings, largely interpreted through ethnohistorical information and comparative stratigraphic analysis from other valleys, became the pillars from which interpretations of the social dynamics in the Lurín Valley were developed. Even more, the data from Pachacamac became the reference from which chronological sequences were established for the Central Coast valleys, therefore directly impacting our understanding of the Wari and Inca presence in the region.

Nonetheless, for a couple of decades now, it has been recognized that the

"Pachacamac-centric" approach has limited the scope of our understanding not only of the site, but of the Central Coast as well. Two major works bring attention to this issue and constitute the basis of our discussion. The first one is "La sombra de Pachacamac" (The Shadow of Pachacamac). In this article, Kaulicke (2000) reminds us that, until then, most of the models and interpretations about the Wari presence in this region were based on the shadow projected from the findings recorded at Pachacamac more than 50 years earlier. More specifically, under this shadow, many findings coming from the surrounding sites were ignored in favor of the idea, now known to be unlikely, of a Wari state directly controlling the Lurín Valley during the Middle Horizon (Kaulicke 2000). The second article, "La sombra de Ychsma" (The Shadow of Ychsma) by Eeckhout (2004b), notes that Kaulicke's idea may apply to every other time period, especially to the late periods in the region, and concludes that:

> Pero Pachacamac no se puede entender sin explicar su entorno y relaciones de contemporaneidad e influencia, es decir, los sitios tardíos que presentan arquitectura y vestigios relacionados con el gran centro costeño. (Eeckhout 2004b: 404) [Pachacamac cannot be understood without understanding its surroundings and contemporary relationships and influence, that is to say, the late sites which present architecture and remains related with the great coastal center (translated by authors)].

More than 15 years after this article was published, the argument still persists within the different models that try to explain the organization of the social landscape of the Lurín Valley during the late periods (for example, Eeckhout 2017; Makowski 2015). Pachacamac´s influence can be understood if we acknowledge that its history is embraced by an archaeological record that spreads not only within the site but also through the rest of the Lurín Valley (see Figure 5.1). Within this context, the study of the rural communities dispersed through the immediate surroundings of the site becomes imperative for such a task.

In this chapter we will focus on Panquilma, a community that grew under the shadow of Pachacamac. In the following pages we will discuss the data within the greater context of regional interactions with Pachacamac to understand the continuities and transformations of power relations in the Lurín Valley during the Late Intermediate Period (LIP) (AD 1000–1400) and the Late Horizon Period (circa AD 1400–1532).

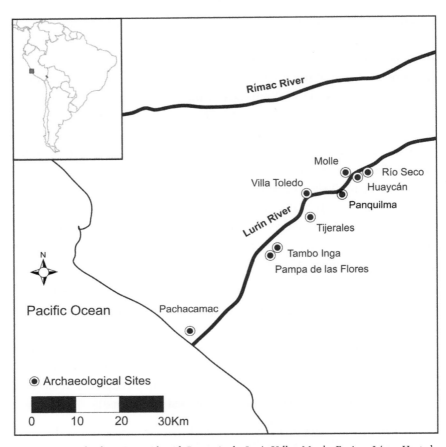

Figure 5.1. Sites that have Pyramids with Ramps in the Lurín Valley. Map by Enrique López-Hurtado 2011: 57.

The archaeological data that supports our discussion comes from three extensive fieldwork seasons at Panquilma. With this research, we aim to contribute to the growing number of works that seek to understand Pacha-camac's religious power within the economic and political dynamics in the surrounding communities from a bottom-up perspective (see Marcone and López-Hurtado 2015).

Power Dynamics during the Late Periods in the Lurín Valley

A major consensus has been reached about the regional importance and power held at Pachacamac during pre-Hispanic times. Nonetheless, when

Enrique López-Hurtado and Andrea Gonzales Lombardi

attempting to characterize such influence, studies based exclusively at this center propose three scenarios: (1) Pachacamac was a pre-Inca spiritual pilgrimage center for a religious confederation; (2) it was the political center of a hierarchical society before the Late Horizon; or (3) it was an outcome of the Inca presence in this region. As stated before, our research at Panquilma (21 km east of Pachacamac) poses that the solution to this controversy lies not only in the center itself but also in the communities that surrounded this important settlement. Thus, our research at Panquilma seeks to offer a new perspective to understand how the religious influence of Pachacamac interacted with economic and political processes in the communities located within its area of influence.

The first scenario was initially proposed by Jiménez and Bueno in 1970; they argue for the LIP:

> Todas las grandes estructuras de la parte baja que son de este periodo, los consideramos "Templos Provinciales," éstos repiten monótonamente el mismo patrón constructivo, con distintas dimensiones. Aledaños a ellos hay canchones cercados, al parecer parcelas listas para ser entregadas a nuevas provincias costeñas que solicitaban tener un templo en la ciudad, pues ello acrecentaba enormemente su prestigio regional. (Jiménez and Bueno 1970: 16) [We consider all the large structures of the lower sector that belong to this period as "provincial temples," all of them constantly repeat the same constructive patter, with different dimensions. There are enclosed patios adjacently, apparently, parcels ready to be distributed to the coastal provinces that [are] required to have a temple within the city (Jiménez and Bueno 1970: 16); translated by authors.]

Under this view, Pachacamac was the ritual center of a religious confederation, one that was composed of different groups that were politically and economically independent, but shared devotion for Pachacamac.

The Pachacamac cult and sanctuary were the main integrating axis of a politically fragmented region. Therefore, the role of Pachacamac in the development of inequality and power relations in the Lurín Valley would have a symbolic value which, despite providing a common cultural frame to the different groups living there, did not influence the development of their political relations (Bueno 1979; Franco 1993, 1998; Jiménez 1985). This first interpretation of the role of Pachacamac within a regional context was followed by the work of Paredes and Franco (1987), who refer to PWRs as "pyramidal temples with ramps." Afterward, Paredes resumes the discussion and redefines PWRs as "religious embassies" (Paredes 1988: 44)

In 1995, Eeckhout published a synthesis of archaeological and ethnohistorical interpretations of Pachacamac's influence. In this article, the author refers to the proposals of Jiménez and Bueno (1970) and Rostworowsky (1972) as hypotheses for understanding the Ychsma occupation of Pachacamac. Later on, Eeckhout presents Jiménez and Bueno's proposal, along with a group of other similar views, under the "embassy model" (2004c, 2008). Specifically, when discussing one of the several perspectives included under this model and its application for understanding Andean pre-Hispanic pilgrimage (for example, Chavín, Pacatnamú and Cahuachi), Eeckhout mentions that:

> Dicha hipótesis [Keatinge 1988] se enmarca en una corriente inspirada en la exégesis de una fuentes etnohistóricas por parte de ciertos autores. Se trata de lo que he designado como "el modelo de las embajadas" y que puede sintetizarse de la manera siguiente: durante el Periodo Intermedio Tardío se establecieron, en diferentes pisos ecológicos, una serie de santuarios dedicados, cada uno, a uno de los miembros de la parentela mítica de Pachacamac. Cada santuario tenía su correspondiente, es decir, su embajada en el sitio, dentro de la Segunda Muralla. (Eeckhout 2008: 169) [This hypothesis (Keatinge 1988) is framed within a group of studies inspired by the exegesis of ethnohistorical sources by certain authors. This is what I have named "the embassy model" and can be summarized as follows: during the Late Intermediate Period a series of dedicated sanctuaries was established in different ecotones, each one was devoted to a member of the mythic family of Pachacamac. Each sanctuary had its corresponding embassy, so to speak, in the site, behind the Second Wall (Eeckhout 2008: 169); translated by authors].

Eeckhout argues that this "embassy model" is mainly based on ethnohistorical sources (Calancha 1974–1981 [1638]; Estete [1533] 1968) and that, while it accurately contemplates cultural aspects common to the Andean area such as the close relationship between religion and power, there are no viable archaeological indicators that help assess their validity (Eeckhout 1995, 2004a, 2008). Alternatively, Eeckhout suggests a second model which presents Pachacamac not only as an important religious center, but also as a center of political and economic power (1999, 2004b). Following this argument, people living in the Lurín Valley would have represented a ranked and politically unified social group whose major center was the site of Pachacamac. Therefore, the lords living at Pachacamac were not only priests but mainly also political leaders. In this case, Pachacamac's influence in the development of power and inequality relationships in the valley was not only of a religious nature but also had a great influence in the political and economic processes of the communities living along this valley.

Like Jiménez Borja and Bueno (1970), Eeckhout based a great part of his argument on data coming from the PWRs at Pachacamac. However, Eeckhout proposes that these pyramids were not religious embassies but power centers and palaces for the Ychsma lords living at Pachacamac. The archaeological evidence that supports this model comes from the excavations conducted by Eeckhout in some of these structures (1999, 2000a, 2000b), which he analyzes to present the chronological sequence between the construction and use of the various pyramids at Pachacamac, and the evidence of feasts carried out at the plazas (2005, 2006, 2008). It is also worth mentioning his findings of elite burials related to evidence of ritual abandonments of the pyramids and large storage areas for agricultural and hand-made products.

Eeckhout also discusses the implications that his model would have for rural communities of the middle lower Lurín Valley settlements that, like Panquilma, have diverse types of pyramids with ramps. Specifically, Eeckhout proposes the hierarchical organization of these sites based on the number and characteristics of the pyramids within each settlement. From this perspective, the site of Pampa de la Flores (only a few miles from Pachacamac) would have been the "dual capital" of Ychsma power in the Lurín Valley (2004c, 2005). This idea certainly fills in the blanks left by the religious embassies model. Nonetheless, if we try to establish some sort of conclusive type of dependency between these communities and Pachacamac—not only political but administrative as well—we should be capable of finding that the activities carried out by the elites of the capital were emulated by the rural groups of the valley. Such activities would have occurred in the pyramids with ramps located at Pampa de las Flores and other similar sites, such as Panquilma.

More recently, Makowski has proposed a novel third point of view. Based on his excavations in the various walls, roads, and main entries to the numerous sectors of Pachacamac, he suggests a different scenario from those that considered Pachacamac a major pre-Inca religious or political center. Makowski proposes that the estimated age of these areas would indicate that the planning of the sanctuary is not from pre-Inca times, but from the Late Horizon under Inca control (2015). According to this view, the main function of Pachacamac within the social organization of Lurín Valley was to reflect not local needs, either ideological or political, but those of the Inca presence in the Central Coast.

From this argument, it is inferred that the ability of Pachacamac to transform or reaffirm power relationships with and within the rural communities of Lurín Valley would have been restricted by a supraregional power. If this is the case, it is appropriate to ask how this would be identified in the archaeological record, and what are the implications of this model for the rest of the valley. More specifically, how would we explain the presence of PWRs in the valley settlements if not constructed under the Inca domain? Would this perspective imply a massive population movement during the Late Horizon? Even more pertinent, would this mean that the limited presence of Inca ceramics in these sites is suggesting a policy of direct control of the Lurín Valley by the Incas, and earlier than we had considered?

On the other hand, if we explore the validity of this model from the point of view of the rural communities in the mid-lower Lurín Valley, we can consider a number of possible archaeological correlates. For example, if part of the power displayed by the rural elites was based on an exclusive religious relationship with Pachacamac, we would expect their control of ritual practices and spaces within their communities. Moreover, if these rural elites were politically and economically independent before the Inca arrival, the settlement pattern in the mid-lower Lurín Valley should not have presented any major hierarchical differentiation, at least during the LIP.

These three perspectives constitute the pillars of the discussion of Pachacamac's complexity within a regional context. All of them are strongly based on the material/historical record recovered from Pachacamac and, to some extent, they all stem from the same material record. This means that, at this point, to prove or discard the validity of these models, it is imperative to expand our horizon to the adjacent rural settlements located in Pachacamac's hinterland. Thus, the aim of our research is not to evaluate the validity or inaccuracy of the models, but to explore them from a different perspective: that of the rural community of Panquilma. The reconstruction of the various power strategies of groups known as intermediates can notably contribute to the analysis of power dynamics in the context of state/imperial expansions (Marcone and López-Hurtado 2015). This is the case in which the rural elites have to adapt to a changing regional context, while maintaining their privileged position within their communities.

In this text, the model of the religious embassies is the center of our analysis. Despite the fact that the idea of PWRs as embassies has been reasonably questioned, this does not mean that Pachacamac was not acting as a major religious referent in the Lurín Valley. As mentioned before, we contend that the archaeological study of the rural settlements near Pachacamac will shed light on the continuities and transformations in power dynamics during the Inca expansion and, more specifically, reveal the ways in which Pachacamac was strategically administrated as a major regional center in the Central Coast.

The Rural Community of Panquilma

The evidence discussed in this chapter focuses on the preliminary findings of our third and fourth fieldwork seasons at the site of Panquilma, located on the left bank of the Lurín River, less than one day's walk from Pachacamac. The site emerged during the Late Intermediate Period as a rural community similar to Tijerales or Molle and was still occupied during the Late Horizon Period. The site is divided into three sectors clearly differentiated from each other: (1) a public sector, composed of three pyramidal cores, each one of them formed by a ramp pyramid and an associated residential area; (2) a domestic sector, composed of 15 residential compounds for extended families; and (3) a funerary sector, located where the gorge becomes narrower, and there is not much evidence of occupation (see Figure 5.2). Panquilma has three PWRs, identified as type B under Eeckhout's analysis of these structures in the Lurín Valley (2004b).

The first season at Panquilma took place during the years 2002 and 2003, with the objective of establishing the limits of the archaeological site, its cultural affiliation, chronology, number of occupations, and the sectoring of the site based on the characteristics and distribution of the architectonic remains on the surface. The second season took place during 2007 and 2008 and the main objective was to identify and characterize the most important activities that took place at Panquilma. This was achieved through the identification of proportional distribution patterns of certain type of artifacts, and excavation units were located randomly across the site.

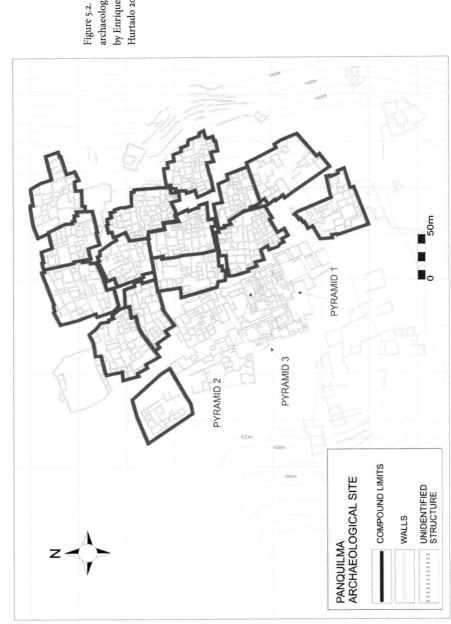

Figure 5.2. Panquilma archaeological site. Map by Enrique López-Hurtado 2011: 32.

For the 2012 season, the aim was to recover contextual information in the public and domestic sectors through the excavation of horizontal units. This data complemented the statistical information recovered from the 2008 season and allowed a better understanding of the use of spaces and dynamics that took place within this rural community.

Excavations carried out in 2008 evidenced that the public sector was isolated from the domestic area by a series of perimetric walls—which probably reached an elevation of 4 m—and by a corridor system that controlled the access to the pyramids' plazas. Results obtained during the excavations at the plaza of Pyramidal Complex 1 suggest that these spaces were the center of ritual practices that consisted of the burial of various types of offerings, figurines, and spondylus shells we recovered from the center of the complex's plaza (López-Hurtado et al. 2014: 19). Further excavation at this complex in 2012 exposed the same sequence of floors previously recorded, but also revealed that the most important offerings were limited to the center of the plaza. The excavations reached 2 m in depth before exposing sterile soil; this revealed that at least the lower floors corresponded to the Late Intermediate occupation at the site before the Inca presence at the region.

The excavations at the plaza of Pyramidal Complex 3 during 2008 revealed what this space was used for under Inca control. For the later archaeological layers, it was found that garbage was being buried and burned in holes in the plaza. This could indicate that once Panquilma was finally under Inca control, the ritual spaces previously administrated by the local elite were desecrated and used as rubbish dumps. This idea about the suppression and ultimate obliteration of local ritual spaces by the Inca was confirmed by our excavations at the main platform of this very same structure, when it was found that the areas surrounding this platform were intentionally burned immediately prior to its abandonment during the Inca occupation of the site (López-Hurtado et al. 2014: 9). Stratigraphy revealed that the fire originated on the structure's cane roof, which then fell on the floor and expanded the flames (López-Hurtado et al. 2014: 30). It is worth noting that similar evidence was recorded in 2008 when the excavation of a test pit in the main platform of Pyramid 1 exposed the same type of event (López-Hurtado 2011: 47).

To address the possibility that these structures with ritual functions were used also as elite dwellings, a rubbish dump contiguous to the back area of Pyramid 3 was excavated, and it exposed a greater ratio of domestic pottery within the total amount of ceramic sherds during the pre-Inca occupation of the site. This has been interpreted as evidence of the presence of an elite group living near the pyramid, at least before the Inca arrival (López-Hurtado 2011). On the other hand, a significant increment in the number of prestige objects was recorded near the moment of abandonment of the structure (López-Hurtado et al. 2014: 30).

As for the Inca material found in the public sector of Panquilma, statistical analysis of the artifacts recovered at this rubbish dump revealed Inca material in both occupation phases. While Inca pottery is present in a relatively small amount, however, there is a significant increment between the first occupational phase (2 percent of the total sherds) and the second phase (5 percent of the total amount). What is also noticeable is the growth of utilitarian pottery during the second phase of occupation, which supports the idea that feasts were held there. Because this data was recovered within areas exclusively used by the elite, it was proposed that both the hosts and participants of such feasts were elite or power groups of Panquilma (López-Hurtado 2011; Marcone and López-Hurtado 2002). Furthermore, the evidence suggests that Panquilma's elite were using Inca pottery during these feasts as a display of power and prestige (López-Hurtado 2011: 102).

In 2012, López-Hurtado proposed two differentiated elite dynamics within Panquilma, occurring prior to the Incas' absolute annexation of the valley. The first one refers to elite-commoner interaction and argues that the elite's power at Panquilma was highly dependent on the control of ritual spaces to validate their economic supremacy and facilitate surplus extraction from the household compounds. The second relates to elite interaction: Panquilma's ruling elite displayed and maintained prestige and power by holding feasts without any special religious significance or ritual component, deliberately displaying their access to Inca goods (López-Hurtado 2011: 194).

The data recorded in 2012 complements the material record from 2008 and allows us to expand the interpretation and argue that, in the struggle for prestige, the use of exotic or foreign material to display a privileged relationship with a supraregional power started to play a more important role during the second occupation phase at Panquilma. Furthermore, regardless of the local acceptance and circulation of Inca goods, once the Inca Empire exerted control over the valley, it desecrated and abandoned the ritual spaces within the plazas and destroyed specific areas of Panquilma's PWRs. This would indicate that the ideological power of the ruling groups at Panquilma was severely damaged by the Inca Conquest of the region. As previously noted, this process would have occurred in parallel with the emergence of Huaycán de Cieneguilla as an Inca administrative center in the Lurín Valley (Capriata and López-Hurtado 2017; López-Hurtado et al. 2014: 9).

Domestic Sector

The domestic sector has 15 residential compounds and is adjacent to the public sector (see Figure 5.3). All the compounds are surrounded by elevated perimeter walls and storage rooms. In 2008, the excavations in one of these areas revealed a great number of goods, especially tools for textile production. The excavation also exposed large plazas or central patios, elevated funerary structures associated with the patio, and, most importantly, constant growth and restructuring of the layout. A small unit placed at a rubbish dump in Residential Compound 2 (see Figure 5.4) revealed a great deal of religious paraphernalia, such as human- and animal-shaped figurines. These characteristics indicate that the domestic compounds were inhabited by extended families that constantly reorganized their domestic spaces as they grew in

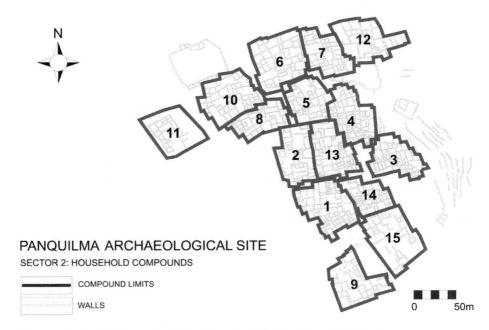

Figure 5.3. Residential compounds at Panquilma. Map by Enrique López-Hurtado 2011: 109.

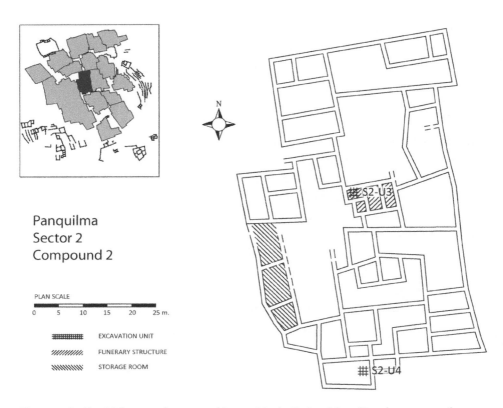

Panquilma
Sector 2
Compound 2

PLAN SCALE

| 0 | 5 | 10 | 15 | 20 | 25 m. |

▦▦▦▦▦▦ EXCAVATION UNIT

//////// FUNERARY STRUCTURE

\\\\\\\\ STORAGE ROOM

Figure 5.4. Residential Compound 2, excavated in 2012. Map by Enrique López-Hurtado 2011, p. 124, fig. 53.

number and had access to certain production goods, as indicated by the findings in the storage rooms.

In 2012, further excavations were conducted in the domestic area to reassess the data of previous seasons. The results revealed that the execution of ritual activities in these domestic spaces went well beyond the public spaces, and they were much more important than previously thought. Specifically, we exposed a mummy bundle associated with animal bones from typical species of the coast, like small ducks and marine mammals. This could indicate the importance of funerary rituals related to collective activities, such as feasts, possibly within the context of ancestor worship.

As mentioned, the excavation of the storage rooms of Compound 2 revealed their alternative use as funerary structures. The peripheral location of these burials in relation to the central patio of the residential compound where they were found suggests they were not necessarily related to ancestor worshipping rituals that might have occurred in the patio. Inside one of the storage rooms (Amb-08) we found the body of a young person (around 20 years old) buried in a very simple bundle that showed signs of disturbance, probably caused by the collapse of the surrounding structure. In the adjacent storage room (Amb-09), we found a small textile bag associated with funerary practices. Inside the bag, there were three small textile bundles holding ritual objects. Specifically, they were figurines of a bird, a feline, and the desiccated head of a snake, which according to the literature, are related to the worlds of the Andean cosmology (López-Hurtado et al. 2014: 41). In another adjacent room, we found a buried pot that also contained animal- and human-shaped stone figurines.

The excavations at the storage rooms of Residential Compound 2 expose the diversity in the use of the rooms within the residential complexes. Evidence suggests that the excavated structures (Amb. 06–09) were initially utilized as storage facilities and, afterward, at least one of them (Amb. 09) was reused as a funerary structure (López-Hurtado 2012: 42). The presence

Figure 5.5. Storage rooms (Amb. 06–09) from Residential Compound 2. Funerary context found inside Amb. 09. Photo by Enrique López-Hurtado (2011: 204).

of associated offerings also supports this idea. Based on the analysis of these findings and their conflict with previous fieldwork seasons at Panquilma, we propose that the execution of ritual practices was not an exclusive right of the elite. On the contrary, it was extended to the domestic areas of all the commoners. This urges us to reevaluate the role of Panquilma's ritual activities in the establishment of power relationships and social hierarchy, as well as their connection to the control and production of goods.

Conclusions

In these pages, we have presented consistent evidence to argue that the execution of ritual activities and feasts in the plazas of the pyramidal complexes at Panquilma occurred prior to the Inca presence in the region, during the Late Intermediate Period. Even though we found Inca material in the residential areas of these public complexes, its low occurrence ratio would indicate that these feasts did not emulate the ones executed by the governing elites at Pachacamac. Therefore, although Panquilma elites had privileged access to sumptuous Inca goods, evidence does not support the idea of a privileged relation with Pachacamac, nor the idea of direct political or economic dependence on it prior to the Inca arrival. It is more feasible that the feast occurring at Panquilma would be related to the internal dynamics of this rural community, and that they were caused by internal processes of local scale, such as the struggle for prestige among elite groups. Nonetheless, it is valid to ask how we can identify a sufficiently representative number of goods flowing from Pachacamac to Panquilma to infer a relevant degree of political and economic dependence of this rural community on the major regional center.

On the other hand, it is inarguable that the Inca presence at the region had significant consequences for the social dynamics of the elites of both Pachacamac and Panquilma. In light of these new findings, what can we say about the shadow of Pachacamac over Panquilma during the Late Intermediate and Late Horizon periods? First, we can conclude that if Panquilma was not directly political or administratively dependent on Pachacamac, the idea of Pachacamac as a predominantly religious center becomes more appealing. However, the fact that the ritual activities at Panquilma occurred well beyond the area controlled by the elite urges us to reexamine this idea. Then, it becomes imperative to explore these dynamics within other settlements that experienced local and Inca occupation, such as Tijerales and Huaycan.

Acknowledgments

The authors wish to thank the Programa de Investigación Arqueológica of the Instituto de Estudios Peruanos (IEP) for their institutional and financial support in conducting our 2012 and 2013 fieldwork seasons.

References Cited

Bueno Mendoza, Alberto

1979   Urbanismo prehispánico tardío en Lurín. *Inca: segunda época* 3(6): 59–66

1982   Antiguo valle de Pachacamac (primera parte). *Boletín de Lima* 4(24): 10–29.

Calancha, Antonio de la, and Ignacio Prado Pastor, ed.

1974–1981 [1638]   *Crónica Moralizada*, 6 vols. Universidad Nacional Mayor de San Marcos, Lima.

Capriata, Camila, and Enrique López-Hurtado

2017   The Demise of the Ruling Elites: Termination Rituals in the Pyramid Complexes of Panquilma, Peruvian Central Coast. In *Rituals of the Past. Prehispanic and Colonial Case Studies in Andean Archaeology,* edited by S. Rosenfeld and S. Bautista, pp. 193–215. University of Colorado Press, Boulder.

Eeckhout, Peter

1995   Pirámide con rampa n°3, Pachacamac. Resultados preliminares de la primera temporada de excavaciones (zonas 1 y 2). *Bulletin de l'Institut Français d'Etudes Andines* 24(1): 65–106.

1999   Pirámide con rampa n°III, Pachacámac. Nuevos datos, nuevas perspectivas. *Bulletin de l'Institut Français d'Etudes Andines* 28(2): 169–214.

2000a   Investigaciones Arqueológicas en la Pirámide con Rampa n. 3 de Pachacamac, Costa Central del Perú. *Estudios Latinoamericanos* 20: 19–40.

2000b   Los Antecedentes Formales y Funcionales de las "Pirámides con Rampa" de la Costa Central del Perú en los Tiempos Prehispánicos. *Boletín Americanista* 50: 39–60.

2004a   Reyes del Sol y Señores de la Luna. Inkas e Ychsmas en Pachacamac. *Chungará* 36(2): 495–503.

2004b   La Sombra de Ychsma. Ensayo Introductorio sobre la Arqueología de la Costa Central del Perú en los Periodos Tardíos. *Bulletin de l'Institut Français d'Etudes Andines* 33(3): 403–424.

2004c   Pachacamac y el proyecto Ychsma (1999–2003). *Bulletin de l'Institut Français d'Etudes Andines* 33(3): 425–448.

2005   Imperial Strategies in a Regional Context: Chimus and Incas at Pachacamac. In *Wars and Conflicts in Prehispanic Mesoamerica and the Andes,* edited by P. Eeckhout and G. L. Fort, pp. 110–127. British Archaeological Reports, Oxford.

2006   Poder y elites en los Andes centrales prehispánicos. In *Y llegaron los Incas. Unidad en la diversidad. Catálogo de la muestra organizada en el Museo de América (2006),* edited by A. Verde and M. J. J. Díaz, pp. 47–67. Ministerio de Cultura, Madrid.

2008   El santuario del Oráculo de Pachacamac y los peregrinajes a larga escala en los Andes prehispánicos. In *Adivinación y Oráculos en las Américas,* edited by M. C. Petrocchi and M. Ziolkowski, pp. 161–180. Pontificia Universidad Católica del Perú and Instituto Francés de Estudios Andinos, Lima.

2017   Ofrendas, rituales, peregrinaciones y ancestros. In *Pachacamac el Oráculo en el Horizonte Marino del Sol Poniente*, edited by D. Pozzi-Escot, pp. 222–237. Banco de Crédito en el Perú, Lima.

Estete, Miguel de
[1533] 1968   Noticia del Perú. In *Biblioteca Peruana; El Perú a través de los siglos, Primera Serie, t.1.*, edited by Editores Técnicos Asociados, pp. 345–402. Editores Técnicos Asociados, Lima.

Franco, Régulo
1993   *Excavaciones en la Pirámide con rampa n°2, Pachacamac.* Unpublished Tesis de Licenciatura, Departamento de Arqueología, Universidad Nacional Mayor de San Marcos, Lima.
1998   *La Pirámide con Rampa n°2 de Pachacamac. Excavaciones y Nuevas Interpretaciones.* s.e., Trujillo.

Jiménez Borja, Arturo
1985   Pachacamac. *Boletín de Lima* 7(38): 40–54.

Jiménez Borja, Arturo and Alberto Bueno Mendoza
1970   Breves notas acerca de Pachacamac. *Arqueología y Sociedad* 4: 13–25.

Kaulicke, Peter
2000   La Sombra de Pachacamac: Huari en la Costa Central. *Boletín de Arqueología PUCP* 4: 313–317.

Keatinge, Richard W.
1988   A Summary View of Peruvian Prehistory. In *Peruvian Prehistory*, edited by R. Keatinge, pp. 303–316. Cambridge University Press, Cambridge.

López-Hurtado, Enrique
2011   Ideology and the Development of Social Hierarchy at the Site of Panquilma, Peruvian central coast. Unpublished Ph.D. dissertation, Department of Anthropology, University of Pittsburgh, Pittsburgh, Pennsylvania.

López-Hurtado, Enrique, Camila Capriata Estrada, Augusto Vásquez Martinez, and Andrea Gonzales Lombardi
2014   *Proyecto de Investigación Arqueológica Panquilma; Informe Final 2012.* Instituto de Estudios Peruanos, Lima.

Makowski, Krzysztof
2015   Pachacamac—Old Wak'a or Inka Syncretic Deity? Imperial Transformation of the Sacred Landscape in the Lower Ychsma (Lurín) Valley. In *The Archaeology of Wak'as; Explorations of the Sacred in the Pre-Columbian Andes*, edited by T. Bray, pp. 127–166. University Press of Colorado, Louisville.

Marcone, Giancarlo, and Enrique López-Hurtado
2002   Panquilma y Cieneguilla en la discusión arqueológica de la Costa Central. *Boletín de Arqueología.*
2015   Dual strategies of the Rural Elites: Exploring the Intersection of Regional and Local Transformations in the Lurín Valley, Peru. *Latin American Antiquity* 26(3): 401–420.

Paredes Botoni, Ponciano
1988   Pachacámac—Pirámide con Rampa n.° 2. *Boletín de Lima* 55: 41–58.

Paredes Botoni, Ponciano, and Régulo Franco
1987   Pachacámac: Las Pirámides con Rampa. Cronología y Función. *Gaceta Arqueológica Andina*, 13: 5–7.

Rostworowski, María

1972   Breve ensayo sobre el Señorío de Ychma o Ychima. *Boletín del Seminario de Arqueología, Instituto Riva Agüero* 13: 37–51.

Strong, William, and John Corbett

1943   A Ceramic Sequence at Pachacamac. In *Archaeological Studies in Peru: 1941–1942,* edited by William Duncan Strong, Gordon R. Willey, and John M. Corbett, pp. 27–122. Columbia University Press, New York.

Uhle, Max

1897   Summary of the Preliminary Report on Pachacamac. *Bulletin of the Free Museum of Science and Art of the University of Pennsylvania* 1(1): 21–23.

6

The Architecture and Spatial Organization of Pachacamac in the Late Horizon

KRZYSZTOF MAKOWSKI

In this chapter, I intend to show how our reading changes when the results of systematic excavations of considerable extension are taken as a starting point and written sources are subject to rigorous internal criticism. Recent archaeological results suggest that Inca imperial policies completely transformed the landscape of the Lurín Valley. The reorganization of the Lurín Valley involved not only the construction of new settlements for populations who had moved from elsewhere in the highlands and possibly the coast, but also the creation of new ceremonial sites. As expected, the largest building activities were conducted in Pachacamac proper. This local ceremonial center, which was originally relatively modest, was transformed during the Late Horizon by the construction of walled streets, new enclosed spaces, and large plazas, in addition to the erection of substantial new temples and an *acllahuasi*. New ramped pyramids were also built during this time period.

Our investigations in the Lurín Valley have focused on issues related to the presence of Inca administration in this zone. The investigations have been carried out as part of the Archaeological Program "Lomas de Lurín," and subsequently the "Valle de Pachacamac" program, both of which were field-school projects of the Pontificia Universidad Católica del Perú conducted with the support of UNACEM (Cementos Lima) S.A. The excavations began here in the 1990s with the monumental entrance to Pachacamac from the north, called the "Third Wall," undertaken in 1994–1995 by Hernán Carrillo and Daniel Guerrero, and with the beginning of long-term excavations carried out in Pueblo Viejo–Pucará in 1999. Judging by the ethnohistoric evidence, burial rites, and architecture typical of the highlands, Pueblo Viejo–Pucará, located near the ceremonial center of Pachacamac, was a major settlement of the Caringa of Huarochirí (Makowski 2002b; Makowski and Vega Centeno 2004; Makowski et al. 2005; Makowski and Lizárraga 2011; Makowski and Ruggles 2011) and the principal abode of the lords of this moiety.

Pachacamac Pre-Inca

Throughout the twentieth century, beginning with Max Uhle (2003 [1903]) to Arturo Jiménez Borja (1985), Thomas Patterson (1966, 1985), María Rostworowski (1999, 2002a), and Peter Eeckhout (1995, 1998, 1999a, 1999b, 2003a, 2003b, 2004a, 2004b, 2004c, 2005, 2008, 2009, 2010a, 2013), multiple interpretive scenarios have been presented for the monumental complex of Pachacamac. Uhle (2003 [1903]), for instance, argued that the planned organization and the erection of the major monumental buildings at the site were associated with the imperial Inca administration. Other scholars subsequently assumed instead that the orthogonal layout of Pachacamac had its origin in the Middle Horizon (Lumbreras 1974: 154, 165; Shimada 1991). These interpretations undoubtedly stemmed from Dorothy Menzel's (1964, 1968a, b; 1976) important work on the stylistic chronology of the Middle Horizon and her convictions regarding the role of this ceremonial center during this period. Some scholars, like Régulo Franco (1993a, 1993b), went even further, positing that the foundations of Pachacamac dated back to the Formative Period and that the ceremonial complex had developed continuously since then.

In recent decades, new interpretive proposals supported by new archaeological evidence have joined the previous ones. Considering both old and new proposals, we now have three completely different interpretations of Pachacamac, which include the following:

The first interpretation is Pachacamac was a ceremonial center with a major temple and several secondary temples, built by faithful communities representing ethnic groups from both the coast and the highlands (for example, Eeckhout 1999b: 405–408; Jiménez Borja 1985; Rostworowski 1999, 2002a), with implicit comparisons being drawn between the site of Pachacamac and Mecca and Delphi, derived in particular from the early Spanish chroniclers.

The second interpretation is Pachacamac was a planned urban administrative and ceremonial center whose layout was defined in the Middle Horizon or slightly earlier (for example, Bueno 1970, 1974–75; Dolorier 1998; Lanning 1967; Patterson 1985).

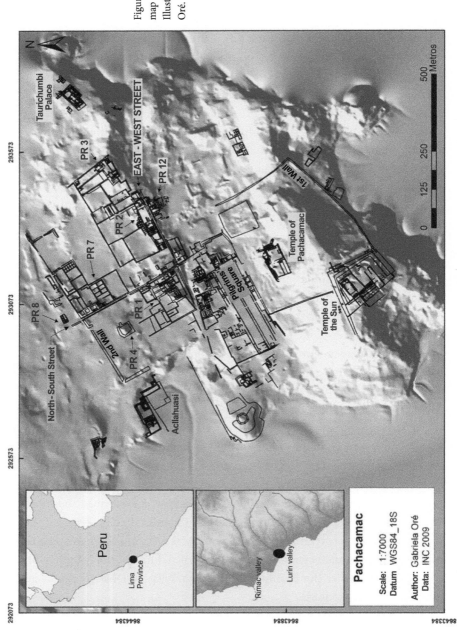

Figure 6.1. Location and map of Pachacamac. Illustration by Gabriela Oré.

The third interpretation is Pachacamac was the capital city of one of the major coastal chiefdoms in the Late Intermediate Period. In this interpretation, the palaces of many successive rulers were built, one alongside the other on the sandy, open field that lies to the northeast of the temple of the god Pachacamac on the valley's high edge (for example, Eeckhout 1999b, 2003a; Tello 1967; Uhle 2003 [1903] had already made similar statements). For Eeckhout (1999b), each king was buried in his palace in similar fashion to Chanchan, the capital of the Chimor state.

The image of Pachacamac which emerges from the review of all these interpretations is contradictory. Furthermore, none of them is consistent with the results of recent excavations, in the opinion of the author (Eeckhout 1995, 1999a, 2004b, 2010a, b; 2013; Makowski 2007, 2013, 2016; Shimada 2003, 2004, 2007; Shimada et al. 2004, 2010). Rather, from the results of recent excavations, a fourth scenario emerges, differing from previous interpretations. There are no firm grounds to believe that Pachacamac was the oracular and pilgrimage center from as far back as the beginning of the Early Intermediate Period (end of the Formative Period). Instead, we observe a long, discontinuous development wherein each of the successive stages of monumental construction was separated by breaks of different duration and each was seen as having a different origin and characteristics. The perceived spatial organization is actually due to the superimposed phases corresponding to the late periods, and particularly to the Late Horizon (Uhle 2003 [1903]). This view can be seen in Hyslop's (1990: 255–261) statement that "Pachacamac is probably the most monumental example of Inka planning that coordinated and adjusted its design to a pre-existing layout." There are three periods manifested in most stratigraphic sequences excavated in all sectors of monumental Pachacamac up to 2013 (see Table 6.1) :

- Lima Period (second half of the Early Intermediate Period and first half of the Middle Horizon; the sequence is subdivided into the Middle Period Lima–Playa Grande [Lima 4–5], and Maranga [Lima 6–9], according to Patterson 1966).
- Ychsma Period (Late Intermediate Period).
- Late Ychsma-Inca Period (Late Horizon).

Whereas construction activities corresponding to each of the three periods left several marks on the architectural landscape of Pachacamac, the characteristics and distribution of buildings are different in each case. Moreover,

Table 6.1. Pachacamac chronology

C 14 Cal. Dates	Periods	Local Styles	Foreign Style, imitations	Main Buildings
1532–1572	Early Colonial Transition	Late Ychsma B	Inca, Chimu-Inca	Cuadrangulo—Tambo
1450–1532	Late Horizon	Late Ychsma A/B	Inca, Chimu-Inca	Walled streets, Sun Temple, Pachacamac; Temple, Acllahuasi, PWR N° 1, 2, 4, 8
1370–1450	Late Intermediate Period	Late Ychsma A		PWR N° 3
1200–1370		Early/Middle Ychsma		Templo del Mono
1000–1200		Early Ychsma	Tricolor	
800–1000	Middle Horizon	Initial Ychsma	Pachamac, Huamanga- Viñaque, Teatino, Epigonal	Huamanga, Casma—Supe
600–800		Late Lima: Maranga Nievería	Wari imitations	Adobitos
300–600	Early Intermediate Period	Early-Middle Lima: Playa Grande		Old Temple
100–300		Villa El Salvador	Topara & Nasca imitations	

Source: Author.

the spatial organization of the whole settlement changes from one period to another. Only larger constructions from the Lima and Ychsma periods are visible on the surface.

Lima architecture is much easier to distinguish from later constructions due to the use of very characteristic types of adobe. These are the parallel-epiped, medium-sized adobe bricks (Makowski and Vallenas 2016) and little mud-bricks (*adobitos*), often arranged like a bookcase (*librero*), as found around the Old Temple (Franco 1993a, 1993b), or as in the structures around the Urpaihuachac Lagoon (Lavallée 1965; Segura Llanos and Shimada 2010; Tello 2009 [1941–1942]). It should be emphasized that during the Lima Period, stone lining is also used in foundations and walls, just as in subsequent periods.

The Middle Lima occupation (4–5) focuses on the hillsides facing the coast and around the pyramid building of the Old Temple (Makowski 2011, 2013; Makowski and Vallenas 2016).

Beginning at the end of the Middle Lima, evidence of settlements moves northward (see Figure 6.1), distributed around Laguna Urpaihuachac that, according to Winsborough (et al. 2012), contained freshwater at the time. The composition of this aquifer has changed significantly over the last 2,000 years following heavy rain events (Paleo-ENSO and tsunamis that caused salinization. One such event caused the abandonment of the Lima settlement around the lagoon circa AD 600. In contrast, the buildings on the upper terraces were still in use during the Late Lima Period (Lavallée 1966; Marcone 2010). Several building activities were also conducted on top of the Old Temple where researchers found ceremonial enclosures and conditions that suggest offerings were made immediately before abandonment (Franco 2004, Franco and Paredes 2000). The Lima buildings were finally abandoned during the Middle Horizon 2, circa AD 800 (C14 cal.). Shortly after the abandonment of the Lima buildings, a period characterized by much drier climatic conditions and heavy rain events began in the tenth century (ENSO Mega) (Winsborough et al. 2012: 611).

For nearly 600 years, between the ninth and fourteenth century AD, the site of Pachacamac lacked a monumental appearance, except for the abandoned ruins of the Pyramid of the Old Temple. The stylistic changes in pottery recorded during excavations at Pachacamac allow for the easy differentiation of at least three stages in this long sequence: the second half of the Middle Horizon, the beginning of the Late Intermediate Period with its highly diagnostic styles, the tricolor and Initial Ychsma (Bazan 2008; Dolorier and Casas 2008; Eeckhout 2018), and the most confusing phase of the three, the Middle Ychsma (Bazan 1990, 1992; Díaz 2002; Falconí 2008; Feltham and Eeckhout 2004; Vallejo 2004, 2009; see review in Makowski and Vega Centeno 2004).

Despite the absence of monumental remains in the first half of the Late Intermediate Period, it is probable that for the inhabitants of the valley, Pachacamac was an exceptional place. Pachacamac was exceptional due to its prime location on the right bank of the mouth of the river to the Pacific Ocean and the particular features of the landscape: several rocky promontories facing the coastline, the guano islands with the abandoned buildings of the Lima era, a lagoon, and several springs and wetlands (Shimada, this volume).

Indications that Pachacamac was an important local place of worship during the first half of the Late Intermediate Period are numerous and are distributed across from the north façade of the Painted Temple in the wide sandy pampa later occupied by the Pilgrims' Plaza and the ramped pyramids. The temple itself during this period was of reduced size, apparently maintaining the same stepped shape that characterizes its last phase (Franco 2004: 472–476; Pozzi-Escot et al. 2013; Uhle 2003 [1903]: 101–129). An extensive cemetery of multiple chamber burials, similar to those Reiss and Stübel (1880–1887) excavated at Ancón (Eeckhout 2005, 2010b; Kaulicke 2001; Shimada et al. 2004, 2010; Uhle 2003 [1903]: 111–207) were formed beginning in the Middle Horizon 2 in front of the northern façade. Around this cemetery ceremonial activities took place. Shimada (1991) has registered a sequence of floors with offerings on the outskirts of the cemetery. These surfaces are probably related to smaller ceremonial structures. The dispersion of ceramic fragments throughout the monumental area of Pachacamac, corresponding to the above periods, is broad and suggests that the ceremonies were performed regularly and massively.

The date construction of the "Painted Temple" has been established in literature by stylistic analysis of the famous Pachacamac Idol (Dulanto 2001). This exceptional venerated sculpture, carved out of wood and two-faced, was found deposited in the construction fill of the last phase of the building. The phase corresponds to the Late Horizon, judging by the findings and the style of figurative painting (Bonavia 1985; Dulanto 2001). Due to the borrowing of iconography from Tiahuanaco and northern Huari, which is present in the relief decoration adorning the figures of two anthropomorphic supernatural beings, the idol is usually assigned to the 2B/3 phases of the Middle Horizon (Shimada 1991: XXXIV; Dulanto 2001: 161; approximately tenth/eleventh century AD). Perhaps fortuitously, this chronological estimate agrees; the only C14 dating carried out was from a sample of the wood base from another idol, a post or column found at the top of the temple platform. In any case, the "Painted Temple" was built, according to Uhle (2003 [1903]: 121–142), subsequent to the oldest chamber burials found in this area of the site. These burials contained grave goods from Middle Horizon 2 (Kaulicke 2001; Segura and Shimada 2010). In a similar vein, Shimada (et al. 2010: 140, figure 30) found a disturbed funerary context with Middle Horizon 3 ceramics, corresponding to the first funereal use of the area in front of the temple, now located under the Pilgrims' Plaza. Other similar contexts were found intact by Eeckhout (2010b: 160–161, figures 7, 8) nearby, to the east.

Recent excavations do not support the influential hypotheses of Menzel (1964, 1968a, 1968b) and Rostworowski (2002a) about the hypothetical rising prestige of the sanctuary beginning in Middle Horizon 2, endorsed by most researchers to date. Arguments based on recent excavations have accumulated against these theories. Compared to the Huaca Malena (Angeles and Pozzi-Escot 2001, 2004), or Castillo de Huarmey (Prümers 2000; Giersz and Pardo 2014; Giersz 2017; Druc et al. 2020), the variety of exotic styles Uhle found in chamber tombs below the Painted Temple of Pachacamac do not seem exceptional (Kaulicke 2001). The funerary contexts from the Middle Horizon 2 are scarce and may be contemporary with Middle Horizon 3 styles (Eeckhout 2018; Makowski 2018; Makowski and Giersz 2016). Most of the findings of ceramics after the abandonment of the Old Temple would be classified in Phase 3 of the Middle Horizon (Franco 2004). Nor is there any evidence of architecture on a monumental scale (Angeles and Pozzi-Escot 2010) or ceremonial activities from Middle Horizon 2, except for occasional Nievería offerings (Franco and Paredes 2000, 2016).

The stylistic evolution of the local pottery from the Middle Horizon 3–4 (Menzel 1964, 1968b) to the Late Ychsma Phase suggests that the valley of Lurín was entering a progressive isolation from other production centers on the coast and in the mountains. In the early Ychsma and Tricolor styles, some interaction is maintained with the north-central coast ("Norte Chico": Vallejo 2004: 602–610; Dolorier and Casas 2008). However, the Middle Ychsma Phase is surprising because of the provincial characteristics and low technology it shows, particularly in comparison with the previous phases

(Bazán 1990, 1992; Díaz 2002; Falconi 2008; Feltham and Eeckhout 2004; Vallejo 2004: 610–621, 2009). The same trends can be observed in the case of textiles. Their designs are a pale, provincial reflection compared to the diversity and sophistication of the pieces from the Chancay Valley (Vanstan 1967; Strelov 1996; Rosenzweig 2006). This situation changed only in the Late Ychsma Phase and, from the point of view of the author, shows a clear relation to changes introduced under the Inca administration (Carmen and Makowski 2019; Makowski et al. 2008: 267–269).

There is a consensus among researchers who have excavated in Pachacamac over the past two decades that, except for the Painted Temple, all the post-Lima monumental buildings visible on the surface were constructed in the aforementioned Late Ychsma Phase (Eeckhout 2010a, 2013, this volume). This style characterizes local pottery production up to the second half of the sixteenth century, when it was replaced by colonial ceramics. The relative timing and origin of the Late Ychsma Phase are the subject of controversy.

According to Bazán (1990) and Vallejo (2004, 2009), most shapes and finishes characteristic of the hypothetical regional Ychsma pottery tradition originated in the Middle Ychsma Phase. Vallejo (2004) proposed subdividing the Middle Ychsma Phase into two subphases: A and B. Subphase A grouped utilitarian vessels designed for food preparation and storage, found in a single context excavated in Armatambo, in the Rímac Valley (Díaz and Vallejo 2002). On the other hand, subphase B is characterized by the repertory of vessels to serve drinks, bottles, and jars.

These same shapes and finishes (for example, cane prints, or dots by area) survived unchanged during the Late Horizon (Feltham and Eeckhout 2004: 654–657) to the end of the sequence, along with the variables considered diagnostic for the Late Ychsma Phase, as the author was able to prove during excavations at Pueblo Viejo–Pucará (Makowski and Vega Centeno 2004) and Pampa Norte Pachacamac, near the Second Wall.

A similar problem occurs in the subsequent phase, the Late Ychsma. Feltham and Eeckhout (2004) followed Vallejo's (2004) proposal to divide the Late Ychsma Phase into two subphases: A and B. The only difference between them is the alleged appearance in subphase B of imitations and imports of the Cuzco Polychrome style, the Chimu-Inca style, and other styles typical of the Late Horizon. Changes in Ychsma style directly relatable to the Inca presence are not very numerous in the perception of Feltham and Eeckhout (2004: 670: table 3), and are limited to:

New types of inclusions in the orange paste; a tendency towards flattened lips and/or strongly beveled on the outside; more orderly and fairly wide vertical bands on a red engobe; a reddish, almost purple, engobe; an increase in black ceramics; incised geometric designs painted after firing; paired snakes modeled horizontally on the upper body and/or neck of the vessel; frogs modeled so as to seem gripped onto the very edge of the neck; other zoomorphic appendages always placed at the very edge of the vessel [translation by author].

The proposals made by both authors are supported by the master stratigraphic sequence, which was formed from the results of their excavations in the monumental complex of the "Pyramid with Ramp No. 3." The sequence comprises five construction phases they assigned to the Late Intermediate Period based on C14 dating and two construction phases that would be located in the Late Horizon. In his seriation "among all types and sub-types that were defined for the Ychsma style, 18% is found exclusively in the Late Intermediate Period and 19% only in the Late Horizon" (Feltham and Eeckhout 2004: 673–675). Paredes and Ramos (1994) previously reached a similar conclusion.

Judging from the experiences of the research project that the author carried out in the Lurín Valley, the recurrence of imitations and imports of imperial Cuzco ceramic is very low in the excavations and directly related to the uses of each area in the given episode of their occupation (Makowski et al. 2005; López-Hurtado 2011; Makowski and Vega Centeno 2004; Ore 2008). In the Late Horizon levels, researchers often find only fragments corresponding to local styles of the Central Coast, even in Pachacamac (Eeckhout and Feltham 2004; Pavel Svendsen 2011).

A similar situation occurs with adobe architecture. The local system of adobe production using parallelepiped molds, the wall framing and the organization of work by tasks that characterize the Pyramid with Ramp No. 3 (Eeckhout 1995, 1999a, 1999b: 128–192, 2000) are fully comparable to the construction modalities in the doorways of the Second Wall, built in the Late Horizon, judging by the recurrent findings of Polychrome A Cuzco style imitations and other diagnostic styles under the foundations (Makowski 2006; Ore 2008; and below). It seems that the new types of adobe bricks, related to imperial technologies, have been introduced without causing the abandonment of the ancient techniques used in the Lurín Valley before their incorporation into Tahuantinsuyu (Presbitero n.d.). In this context, large discrepancies between researchers should not be surprising when discussing the construction date of a structure of the Late periods. As an example, one can cite the case of Palmas, a complex located on the upper side of the Lurín Valley, south of Pachacamac and the level of the Third Wall (see Figure 6.1). Díaz and Vallejo (2002: figure 9) classified the pottery of this site in its Middle Ychsma phase. Paredes and Ramos (1994), who excavated some cuts in this system of monumental walls, have put forward a full occupational sequence from the Middle Horizon through the Late Horizon. For Feltham and Eeckhout (2004: 649) several pieces in the Palmas collection are diagnostic for the Late Ychsma phase. From the point of view of the author, almost all illustrated and described fragments could come from the Late Horizon Period as they have direct counterparts in the material from Pueblo Viejo–Pucará.

Pachacamac Inca

When the author began the systematic excavations at Pachacamac in 2005 within the framework of the "Lomas de Lurín" (ex PATL) project, then called the "'Pachacamac Valley' Archaeological Program and Field-School," he focused on the set of questions related to the architectural organization of the sanctuary under Inca rule. According to completely reliable Spanish sources from the sixteenth century AD, Pachacamac became one of the three main temples of the Inca Empire, together with Koricancha and the Temple of the Sun and Moon islands (Lake Titicaca). Most questions are concerned with how the architecture of Pachacamac responded to the multiple functions of the great ceremonial center:

- What types of accesses were there to the temples and monumental area when you entered from the outside, and where were they located?
- What was the circulation pattern of those who entered the monumental area and where did they direct their steps?
- Regarding pilgrims and workers responsible for the construction of new buildings and expansion of existing ones, where did they camp?
- What role did the pyramids with ramps play in the new political and religious context?

As a starting point, the author has found it necessary to obtain reliable evidence of the relative chronology of the three walls that separate one sector of the site from another. We also needed to temporally place the construction of the entrances through the Second Wall from the north side of the Lurín Valley, and through the First Wall from the southern, coastal side. Michczyński's experience (et al. 2003, 2007) has shown that C14 dating is an imperfect source of chronological information despite fine Bayesian analysis because of the short duration of Inca occupation and the wide range of standard deviation. It has also been seen that local masonry bonding and the presence of pottery in exclusively or mostly local styles (Late Ychsma) are not sufficient evidence to assign the context or structure to the Late Intermediate Period and discard a later date. For this reason, we have based the chronology of the doorways, walls, entrances, and paths on the record of the imitations of Cuzco ceramics and other foreign styles, diagnostic elements for the Late Horizon, in primary contexts associated with the first level use of the structures or found in the foundations. With this method we have successfully demonstrated that the three walls (see Figures 6.1, 6.2), the façades of the Second Wall and the N-S Causeway, as well as large areas of camps between the Second and Third Walls (Figure 6.5), were built during the Late Horizon.

Most of the researchers who have conducted excavations at Pachacamac have assumed that the Inca Period corresponds to the last layer below the surface in the complex stratigraphy of the site and that it is distinguished by the abundance of pottery fragments that imitate the Cuzco ceramic style and other foreign styles of the time. The presence of these fragments in the lower layers was implicitly regarded as the effects of intrusion. During the excavation of more than 10,000 m² in Pueblo Viejo–Pucará (Makowski 2002b; Makowski and Vega Centeno 2004; Makowski et al. 2005; Makowski and Ruggles 2011; Makowski and Lizárraga 2011, Makowski 2016), a stratigraphic sequence with two to three phases on the sterile level, all corresponding to the Late Horizon, has been documented in several sectors of this urban settlement of *mitmaquna* from the high valley, probably Huarochirí Caringas. The two main phases were separated by evidence of a strong earthquake followed by episodes of intense rainfall. The destruction, in various parts of the settlement (for example, Sector III, Makowski et al. 2005) was such that they had to level the damaged structures and construct new buildings on top. It seemed more than likely that this situation could have been repeated in Pachacamac.

Moreover, the descriptions and comments made by Uhle (2003 [1903]) and

Figure 6.2. The units excavated in the south area of Pachacamac, in the Sun Temple and outside the First Wall. Illustration by Gabriela Oré.

Within the figure:

N

Sector IF

Primera Muralla

Templo Viejo

Sector IE

Templo del Sol

120   60   0   150 m

PROGRAMA ARQUEOLÓGICO ESCUELA DE CAMPO
VALLE DE PACHACAMAC
Pontificia Universidad Católica del Perú

Región:	LIMA	Pampas Sur - Temporada 2012		Código:	Wak'a 03
Provincia / Distrito	Lima / Lurín	Fecha: 29/06/2013	Escala: 1:3.000	Datum: WGS84-18S	Autor: Gabriela Oré M.

Tello (2009) gave evidence of heavy use of the entire space of the sanctuary during the Late Horizon, both inside and outside the monumental area on the vast sandy plain. The excavations we have conducted in different parts of the ceremonial complex of Pachacamac, including areas without monumental architecture, have fully confirmed the validity of this assessment. In many areas we found a complex stratigraphic sequence with materials diagnostic of the Late Horizon in several layers and overlying levels. Such evidence corresponds to the effects of leveling work done before construction, as well as the work required after a seismic event of considerable magnitude, such as floor renovation, removal and reconstruction of walls, garbage disposal, and building structures with walls and ceilings made of thatch and rush mats. Episodes of occupation and construction were often separated by layers of aeolian sand and colluvial deposits on slopes. The complexity of the stratigraphy and the thickness of all deposits, which often exceeds 2 m, are explained by the high intensity of human activities in a relatively short period of time.

The most important evidence for the stratigraphic sequence of Inca occupation in Pachacamac comes, of course, from the Sun Temple. Excavations at the northeast façade of this pyramid were carried out with a dual purpose:

- revising the stratigraphic sequence, documented for the first time by Strong and Corbett (1943) as a frequency diagram of ceramic styles based on the findings in this famous trench;
- defining the eventual entrance that gave access to the set of stairs leading to the top of the pyramid and was located near the axis of symmetry of the façade.

Four of the units excavated between 2010 and 2012 (Figure 6.2) were located along a suspicious spur that projected transversely to the slope and below the trench made by looters. This trench was dug at the site where two large projections were attached, bastion-like, to the first terrace of the stepped pyramid-shaped body and created a likely foyer for the main entrance to the temple. The almost rectangular shape of the buttress led us to suspect that some sort of pre-Hispanic architecture was hiding under the sand but was disassembled by looters in the period between the world wars. The looters' trench has affected part of the architecture of the foyer that opens onto the first terrace.

It is noteworthy that on Uhle's map (2003 [1903]: Figure 16) the bastions and hypothetical hallway appear completely covered by sand under the surface of a wide terrace that shows no walls. However, the shape of the buttress is marked on Uhle's map, although it is slightly smaller in size. We expected to find under this suggestive promontory a stairway or ramp that would lead through the hallway to the stairs recorded by Uhle. These stairs would have connected the entrance of the first terrace with the main entrance to the courtyard at the top of the pyramid.

Our suspicions were confirmed only partially, since we have found no traces of a Late Horizon ramp or stairway. However, the buttress hid traces of monumental architecture as we thought, but not from Inca times, rather from the Middle Lima Period (Lima 4.5: Makowski 2011, 2013; Makowski and Vallenas 2016; Patterson 1966). The foyer formed the single entryway to the stairs of the upper terraces. To our great surprise, further down the slope, we found a tall, wide mound of rubbish that stretched downhill in front of the entrance, instead of a monumental staircase. Judging by the complex stratification, this midden had accumulated over several decades, from the first years after the construction of the temple until the time of its abandonment in the Early Colonial Period. This is not simple household garbage. The reed mats from roofs and walls make up the majority of waste. Fine Cuzco polychrome pottery imitations abound, and there may also be some imports.

During our excavations we have successfully established a direct relationship between the stratigraphy of the midden and the architectural sequence of three phases in the retaining walls that line the entrance to the first terrace of the Temple of the Sun. The walls of the first phase were constructed using large parallelepiped adobes on the E/F interface (I-E-3 Unit, see Figure 6.2). The outer side wall is lined with partially quarried slabs. After a seismic event that left traces of the destruction of masonry in the E layer, the space between two projecting bastions was reduced. Apparently, the intent was to rebuild the fallen segments of the façade and also restrict access to the top of the pyramid with the construction of new adobe walls, this time uncoated and of a lesser quality than the previous ones. The last and third construction episode relates to the building of a thin wall of quickly made adobes that were tempered with a lot of grit. The discernible function of this wall that abuts the southern projection of the hallway was to definitively close the access to the top of the pyramid. This wall, probably built in the first decades of the colonial era, has been cut by the looters' trench.

The entire stratigraphy of the midden mentioned above was recorded in the I-G-1 unit; several levels of deposits and the dragging of organic and inorganic materials (Figure 6.4, right) form two superimposed layers of significant thickness, separated by a layer of wind-blown sand (A–G and I, J). The layers I and J have an average thickness of more than 1 m, and are composed of fragments of adobe, mortar, and plaster mixed with fragments of mats. The layers lie on the unpaved surface slope of the hill (Figure 6.4: layer K). This is the continuation of the I layer in the I-E-3 unit (Figure 6.4, left). There is no doubt that the accumulation of waste was created by the renovation of structures built of perishable materials on the terraces of the Temple of the Sun as well as the removal of debris after a strong seismic event. The B, D, F layers of the I-G-1 unit (Figure 6.3) have a higher concentration of reed mat fragments used for walls and roofs than the previous one. Many of the architectural elements of perishable materials were partially burned and the midden contains multiple levels of ash lenses. In the I-E-4 cut (Figure 6.4, center) we found that the G and H layers of the midden had accumulated over the walls of the second phase, when the walls were partially destroyed by human action and precipitation. Therefore, it is assumed that this layer was formed as a result of the deliberate destruction of the reed mat architecture after the abandonment of the Temple of the Sun in the Early Colonial Period. In both cases, the layers of dismantlement were formed using organized labor whose participants descended the staircase and hallway at the foot of the first terrace of the temple to dispose of waste on the slope of the hill.

Middens formed by rubble and garbage, similar to the one excavated, have accumulated along the northwest façade of the first terrace. The Strong and Corbett (1943) Trench goes through one of the largest accumulations of its kind. The waste was dumped, in this case, from the top of the first terrace down the slope of the hill. We conducted a survey of the southern profile of this trench (I-E-5 unit, see Figure 6.3) and we found that the stratigraphic situation is very similar to that registered in the entrance area. Had one found this stratigraphic situation elsewhere in Pachacamac, one would have surely thought that only the C layer, made up of burnt waste, corresponds to the Late Horizon, since in this layer the highest concentration of Cuzco pottery and diagnostic textiles are found. The lower strata in this profile, over 4 m high, would have been dated to the Late Intermediate Period. In this case there is, happily, no doubt that the first five layers (A–E) are from the Late Horizon, due to the direct association with the architecture of the Temple of the Sun. The relative chronological sequence for this sector of Pachacamac, assembled from our stratigraphic research is as follows:

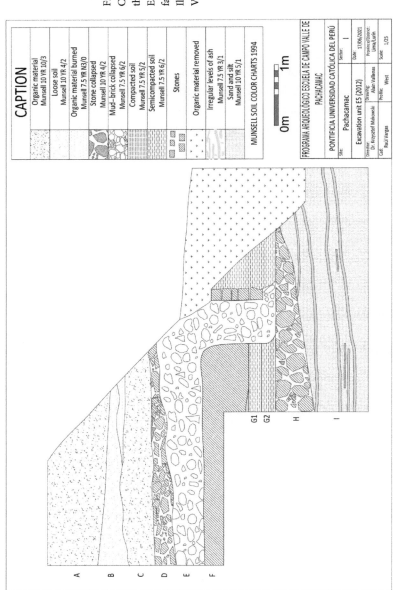

CAPTION

Organic material
Munsell 10 YR 10/3

Loose soil
Munsell 10 YR 4/2

Organic material burned
Munsell 7.5 YR N3/0

Stone collapsed
Munsell 10 YR 4/2

Mud–brick collapsed
Munsell 7.5 YR 6/2

Compacted soil
Munsell 7.5 YR 5/2

Semicompacted soil
Munsell 7.5 YR 6/2

Stones

Organic material removed

Irregular levels of ash
Munsell 7.5 YR 3/1

Sand and silt
Munsell 10 YR 5/1

MUNSELL SOIL COLOR CHARTS 1994

0m   1m

PROGRAMA ARQUEOLÓGICO ESCUELA DE CAMPO VALLE DE PACHACAMAC

PONTIFICIA UNIVERSIDAD CATÓLICA DEL PERÚ

Site: Pachacamac		Sector: I
Excavation unit E5 (2012)	Drawing: Alain Vallenas	Date: 17/06/2021
Director: Dr. Krzysztof Makowski		Province/District: Lim.q/Lurín
Cad: Raúl Vargas	Profile: West	Scale: 1/25

Figure 6.3. Strong and Corbett Trench revisited: the south profile of our E-5 unit in the northeast façade of the Sun Temple. Illustration by Alain Vallenas.

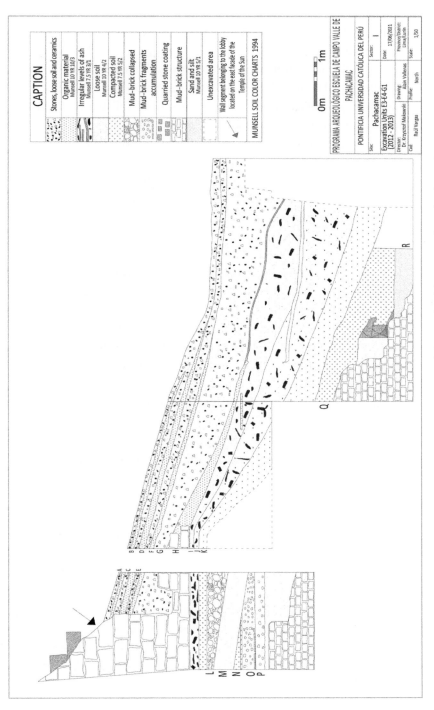

Figure 6.4. Stratigraphy at the main entrance of the Temple of the Sun, northeast façade: north profiles of the 1-E3, 3,4, and 1-G1 units—"A to "L," Late Horizon levels; N-R strata, use and abandonment of the Early Intermediate Period architecture. Map by Alain Vallenas and Raúl Vargas Abanto.

1. Brief and repeated episodes, prior to construction activities, related to the "Villa el Salvador" ceramic type (Stothert and Ravines 1977; Makowski et al. 2013).
2. Construction of monumental architecture with medium-sized parallelepiped adobes during the Middle Lima occupation (Lima 4.5, Paterson 1966; Vallenas 2012; Makowski and Vallenas 2016); in some cases, the walls are coated with stones.
3. Hiatus marked by the gradual destruction of the Middle Lima architecture.
4. Construction of the northeastern terraces of the Temple of the Sun, with the entrance between two bastions on the façade of the first terrace, at the beginning of the Inca occupation, perhaps by the Inca Tupac Yupanqui mandate.
5. Earthquake, with subsequent debris removal and reconstruction. The effects of this earthquake were easy to distinguish in the stratigraphy of Pachacamac from the later ones, including the Lima great earthquake of 1687 (see Pozzi-Escot and Bernuy, this volume), because their evidence is below another level of occupation with the pottery of the Late Horizon, and of course also below levels corresponding to the reuse of space in the Early Colonial Period and/or to definitive abandonment.
6. Intentional destruction of the architecture made of perishable materials, the foyer and waste disposal at the foot of the façade.
7. Closing of the hallway entrance through the construction of the north-south wall, probably at the beginning of the Colonial Period.

The Date of Construction of the First Wall

All researchers, without exception, agree with Uhle's preliminary observations (2003 [1903]: 92) when he stated, "The dilapidated wall that Estete talks about is inside, the oldest, as the outside is, even now, almost intact." The First Wall starts at the southeast corner of the Temple of the Sun and goes around the Old Temple and the Painted Temple to reach the north façade of this building (see Figure 6.2). The wall encloses two temples, a large quadrangular precinct, and some funerary areas, separating these from the Plaza of the Pilgrims and the precincts of the pyramids with ramps. For this reason, scholars agree to consider this the wall of the sacred enclosure of Pachacamac.

The date of construction for the wall has never been clarified, but researchers suspect it might be related to one of the phases of construction of the Old Lima Temple in the Early Intermediate Period (Patterson 1966, 1985) or the Middle Horizon (Bueno 1974–1975). That date seemed unlikely to us given that the wall at both ends is attached to the walls of the first terrace of the Sun Temple, built during the Late Horizon. However, without clear evidence, one should not rule out the possibility that the oldest walls remained covered under the foundations of those seen on the surface. To test this hypothesis, in 2009 we opened eight survey trenches (Makowski 2010b) along different parts of the southern segment of the enclosure that faces the coast of the Pacific Ocean (Figure 6.2). Other excavations were also carried out in the eastern segment with a unit open during the 2013 campaign. All cuts and trenches were located in those short sections of the wall where the mud-brick fabric was not visible on the surface and therefore access to the interior of the enclosure could have existed in the past.

Thanks to the results of our excavations, we have ruled out the existence of traces of earlier walls. Besides the above-mentioned trenches and cuts, we opened another trench through the flat part of the pampa, reaching sterile soil without any vestiges of an eventual parallel wall under the surface. In all units researched we found pottery that is very diagnostic for the Late Horizon, including Cuzco Polychrome A and Cuzco Figurative, in direct association or under the foundation. For much of its path, the wall was built on sterile soil. Only in the vicinity of the Old Temple did we find a Middle Lima (Lima 4–5; Patterson 1966; Makowski and Vallenas 2016) occupancy level.

A variety of evidence suggests that the construction of the First Wall was started at the end of the Late Horizon and was never completed. The differences in height between the sections in all probability are related, among other factors, to the progress of construction. There are differences in the progression of construction between sections and between tasks in each section. In the northern parts we recorded some sections in which the work progressed only to the stage of construction of the wall base. In some cases, the foundation design was ambitious and required a large investment of work. For example, a wide-based platform runs parallel to the wall, supporting the slope of the hill next to the "South-West building." This measure apparently did not prevent the collapse of the wall in the section that rises to the Temple of the Sun. The way the wall is attached to the lower terrace of the temple suggests that the idea of building the wall occurred after the earthquake and the rebuilding of the pyramid. This is confirmed by the complex stratigraphy recorded in the northeast corner of the enclosure. The wall is superimposed upon another level of apparently domestic constructions, also from the Late Horizon. Repeated rains seriously affected the adobe and thatch buildings on this level. The superimposed layered sediments covering the adobe foundations of the wall are unmistakable. It seems very likely that these are traces of El Niño–ENSO 1925/26, considered particularly strong on a regional scale. Other relatively intense events occurred in 1500, then again in 1525–26, 1540–41, and 1544 (Kiracofe and Marr 2008: 161–162; Gergis and Fowler 2008; Couper-Johnston 2000; Quinn et al. 1987). However, the first strong event that is historically well documented only occurred in 1578 (Ortlieb 2000, Huertas 2001). Below the adobe and thatch constructions affected by the rains are vestiges of a platform, probably from the Late Intermediate Period. The platform is built with layers of clay soil and boulders. On its surface there are traces of thatch (*quincha*) architecture whose outline was changed very often. Levels with Early Intermediate Period pottery, underlying the platform, complete the stratigraphic sequence.

It is necessary to emphasize the fact that despite having excavated all possible points of an entry location, we have not found any doorway, whether completed or at advanced levels of foundation work. The examination of all sections preserved to a height of 1 m or more suggests that it was the intention of the builders to prevent access to the enclosure from all sides. However, part of the northern section of the First Wall has been destroyed and hidden by the current east-west visitors' path, which already existed as a bridle path at the beginning of the twentieth century. Almost all of this northern section, now destroyed, can be seen, however, on Uhle's plans (2003 [1893]: annex). Only some interruptions are seen at the height of the Pilgrims' Plaza and Sunken Patio. According to Uhle (2003 [1903]: annex), the structure today interpreted as ushnu (Hyslop 1990: 259; Shimada 1991) was the "porters lodge" and therefore functioned as the door from the Pilgrims' Plaza to the inside of the *témenos* enclosure. Given the very late date and the unfinished state of the First Wall, two alternatives of interpretation, perhaps complementary, remain open:

1. The First Wall was part of a reorganizational plan of the ceremonial space conceived a few years before the arrival of Pizarro, and the plan was never completed.
2. The construction was initiated or taken up rigorously after the Spanish Conquest to seal access to the temple.

The relationship observed between the consolidation work of the First Wall slope and the construction of the southwest building suggests that work began even before the Spanish Conquest. In any case, it is clear that the Old Temple, the Painted Temple, and the Temple of the Sun did not share the same enclosure, similar to the temenos in the Greco-Roman tradition. The first wall was added belatedly and never finished. Thus, each of the temples has an independent access.

Entries through the Second Wall and N-S Street

Unlike the First Wall and Third Wall, the Second Wall was not part of a single architectural project nor was it necessarily built in a short period. This wall is actually composed of parts of perimeter fences of several pyramids with ramp numbers 4, 6, and 7. Only a few segments to the northwest and northeast could have been traced as a separate fence, or as part of a project of an unfinished monumental building. Surveys, reviews of aerial and satellite photos, and the results of our excavations have left no doubt that only two gateways in the Second Wall provided access from the sandy *pampa* extending between the Second and Third walls into the monumental complex. One of them was in the visual axis extending between the Gateway of the Third Wall and the main ramp of the Pyramid with Ramp Number 1 and facing the courtyard in front of Pyramid with Ramp Number 4 (Figure 6.5). The other entrance is opened in the middle of the North-South Street whose side walls were projecting outward from the Second Wall. Both gateways were built during the Late Horizon. This conclusion is supported by the results of our excavations in four units located in strategic places, where we could record the stratigraphic relations between the roadway(s), the side walls of the street, and the sequence of construction and abandonment of other buildings or adjacent architectural components. These units were located in:

- The entrance through the Second Wall (SW) (Figure 6.5: SW-E1).
- The intersection of the North-South Street with the East-West unfinished street, which runs along the external façade of the second wall (Figure 6.5: SW-E2).
- The final segment of the North-South Street on the outskirts of the Second Wall and the space between the west lateral wall of this street and the rear face of the Pyramid with Ramp No. 8 (Figure 6.5: SW-A1,2,3).

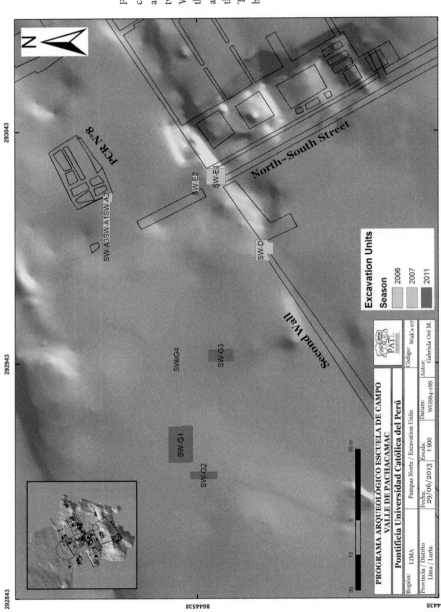

Figure 6.5. The units excavated in the northern area of Pachacamac, the two gates in the Second Wall, the beginning of the North-South Street, and the camps between the Second and the Third Wall. Illustration by Gabriela Oré.

- The north end of the roadway from the North-South Street and the encampment area.

In all four units we have found matching sequences, and in some cases complementary ones. The cut made between the doorjambs of the gate (Figure 6.6) has been particularly revealing. The two jambs of the gate, the street surface (a remarkably thick and hard roadway made of mud and crossed midway by a canal), and the outer walls of the Pyramid with Ramp No. 4, are part of the same construction episode. This episode clearly occurred after construction of the perimeter enclosure of the Pyramid with Ramp No. 7. The second segment of the wall that abuts the doorjamb that belongs to this enclosure and its foundation is deeper than the west doorjamb (Figure 6.6). In addition, two affirmed surfaces were destroyed to build the canal and the causeway, which are directly related to the foundation of the jambs. The eastern jamb of the doorway was built on a stone base in the trench dug in order to reach the foundation level corresponding to the corner of the enclosure of Pyramid with Ramp No. 7, and thus save the gap regarding the foundation of the western wall of the street (enclosure of Pyramid with Ramp No. 4). The channel with stone-covered walls and rectangular walls, constructed to ensure cleanliness, has characteristics similar to channels recorded elsewhere in Inca Pachacamac, in particular in the vicinity of the *acllahuasi*. This channel turns west after a few meters and traverses the western side wall of the road, then crosses the courtyard of Pyramid with Ramp No. 4 in the direction of the *acllahuasi*. Up to three levels of thin mud floors, separated by thin layers of aeolian sand, were formed during the use of the road in the Late Horizon. Then a strong earthquake caused the collapse of the side walls and the permanent abandonment of that section of the street (Figure 6.6). The stratigraphic sequence described above was covered under thick depositions of wind sand alternating with lateral wall collapses that originated from earthquakes in the Colonial and Republican periods. These depositions and landslides of adobes were excavated by Pozzi-Escot and Bernuy (this volume) throughout the street until the last level of use of the road, except for the part of the entrance from the north, investigated by us.

The validity of this scenario has been fully confirmed with the excavations of the section of the street located outside the Second Wall. With the SW-A1, 2, 3 trench (Figure 6.5), we transversely cut the street with its two side walls and the space between the street and the front face of the Pyramid with Ramp No. 8. The cut exposed the roadway and the foundations of the side

Figure 6.6. Profile through the North-South Street at the gateway of the Second Wall, view from the north: stratigraphy beneath the roadway crossed by a canal with many wells for cleaning. On the road: levels of sanding and floors covered by collapse caused by the earthquake. Photo by Krzysztof Makowski.

walls of the street. The roadway and the side walls were built in the initial stages of the Late Horizon, like the doorway. The accumulation of various levels of tamped sand shows that the street was in use some time before a strong earthquake demolished entire sections of side walls. These were never rebuilt. Several sections of the walls had been dismantled, in some cases down to their foundations, and a trench was dug for this purpose. In all probability, the attempt was to recover bricks and facing stones.

After the earthquake, the construction of the Pyramid with Ramp No. 8 started. The roadway of the street at this time was invaded by thatch (*quincha*) orthogonal structures and by stratified mounds of garbage. Many of these structures have made use of bricks and quarried stones from the earthquake-damaged structures, reused here to strengthen the foundation. There is no doubt that the front entrance on the North-South Street was completely closed at the end of the Late Horizon. We have more than sufficient grounds to believe that after the closing of the North-South Street, access through the Second Wall was through the second gate, open to the large patio in front of the Pyramid with Ramp No. 4. This gate is located in the visual axis connecting the central ramp of Pyramid with Ramp No. 1 with the only doorway that opened in the Third Wall. Everyone who came from the north entered Pachacamac through this gate (see Figure 6.1). The ceramic material found in the leveling layer, next to large pitcher-*paicas* that provided water for the builders, leaves no doubt that the gate and the wall were built in the Late Horizon.

In the second section of the wall adjacent to the doorway we have not found clear traces of destruction by earthquake damage, but rainfall damage is visible. The fact that one of the decorated fragments found in the foundations of the entry matched up with another found in the roadway of the North-South Street reinforces the idea that the new entry was enabled after the abandonment of the street or shortly before. Note that the courtyards off Pyramids with Ramps Nos. 1 and 4 communicated with the North-South Street via two entries in the wall separating the courtyard from the street. The results of our excavations throw new light on the chronology of use of the largest among the pyramids with ramps and the reason for the North-South Street construction. Initially we suspected (Makowski 2012) that said street specifically led, in a ceremonial manner, to Pyramid with Ramp No. 2 and further provided access to Pyramids with Ramps Nos. 1 and 12. The presence of a depression left perhaps by the old quarry, more than 4 m deep, which seemed to interrupt the path just south of the intersection of the North-West and East-West streets, is the origin of our suspicion. Several researchers, from Uhle (2003 [1903]: map, annex) to Patterson (1985) and Eeckhout (1999b: 116), considered, however, that the road bridged this gap and continued southward to a sunken patio, there joining the system of corridors and passages that led to the Pilgrims' Plaza. Excavations and cleaning work undertaken for the preservation and enhancement of the site by Pozzi-Escot and Bernuy (this volume) are providing concrete evidence to clarify this issue. During the 2016–2019 seasons we have managed to verify that the North-South Street continued to the Quadrangle and ended inside. This extension was under construction shortly before the Spanish Conquest and was never finished. Significantly, the East-West Street does not continue to the west, as the *decumanus* of Roman cities do, contrary to Uhle's considerations.

Ravines (1996) rightly observed that instead of a street, it is more a series of triangular and unleveled open spaces, without roadways and covered with pre-Hispanic trash behind adjacent enclosures. These enclosures lack access to the adjacent triangular spaces. Compared to the western section, the eastern section is characterized by a roadway—now covered by protective layers laid to enhance the site—which runs on top of the oldest buildings that must have been leveled and covered for this purpose. The eastern section of the road ends with the access to the Pyramid with Ramp No. 2.

Final Discussion and Conclusions

In light of the results of excavations carried out under the direction of the author since 2005, it was established that Pachacamac has acquired its planned appearance by the successive realization of various construction projects carried on by the Inca administration. The reconstruction of what was Pachacamac in the Late Intermediate Period depends on the size of future excavations, since the Ychsma vestiges are largely covered or transformed by the architecture of the Late Horizon. In almost all surveyed sectors we found more than three stratigraphic levels with Late Horizon material. A simple comparison of waste deposition thickness is sufficient to note that only in the latter period was Pachacamac the scene of mass activities. The thickness of laminate waste levels often exceeds 2 m. In comparison, Late Intermediate Period levels do not exceed 0.50 m, and the density of cultural content in them is relatively low. There is no doubt that the earthquake and torrential rains have further contributed to the creation of this particular stratigraphic situation.

Contrary to widespread opinion, the pyramids with ramps, a local architectural form but possibly inspired by the north, were still being built after the transformation of the local Ychsma ceremonial center into an Inca sanctuary and oracle. These structures have played an important role as places for the reception of visitors, also designed for various rituals requiring mass participation. Two of the pyramids were part of the complex reception for all those visitors who came through the monumental gates aligned in the Second and Third walls. The walled streets running through the grouping of pyramids with ramps led the visitors on foot to the large courtyards of the pyramids with ramps and the restricted access system of the Pilgrims' Plaza. The space between the two outer walls was not occupied by spacious and organized residential neighborhoods as previously thought by many scholars. This area was occupied by camps and workshops producing building materials during the Late Horizon. Some dispersed clusters of residential architecture are found at the foot of Gallinazo Hill and along the high sandy edge that faces the Lurín Valley. The term "populated ceremonial center" best summarizes these characteristics rather than urban center.

During Cuzco imperial administration, Pachacamac lacked the characteristics of other populous cities from the Middle Ages or the Renaissance in Europe or Asia, according to the results of our investigations. There were no residential areas *sensu stricto*. The complex lacked perimeter walls. Nothing prevented access to the sanctuary from the sea coast. However, the roads coming from the Rímac Valley or following the branch of the Qhapaq Ñan along the Lurín River definitely headed toward the two symbolic gates, one in the sector of Las Palmas (Paredes and Ramos 1994) and another in the Third Wall. Visitors had to go through lengthy and messy camps to reach one of the two doors in the Second Wall, built and enabled sequentially, one after another. After going through one of the gates, visitors were directed toward certain precincts. The complex of the Pyramids with Ramps Nos. 1 and 4 suggests that the division into two to three groups was one of the principles used to organize the visitors. Three pyramids with ramps (numbers 1a, 1b, 4) and their outer patios share a common area with a source of fresh water today covered with rubble. After having prepared themselves by fasting, some pilgrims could access one of the temples after gathering in the Pilgrims' Plaza in front of the Painted Temple.

There is an interesting difference in the mode of access to the holy places, including the oracle. Those who went to the Painted Temple could apparently be seen in their ascent to the top patios. This was not the case with the Temple of the Sun. The chosen had to climb up seemingly half the slope of the mountain, where entries to the first and second terraces were located. At the entrance we have excavated a surface of rammed earth leading to the door flanked by two bastion-like projections on the terrace. There was no ramp or staircase. While the full communication circuit from the entrance remains to be discovered, it is quite clear that visitors to the temple disappeared from the sight of the people gathered in the square and no one could see the top of the temple, the final destination of the climb.

Labyrinthine corridors and stairs, partially uncovered first by Tello and then during subsequent cleaning and maintenance work carried out during the last century, led from one terrace to the next, until one reached the entrance that was located symmetrically in the center of the northeastern wall of the top courtyard. Structures containing, among other things, the object of worship were in the center of this courtyard. This is where the main rituals were performed and where the oracle gave her premonitions.

The intensity of the construction work realized by the Cuzco administration, and the apparent absence of a single plan regulating the whole, suggests that each Sapa Inca contributed to transforming the design of the ceremonial center of Pachacamac and to commanding new buildings. The roads and entrances were also frequently modified. The image of the role of the Incas in the history of the sanctuary, formed from the results of excavations, do not necessarily agree with the reconstruction of events from historical sources (Rostworowski 1972, 1999, 2002a, 2002b). According to these sources, the incorporation of the seigniory (*curacazgo*) Ychsma to the Tahuantinsuyu Empire would have happened peacefully in times of Tupac Inca Yupanqui. The Inca administration would not have altered the political organization of this dominion.

The results of the excavations carried out over the past 20 years suggest a different scenario. The great investment the Incas made in transforming the political and economic organization of the three valleys of the Central Coast is evident. This investment does not refer only to new monumental buildings in ceremonial and administrative centers such as Pachacamac, Armatambo, Maranga, and Mateo Salado. Judging by the Rímac (Lati-Ate: Villacorta 2004, 2010) and Lurín (Eeckhout 1999b; López-Hurtado 2011; Makowski 2002b) valleys, the majority of large settlements with elite residences and palace complexes, which previously were dated to the Late Intermediate Period, were built during the Late Horizon. The settlement network is related to the parts of the basin suitable for cultivation of highly prized crops, such as corn, pepper, and coca (Rostworowski 1988). Among these settlements, one has the characteristics of a military colony and was founded by *mitimaes* Huarochirí: Pueblo Viejo–Pucará (Makowski 2002b; Makowski et al. 2005; Makowski and Lizárraga 2011; Makowski and Ruggles 2011). Archaeological evidence suggests that the Cuzco administration had developed a system of territorial control rather than a hegemonic incorporation. Archaeological evidence—the complex stratigraphy of the Late Horizon recorded at all sites excavated systematically in the Lurín Valley, and

C14 dating of the Ychsma Late Period—also contradicts the chronological hypothesis formulated with historical criteria regarding the short duration of the Inca domination in the Central Coast: AD 1470–1533. Maybe we should move this date for Inca domination back at least a few decades to the reign of Pachacuti Inca?

References Cited

Ángeles, Rommel, and Denise Pozzi-Escot

2001　Textiles del Horizonte Medio. Las evidencias de Huaca Malena, Valle de Asia in Huari y Tiwanaku. Modelos vs. Evidencias. Primera Parte. *Boletín de Arqueología PUCP* 4(2000): 401–424.

2004　Del Horizonte Medio al Horizonte Tardío en la costa sur central: El caso del valle de Asia. *Bulletin de l'Institut Français d'Études Andines* 33(3): 861–886.

2010　El Horizonte Medio en Pachacámac. In *Arqueología en el Perú. Nuevos aportes para el estudio de las sociedades andinas prehispánicas*, edited by Rubén Romero Velarde and Trine Pavel Svendsen, pp. 175–196. Anheb Impresiones, Lima.

Bazán, Francisco

1990　*Arqueología y etnohistoria de los periodos prehispánicos tardíos de la costa central del Perú*. Tesis de licenciatura. Universidad Nacional Mayor de San Marcos, Lima.

1992　*Arqueología de Lima: Evaluación del término huancho. Los estilos de cerámica de Lima a fines del Horizonte Medio*. CREarte, Centro de Estudios y Difusión de Arte, Lima

2008　Los contextos funerarios Ichma Inicial de Conde de Las Torres. *Arqueología y Sociedad* 19: 9–22.

Bernuy, Katiusha, and Rocío Villar

2009　Por estas calles. Investigación arqueológica en la Calle Norte-Sur de Pachacamac. *Gaceta Cultural del Perú* 39: 26–27.

Bonavía, Duccio

1959　Cerámica de Puerto Viejo (Chilca). In *Actas del 2do Congreso Nacional de Historia del Perú, 1958*, pp. 137–168. Lima.

1985　*Mural Painting in Ancient Peru*. Indiana University Press, Bloomington.

Bueno, Alberto

1970　Breves notas acerca de Pachacamac. *Arqueología y Sociedad* 4: 13–24.

1974–1975　Cajamarquilla y Pachacamac: Dos ciudades de la costa central del Perú. *Boletín Bibliográfico de Antropología Americana* 37(46): 171–193.

1982　El antiguo valle de Pachacamac. Espacio, tiempo y cultura. *Boletín de Lima* 24: 1–52.

Carmen Castillo, Mayra, and Krzysztof Makowski

2019　La cerámica provincial inca como producto y como expresión de estatus en la población *mitmaquna* de Pueblo Viejo-Pucará. *Boletín de Arqueología PUCP* 27: 7–26. https://doi.org/10.18800/boletindearqueologiapucp.201902.001.

Cerrón Palomino, Rodolfo

2000　"Hurín": un espejismo léxico opuesto a "Hanan." In *El hombre y los Andes. Homenaje a Franklin Pease*, edited by Javier Flores Espínosa and Rafael Varón Gabaï, pp. 219–235. Fondo Editorial de la Pontificia Universidad Católica del Perú, Lima.

Couper-Johnston, Ross

2000 *El Niño: The Weather Phenomenon that Changed the World*. Hodder Headline, Sidney.

Díaz, Luisa

2008 Aproximaciones hacia la problemática del territorio Ychsma. *Arqueología y Sociedad* 19: 115–127.

Díaz, Luisa, and Francisco Vallejo

2002 Armatambo y el dominio incaico en el valle de Lima. *Boletín de Arqueología PUCP* 6: 355–374.

Dolorier, Camilo

1998 Pirámides con rampa en Pachacamac. Análisis espacial, crecimiento y evolución de la ciudad. *Arkinka* 32: 102–112.

Dolorier, Camilo, and Lyda Casas

2008 Caracterización de algunos estilos locales de la Costa Central a inicios del Intermedio Tardío. *Arqueología y Sociedad* 19: 23–42.

Druc, I., M. Giersz, M. Kałaska, R. Siuda, M. Syczewski, Nita R. Pimentel, J. M. Chyla, and K. Makowski

2020 Offerings for Wari Ancestors: Strategies of Ceramic Production and Distribution at Castillo de Huarmey, Peru. *Journal of Archaeological Science: Reports* 30: 1–9. https://doi.org/10.1016/j.jasrep.2020.102229

Dulanto, Jalh

2001 Dioses de Pachacamac: el ídolo y el templo. In *Dioses del Antiguo Perú*, Vol. II, edited by Krzysztof Makowski, pp. 159–181. Banco de Crédito del Perú, Lima.

Eeckhout, Peter

1995 Pirámide con rampa n° 3 de Pachacamac, costa central del Perú. Resultados preliminares de la primera temporada de excavaciones (zona 1 y 2). *Bulletin de l'Institut Français d'Études Andines* 24(1): 65–106.

1998 Le temple de Pachacamac sous l'Empire Inca. *Journal de la Société des Américanistes* 84(1): 9–44.

1999a Pirámide con rampa N° III, Pachacamac. Nuevos datos, nuevas perspectivas. *Bulletin de l'Institut Français d'Études Andines* 28(2): 169–214.

1999b Pachacamac durant l'Intermédiaire Récent. Étude d'un site monumental préhispanique de la Côte centrale du Pérou. *BAR International Series*, 747.

2000 Investigaciones arqueológicas en la pirámide n° III de Pachacamac, costa central del Perú. *Estudios Lationamericanos* 20: 19–40.

2003a Diseño arquitectónico, patrones de ocupación y formas de poder en Pachacamac, Costa central del Perú. *Revista Española de Antropología Americana* 33: 17–37.

2003b Ancient monuments and patterns of power at Pachacamac, central coast of Perú. *Beiträge zur allgemeinen und vergleichend archäologie*, 23: 139–182.

2004a Pachacámac y el proyecto Ychsma (1999–2003). *Bulletin de l'Institut Français d'Études Andines* 33(3): 425–448.

2004b Reyes del sol y señores de la luna. Inkas e Ychsmas en Pachacámac. *Chungará* 36(2): 495–503.

2004c La sombra de Ychsma. Ensayo introductorio sobre la arqueología de la costa central del Perú en los periodos tardíos. *Bulletin de l'Institut Français d'Études Andines* 33(3): 403–423.

2005 Ancient Peru's Power Elite. *National Geographic* 207(3): 52–57.

2008   El oráculo de Pachacamac y los peregrinajes a larga distancia en el mundo andino antiguo. In *Adivinación y oráculos en el mundo andino antiguo*, edited by Marco Curatola and Mariusz S. Ziolkowski, pp. 161–180. Institut Français d'Études Andines, Fondo Editorial PUCP, Lima.

2009   Poder y jerarquías ychsmas en el valle de Lurín. *Arqueología y Sociedad* 19: 223–240.

2010a Las pirámides con rampa de Pachacamac durante el Horizonte Tardío. In *Arqueología en el Perú: Nuevos aportes para el estudio de las sociedades andinas prehispánicas*, edited by Rubén Romero Velarde and Trine Pavel Svendsen, pp. 415–434. Anheb Impresiones, Lima.

2010b Nuevas evidencias sobre costumbres funerarias en Pachacamac. In *Max Uhle (1856–1944). Evaluaciones de sus investigaciones y obras*, edited by P. Kaulicke, M. Fischer, P. Masson, and G. Wolff, pp. 151–164. Fondo Editorial PUCP, Lima.

2012   Absolute Chronology, Monumental Architecture and Social Complexity at Pachacamac. Paper presented at the Roundtable on the Pachacamac Sanctuary, Dumbarton Oaks Library and Collection, Harvard University, Washington, D.C.

2013   Change and Permanency on the Coast of Ancient Peru: The Religious Site of Pachacamac. *World Archaeology* 45(1): 137–160.

2018   The Middle Horizon and Southern Andean Iconographic Series on the Central Coast of Peru. In *Images in Action. The Southern Andean Iconographic Series*, edited by William H. Isbell, Mauricio I. Uribe, Ann Tiballi, and Edward P. Zegarra, pp. 529–570. UCLA, Cotsen Institute of Archaeology Press, Los Angeles.

Estete, Miguel de

1968 [1535]   Noticia del Perú. In *Biblioteca Peruana. Primera Serie*, Vol. I, pp. 345–404. Editores Técnicos Asociados S.A., Lima.

Falconí, Iván

2008   Caracterización de la cerámica de la fase Ychsma Medio del sitio de Armatambo, Costa Central del Perú. *Arqueología y Sociedad* 19: 43–66.

Farfán, Carlos

2004   Aspectos simbólicos de las pirámides con rampa; ensayo interpretativo. *Bulletin de l'Institut Français d'Études Andines* 33(3): 449–464.

2010   Poder simbólico y poder político del estado Inca en la cordillera del Pariacaca. In *Arqueología en el Perú: Nuevos aportes para el estudio de las sociedades andinas prehispánicas*, edited by R. R. Velarde and T. P. Svendsen, pp. 377–413. AnhebImpresiones, Lima.

Feltham, Jane, and Peter Eeckhout

2004   Hacia una definición del estilo Ychsma: Aportes preliminares sobre la cerámica Ychsma tardía de la pirámide III de Pachacamac. *Bulletin de l'Institut Français d'Etudes Andines* 33(3): 643–679.

Franco, Régulo

1993a Los dos templos principales de Pachacamac. *Revista del Museo de Arqueología* 4: 55–77.

1993b El centro ceremonial de Pachacamac: Nuevas evidencias en el Templo Viejo. *Boletín de Lima* 86: 45–62.

1998   *La pirámide con Rampa N° 2 de Pachacamac. Excavaciones y nuevas interpretaciones.* Trujillo.

2004   Poder religioso, crisis y prosperidad en Pachacamac: del Horizonte Medio al Intermedio Tardío. *Bulletin de l'Institut Français d'Études Andines* 33(3): 465–506.

Franco, Régulo, and Ponciano Paredes

2000   El Templo Viejo de Pachacamac: Nuevos aportes al estudio del Horizonte Medio. *Boletín de Arqueología PUCP* 4: 607–630.

Gergis, Joelle L., and Anthony M. Fowler

2008   A History of ENSO Events since 1525: Implications for Future Climate Change. *Climatic Change* 92: 343–387.

Giersz, Milosz

2017   *Castillo de Huarmey. Un centro del imperio Wari en la costa norte del Perú.* Ediciones del Hipocampo, Lima.

Huertas, Lorenzo V.

2001   *Diluvios andinos a través de las fuentes documentales,* Pontificia Universidad Católica del Perú, Fondo Editorial, Lima.

Hyslop, John

1990   *Inka Settlement Planning.* University of Texas Press, Austin

Jiménez Borja, Arturo

1985   Pachacamac. *Boletín de Lima* 38: 40–54.

Kaulicke, Peter

2001   La sombra de Pachacamac: Huari en la costa central. *Boletín de Arqueología PUCP* 4: 313–358.

Kiracofe, James B., and John S. Marr

2008   Marching to Disaster: The Catastrophic Convergence of Inca Imperial Policy, Sand Flies and El Niño in the 1524 Andean Epidemic. In *El Niño, Catastrophism, and Cultural Change in Ancient America,* edited by Daniel H. Sandweiss and Jeffrey Quilter, pp. 145–164. Dumbarton Oaks Library and Collection, Washington, D.C.

Knobloch, Patricia

2001   La cronología del contacto y encuentros cercanos de Wari. *Boletín de Arqueología PUCP* 4: 69–88.

Lanning, Edward P.

1967   *Peru before the Incas.* Prentice-Hall, Englewood Cliffs, New Jersey.

Lavallée, Danielle

1965   Una colección de cerámica de Pachacamac. *Revista del Museo Nacional* 34: 220–246.

López-Hurtado, Luis Enrique

2011   *Ideology and the Development of Social Hierarchy at the Site of Panquilma, Peruvian Central Coast.* Ph.D. dissertation, Department of Anthropology, University of Pittsburgh. University Microfilms, Ann Arbor, Michigan.

López-Hurtado, Enrique, and Jason Nesbitt

2010   Centros religiosos provinciales en el imperio Incaico: ¿Difusores de la ideología oficial o espacios de resistencia local? In *Perspectivas comparativas sobre la arqueología de la costa sudamericana,* edited by Robin E. Cutright, Enrique López-Hurtado, and Alexander J.Martin, pp. 213–229. Center for Comparative Archaeology/Fondo Editorial de la PUCP/Ministerio de Cultura del Ecuador, Pittsburgh, Lima.

Lumbreras, Luís Guillermo

1974   *The Peoples and Cultures of Ancient Perú.* Smithsonian Institution, Washington, D.C.

Makowski, Krzysztof

2002a   Los Personajes frontales de báculos en la iconografía tiahuanaco y huari: ¿tema o convención? *Boletín de Arqueología PUCP* 5: 337–373.

2002b   Arquitectura, estilo e identidad en el Horizonte Tardío: el sitio de Pueblo Viejo–Pucará, valle de Lurín. *Boletín de Arqueología PUCP* 6: 137–170.

2006   Proyecto Arqueológico-Taller de Campo "Lomas de Lurín" PATL (antes Tablada de Lurín), Informe de la temporada de trabajo 2005/2006, report presented to the Instituto Nacional de Cultura (INC), Lima.

2007   The Transformation of Pachacamac Layout during Inca Occupation and the Network of Entrances to the Pyramids with Ramp. Paper presented at the Institute of Andean Studies Meeting, January 2007, Berkeley. Manuscript on file.

2008   Proyecto Arqueológico-Taller de Campo "Lomas de Lurín" PATL (antes Tablada de Lurín), Informe de la temporada de trabajo 2007/2008, report presented to the Instituto Nacional de Cultura (INC), Lima.

2010a   Vestido, arquitectura y mecanismos del poder en el Horizonte Medio. In *Señores de los Imperios del Sol*, edited by Krzysztof Makowski, pp. 57–71. Banco de Crédito del Perú, Lima.

2010b   Programa Arqueológico-Escuela de Campo "Valle de Pachacamac" PATL (antes Tablada de Lurín, Valle de Lurín), Informe de la temporada de trabajo 2008/2009, report presented to the Instituto Nacional de Cultura (INC), Lima.

2011   Programa Arqueológico-Escuela de Campo "Valle de Pachacamac" PATL (antes Tablada de Lurín, Valle de Lurín), Informe de la temporada de trabajo 2010/2011. Report presented to the Ministerio de Cultura, Lima.

2012   City and Ceremonial Center: Conceptual Challenges on Andean Urbanism. *Annual Papers of the Anthropological Institute* 2: 1–66 (in Spanish and Japanese: translated by Shinya Watanabe); in Spanish: http://www.ic.nanzan-u.ac.jp/JINRUIKEN/publication/index.html.

2013   Programa Arqueológico-Escuela de Campo "Valle de Pachacamac" PATL (antes Tablada de Lurín, Valle de Lurín), Informe de la temporada de trabajo 2011/2012, report presented to the Ministerio de Cultura, Lima.

2016   *Urbanismo andino: centro ceremonial y ciudad en el Perú prehispánico*, Apus graph, Lima.

2018   Huari, Tiahuanaco and SAIS: The Local and Foreign in the Iconography of the Empire. In *Images in Action. The Southern Andean Iconographic Series*, edited by William H. Isbell, Mauricio I. Uribe, Ann Tiballi, and Edward P. Zegarra, pp. 631–658. UCLA, Cotsen Institute of Archaeology Press, Los Angeles.

Makowski, Krzysztof, Pamela Castro de la Mata, Glenda Escajadillo, Milagritos Jímenez, and Elsa Tomasto

2012   Ajuares funerarios de los cementerios prehispánicos en Tablada de Lurín (Periodo Formativo Tardío, Lima, Perú). Corpus Antiquitatum Americaniensium Polonia-Perú, Union Académique Internationale, Academia Polaca de Ciencias y Letras, Pontificia Universidad Católica del Perú, Cracovia.

Makowski, Krzysztof, María Fe Córdova, Patricia Habetler, and Manuel Lizárraga

2005   La plaza y la fiesta: Reflexiones acerca de la función de los patios en la arquitectura pública prehispánica de los periodos tardíos. *Boletín de Arqueología PUCP* 9: 297–333.

Makowski, Krzysztof, Iván Ghezzi, Daniel Guerrero, Héctor Neff, Milagritos Jimenez, Gabriela Oré, and Rosabella Álvarez Calderón

2008   Pachacamac, Ychsma y los Caringas: Estilos e identidades en el valle de Lurín Inca. In *Arqueología de la costa centro sur peruana*, edited by Omar Pinedo and Henry Tantaleán, pp. 267–316. Avqi Ed., Lima.

Makowski, Krzysztof, and Miłosz Giersz

2016   El Imperio en debate: hacia nuevas perspectivas en la organización política Wari. AN-
        DES. *Boletín del Centro de Estudios Precolombinos de la Universidad de Varsovia* 9: 5–38.

Makowski, Krzysztof, and Manuel Lizárraga

2011   El rol de *Spondylus princeps* en los rituales intracomunitarios de Pueblo Viejo-Pucará.
        Estudios del Hombre 29: 333–366.

Makowski, Krzysztof, and Clive Ruggles

2011   Watching the Sky from the Ushnu: The Sukanka-like Summit Temple in Pueblo Viejo-
        Pucara (Lurin Valley, Peru). In *Archaeostronomy and Ethnoastronomy: Building Bridges
        between Cultures*, Proceedings of the 278th Symposium of the International Astro-
        nomical Union and "Oxford IX" International Symposium of Archaeoastronomy held
        in Lima, Peru, January 5–14, 2011, edited by Clive Ruggles, pp. 169–177. Cambridge
        University Press, Cambridge.

Makowski, Krzysztof, and Alaín Vallenas

2016   La ocupación lima en el valle de Lurín: en los orígenes de Pachacamac monumental,
        Boletín de Arqueología PUCP 19 (2015): Avances en la Arqueología de la Cultura Lima
        (Segunda Parte): 97–143.

Makowski, Krzysztof, and Milena Vega Centeno

2004   Estilos regionales en la costa central en el Horizonte Tardío. Una aproximación desde el
        valle del Lurín. *Bulletin de l'Institut Français d'Etudes Andines* 33(3): 681–714.

Marcone, Giancarlo

2010   What Role Did Wari Play in the Lima Political Economy? The Peruvian Central Coast
        at the Beginning of the Middle Horizon. In *Beyond Wari Walls*, edited by Justin Jen-
        nings, pp. 136–153. University of New Mexico Press, Albuquerque.

Menzel, Dorothy

1964   Style and Time in the Middle Horizon. *Ñawpa Pacha* 2: 1–105.

1968a   New data on the Huari Empire in Middle Horizon Epoch 2A. *Ñawpa Pacha* 6: 47–114.

1968b   *La cultura Huari. Las grandes civilizaciones del antiguo Perú 6*. Compañía de Seguros y
        Reaseguros Peruano-Suiza, Lima.

1976   *Pottery Style and Society in Ancient Peru. Art as a Mirror of History in the Ica Valley,
        1350–1570*. University of California Press, Berkeley.

Michczyński, Adam, Peter Eeckhout, and Anna Pazdur

2003   14C Absolute Chronology of Pyramid III and the Dynastic Model at Pachacamac, Peru.
        Radiocarbon 45(1): 59–73.

Michczyński, Adam, Peter Eeckhout, Anna Padur, and Jacek Pawlyta

2007   Radiocarbon dating of the Temple of the Monkey—The Next Step towards a Compre-
        hensive Absolute Chronology of Pachacamac, Perú. *Radiocarbon* 49(2): 565–578.

Oré Menedez, Gabriela

2008   *Aspectos cronológicos y funcionales de la ocupación Inca a lo largo de la segunda mu-
        ralla: excavaciones en los sectores SE-A, SW-B y SW-D en Pachacamac*. Tesis de licen-
        ciatura. Facultad de Letras y Ciencias Humanas, especialidad de Arqueología, PUCP,
        Lima.

Ortlieb, Luc

2000   The Documentary Historical Record of El Niño Events in Peru: An Update of the
        Quinn Record (Sixteenth through Nineteenth Centuries). In *El Niño and the Southern
        Oscillation: Variability, Global and Regional Impacts*, edited by H. Díaz and V. Markgraf,
        pp. 207–295. Cambridge University Press, Cambridge.

Paredes, Ponciano

1988   Pachacamac—Pirámide con rampa n° 2. *Boletín de Lima* 55: 41–58.

1991   Pachacamac: Murallas y caminos epimurales. *Boletín de Lima* 74: 85–95.

Paredes, Ponciano, and Jesús Ramos

1994   Excavaciones Arqueológicas en el Sector Las Palmas, Pachacamac. *Boletín de Lima*, 16 (91–96): 313–349.

Patterson, Thomas C.

1966   *Pattern and Process in the Early Intermediate Period Pottery of the Central Coast of Peru*, University of California Press. Berkeley.

1985   Pachacamac: An Andean Oracle under Inca Rule. In *Recent Studies in Andean Prehistory and Protohistory*, edited by Peter Kvietok and Daniel Sanweiss, pp. 159–175. Cornell University Press, Ithaca.

Pavel Svendsen, Trine

2011   *La presencia inca en las pirámides con rampa de Pachacamac: una propuesta para su cronología y función desde la perspectiva de la cerámica.* Tésis para optar el grado de Magister en Arqueología, Programa de Estudios Andinos, Escuela de Graduados, Pontificia Universidad Católica del Perú, Lima.

Pillsbury, Joan

2004   The Concept of the Palace in the Andes. In *Palaces of the Ancient New Word*, edited by Susan Toby Evans and Joan Pillsbury, pp. 181–190. Dumbarton Oaks, Washington, D.C.

2008   Los Palacios de Chimor. In *Señores de los reinos de la Luna*, edited by Krzysztof Makowski, pp. 201–222. Banco de Crédito del Perú, Lima.

Pozzi-Escot, Denise, Gianella Pacheco, and Carmen Rosa Uceda

2013   *Pachacamac: Templo Pintado, Conservación e investigación.* Ministerio de Cultura, Lima.

Presbitero, Gonzalo

n.d.   *Definición del proceso constructivo: análisis de la mampostería. Sitio Arqueológico de Pachacamac. Informe interno del Proyecto Arqueológico-Escuela de Campo "Valle de Pachacamac,"* dir. Krzysztof Makowski. Manuscript on file.

Prümers, Heiko

2000   El Castillo de Huarmey: una plataforma funeraria del Horizonte Medio. *Boletín de Arqueología PUCP* 4: 289–312.

Quinn, William, Victor Neal, and Santiago Antúnez de Mayolo

1987   El Niño Occurrences over the Past Four and a Half Centuries. *Journal of Geophysical Research* 92(c13): 1449–1461.

Ramos Giraldo, Jesús A., and Ponciano Paredes Botoni

2010   Excavaciones en la segunda muralla-sector Puente Lurín. Correlación estratigráfica de los estilos cerámicos durante el Horizonte Tardío en el santuario Pachacamac. *Bulletin de l'Institut Francais d'Études Andines* 39, 1: 105–166.

Ravines, Rogger

1996   *Pachacámac. Santuario universal.* Editorial Los Pinos, Lima.

Reiss, Wilhelm, and Stübel, Alphons

1880–1887   The Necropolis of Ancón in Perú: A Contribution in Our Knowledge of the Culture and Industries of the Empire of the Incas, Being the Results of Excavations Made on the Spot. Translated by A. H. Keane, 3 Vols. A. Ascher, Berlín.

Rosenzweig, Alfredo

2006   Weaving for the Warrior Kings and Nobles. The Late Intermediate Period Textiles. In *Weaving for the Afterlife. Peruvian Textiles from the Maiman Collection*, Vol. 2, edited by

Krzysztof Makowski, Alfredo Rosenzweig, and Maria Jesús Jiménez Diaz, pp. 68–102. Ampal, Merhav, Tel Aviv.

Rostworowski, María

1972 Breve informe sobre el Señorío de Ychma o Ychima. *Arqueología PUCP* 13: 37–51.

1988 Conflicts over Coca Fields in Sixteenth-Century Peru, *Memoirs of the Museum of Anthropology* No. 21, University of Michigan, *Studies in Latin American Ethnohistory & Archaeology*, No. 4, Ann Arbor.

1991 *The Huarochiri Manuscript: A Testament of Ancient and Colonial Andean Religion (Often Atributed to Francisco de Avila)*. University of Texas Press, Austin.

1999 *El Señorío de Pachacamac: el informe de Rodrigo Cantos de Andrade de 1573*. Instituto de Estudios Peruanos (IEP), Banco Central de Reserva del Perú, Lima.

2002a Pachacamac y el Señor de los Milagros. Una trayectoria milenaria [1992]. In *Obras completas*, Vol. II, pp. 15–171. Instituto de Estudios Peruano (IEP), Lima.

2002b Señoríos indígenas de Lima y Canta [1978]. In *Pachacamac, Obras completas*, Vol. II, pp. 189–376. Instituto de Estudios Peruano (IEP), Lima

2004 Guarco y Lunahuaná: Dos señoríos prehispánicos de la costa sur central del Perú [1978–80]. Costa peruana prehispánica. *Obras completas*, Vol. III, pp. 83–139. Instituto de Estudios Peruanos (IEP), Lima.

Salomon, Frank, and George L. Urioste [Translation from the Quechua]

1991 *The Huarochiri Manuscript: A Testament of Ancient and Colonial Andean Religion* (Often Atributed to Francisco de Avila). University of Texas Press, Austin.

Salomon, Frank, and Sue Grosboll

2009 Una visita a los hijos de Chaupiñamca en 1588: desigualdad de género, nombres indígenas y cambios demográficos en el centro de los Andes posincas. In *La revisita de Sisicaya, 1588. Huarochirí veinte años antes de Dioses y Hombres*, edited by by Frank Salomon, Jane Feltham, and Sue Grosboll, pp. 17–55. Fondo Editorial PUCP, Lima.

Segura Llanos, Rafael, and Izumi Shimada

2010 The Wari Footprint on the Central Coast: A View from Cajamarquilla and Pachacamac. In *Beyond Wari Walls*, edited by Justin Jennings, pp. 113–135. University of New Mexico Press, Albuquerque.

Shimada, Izumi

1991 Pachacamac Archaeology: Retrospect and Prospect. In *Pachacamac: Report of the William Pepper, MD, LL.D., Peruvian Expedition of 1896*, edited by Max Uhle, pp. XV–LXVI, University of Pennsylvania, University Museum of Archaeology and Anthropology, Philadelphia.

2003 Preliminary Results of the 2003 Fieldwork. Electronic document, http://www.pachacamac.net/papers/ PAP_RESULTS2003.pdf.

2004 Summary Report of the 2004 Season of the Pachacamac Archaeological Project. Electronic document, http://www.pachacamac.net/papers/PAP_RESULTS2004.pdf

2007 Las prospecciones y excavaciones en Urpi Kocha y Urpi Wachaq: Estudio preliminar. *Cuadernos de investigación del Archivo Tello* 5: 13–18.

Shimada, Izumi, Rafael A. Segura, María Rostworowski de Diez Canseco, and Hirokatsu Watanabe

2004 Una nueva evaluación de la Plaza de los Peregrinos de Pachacamac: aportes de la primera campaña 2003 del Proyecto Arqueológico Pachacamac. *Bulletin de l'Institut Français d'Études Andines* 33(3): 507–538.

Shimada, Izumi, Rafael Segura Llanos, David J. Goldstein, Kelly J. Knudson, Melody J. Shimada, Ken-ichi Shinoda, Mai Takogami, and Ursel Wagner

2010   Un siglo después de Uhle: Reflexiones sobre la arqueología de Pachacamac y Perú. In *Max Uhle (1856–1944). Evaluaciones de sus investigaciones y obras,* edited by Peter Kaulicke, Manuela Fischer, Peter Masson, and Gregor Wolff, pp. 109–150. Fondo Editorial PUCP, Lima.

Spalding, Karen

1984   *Huarochirí: An Andean Society under Inca and Spanish Rule.* Stanford University Press, Stanford, California.

Stothert, Karen, and Rogger Ravines

1977   Investigaciones arqueológicas en Villa El Salvador. *Revista del Museo Nacional* 43: 157–226.

Strelov, Renate

1996   *Gewebe mit Unterbrochenen Ketten aus dem Vorspanischen Peru (Peruvian Prehispanic Textiles with Discontinous Warp).* Veroffentilichungen des Museum für Volkerkunde, Anteilung Amerikanische Archäologie, Neue Folge 61, Berlin.

Strong, William Duncan, and John M. Corbett

1943   A Ceramic Sequence at Pachacamac. *Columbia Studies in Archaeology and Ethnology* 1(2): 27–122.

Taylor, Gérald

1999   *Ritos y tradiciones de Huarochirí.* Instituto Francés de Estudios Andinos, Banco Central de Reserva del Perú, Universidad Particular Ricardo Palma, Lima.

Tello, Julio C.

1967   *Páginas escogidas.* UNMSM, Lima.

2009 [1941–1942] *Arqueología de Pachacamac: Excavaciones en el Templo de la Luna y Cuarteles, 1940–1941,* edited by Rafael Vega Centeno Sara-Lafosse. Cuaderno de investigación del Archivo Tello 6. Museo de Arqueología y Antropología, Universidad Nacional Mayor de San Marcos, Lima.

Uhle, Max

2003 [1903]   *Pachacamac: Informe de la expedición peruana William Pepper de 1896,* Universidad Nacional Mayor de San Marcos, Lima.

Vallejo Berriós, Francisco

2004   El estilo Ychsma: Características generales, secuencia y distribución geográfica. *Bulletin de l'Institut Français d'Études Andines* 33(3): 595–642.

2008   Desarrollo y complejización de las sociedades tardías de la Costa Central: El caso de Ychsma. *Arqueología y Sociedad* 19: 83–114.

2009   La problemática de la cerámica ychsma: El estado de la situación y algunos elementos de discusión. *Revista Chilena de Antropología* 20: 133–168.

Vallenas, Alaín

2012   Ocupación Lima y la construcción del Templo Viejo de Pachacamac, Tesis de Licenciatura, Facultad de Letras y Ciencias Humanas, Pontificia Universidad Católica del Perú, Lima.

Vanstan, Ina

1967   *Textiles from Beneath the Temple of Pachacamac. Peru.* A part of the Uhle Collection. University of Pennsylvania, Philadelphia.

Villacorta, Luis Felipe

2004   Los palacios en la costa central durante los Periodos Tardíos: de Pachacamac al Inca, *Bulletin de l'Institut Français d'Études Andines* 33(3), 539–570.

2010   Palacios yungas y racionalidad andina en la costa central prehispánica. In *Señores de los Imperios del Sol*, edited by Krzysztof Makowski, pp. 163–172. Banco de Crédito del Perú, Lima.

Winsborough, Barbara M., Izumi Shimada, Lee A. Newsom, John G. Jones, and Rafael A. Segura

2012   Paleoenvironmental Catastrophies on the Peruvian Coast Revealed in Lagoon Sediment Cores from Pachacamac. *Journal of Archaeological Science* 39(3): 602–614.

7

Pachacamac

Contributions to the Study of the North-South Street
and the Main Temples

DENISE POZZI-ESCOT AND KATIUSHA BERNUY

The Pachacamac Site Museum has been executing, through the Qhapaq Ñan Project–Ministry of Culture, a series of tasks to boost the social use of the Pachacamac Sanctuary, one of the main pilgrimage centers in the pre-Hispanic Andean world. These tasks are divided into three main components: research, conservation, and relationship with the community; these components are included in the Sanctuary Management Plan, an important site management document (Ministerio de Cultura and Ministerio de Comercio Exterior y Turismo 2012) that allows us to plan and organize our work.

One of the guiding principles of this Management Plan (approved by 2014), is to preserve and conserve the exceptional values of the sanctuary, promoting integration and a greater commitment by the community with the preservation of its archaeological heritage.

• • •

For some years we have managed to implement a community development project that includes work with schools and cultural activities sustained with the community, and aims to:

> develop programs and projects so that the population and interest groups are committed to the conservation of the site and its values. (Ministerio de Cultura and Ministerio de Comercio Exterior and Turismo 2012)

The archaeological sanctuary today covers some 465 ha, including the monumental area that covers about 250 ha (approximately 40 percent of the entire area) and is made up of a series of structures, streets, and squares whose cultural affiliation and construction sequence have not been investigated in their entirety.

If we consider the long occupational history of the site, more than 1,200 years, it becomes clear that the construction sequence is more complex than we know today. Accordingly, in order to specify the characteristics of the site in each occupational period, a primary need was identified: establish when the different structures were built, when the renovations or extensions were carried out, and what their chronological relationship was with other structures.

North-South Street Research and Conservation Project (PIA-CNS, acronyms in Spanish)

This project is part of the research that will allow us to highlight the original access routes and internal circulation of the sanctuary. The investigations began in 2009 and ended in 2013. The main objective was to determine the occupational and constructive sequence of the area occupied by the main access route and the internal circulation of the sanctuary: North-South Street (Uhle 2003 [1903]: 240–241).

The drawing published by Max Uhle in 1903 records the existence of two streets that intersect and divide the site into four sectors. These were named according to their orientation, North-South and East-West. Uhle describes that at the point where the streets intersect there is a kind of open plaza, and at the culmination point of the North-South Street is a quadrangular plaza (Central Hall) (see Figure 7.1).

To facilitate the description of our excavations, we have divided our study area into two sections. The first, North Section, covers from the access to the North-South Street located in the second wall to the intersection with the East-West Street. The second, Southern Section, runs from the junction with East-West Street to the Central Hall.

As a result of our investigations, we can affirm that the street stopped being used when it was closed due to the collapse of the walls that delimit it, due to an intense seismic movement that occurred during the Colonial Era.

When removing the wind-deposited sand from the street as part of our investigations, we found collapses made up of thousands of adobes and stone blocks that form the walls, confirming that most of the walls had collapsed in a single moment over a layer of dark sand with little cultural material.

The finding of glass beads and glazed ceramics on the last traffic surface of

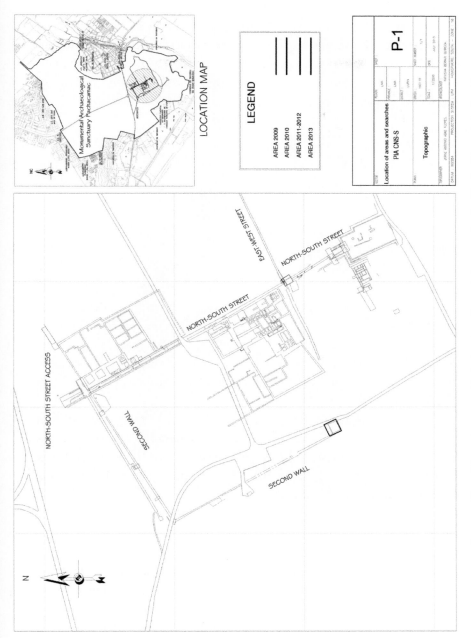

Figure 7.1. Plan of the entire street with the location of excavated areas and wells. Map by "Proyecto de Investigación y Conservación de la Calle Norte-Sur Temporada 2013 (PIA CNS 2013)."

Figure 7.2. Evidence of the earthquake. Photo by "Proyecto de Investigación y Conservación de la Calle Norte-Sur Temporada 2010 (PIA CNS 2011–2012)."

the street, together with the finding of horse coprolites attached to that surface, would confirm that the street continued to be used until colonial times.

Obtaining a date of AD 1680–1740 (2 sigma KIA-42130) from a sample of horse coprolites allowed us to point out that the earthquake that caused the closure of the street occurred during the Colonial Era. Possibly the earthquake that occurred in 1687, which was rated as the most intense earthquake occurring in Lima in the sixteenth and seventeenth centuries (Seiner 2009: 382).

North Section

Based on the stratigraphic sequence established with targeted excavations located at strategic points in the Northern Section, we were able to define that there were occupations prior to the construction of this street. The first occupation is transitory, since it occurred on dunes, without the presence of rammed earth or a floor. The second presented evidence of permanent occupation: such as rammed earth, small, flat adobe walls, construction ditches, and so forth; and it is possible that it was related to the beginning of the construction of the Pyramid with Ramp No. 7 since most of the building was constructed before the east wall that defines the street.

The recovered data revealed that the Northern Section was built during the Ychsma occupation (AD 1380 to 1440, 2 sigma UBA-17116). The construction of the street involved the construction of two walls that delimited it and, at the same time, demarcated the squares of the groups of Pyramids with Ramps located on its margins, so planning and construction of the street involved implementation of access to Pyramid with Ramp No. 4 and Pyramid with Ramp No. 7, discovered during excavation of the first 160 m of the North Section.

After the Inca Conquest of the sanctuary, the North Section continued to be used and underwent some renovations, mainly focused on the area of the access to the street and the accesses to the Pyramids with Ramps. The extensive excavation carried out at the northern access of the street, located on the Second Wall, revealed that two main roads converged at this point. Both were part of the Qhapaq Ñan, the Inca Highway system, one coming down from the highlands, the other running along the coast. Excavations at the entrance of the Pyramids with Ramps revealed that these were open during the Ychsma and Inca occupations, but were intentionally closed by middens and small walls toward the end of the Inca occupation. Despite this closure, the street continued being used, even until colonial times.

The data described was obtained thanks to the use of areal excavation, which in addition to allowing a broad vision of the characteristics of the architecture that makes up the street, was essential to locating targeted excavations in strategic places. In this way we have been able to corroborate that the

North Section of the North-South Street constituted, since its construction, and during much of its use, the main means of communication between the groups of Pyramids with Ramps. Furthermore, the excavations made clear that, since its construction, the street was the main access to the sanctuary and that, at least during the Inca occupation, this access was the culmination of two important roads that were part of the Inca road network.

The closure of the access to Pyramid with Ramp No. 4 seems to be related not only to the opening of a new access in the Second Wall, discovered by the team led by Krzysztof Makowski (Oré 2008: 122), but also with the removal of the wall that demarcates the front plaza of Pyramid with Ramp No. 4 (Eeckhout and Farfán 2004: 33); this wall joined the front plaza to the front space of Pyramid with Ramp No. 1.

This reorganization of the space that occurred during the Inca occupation must have been a planned process that responded to new needs of the administrators of the sanctuary. Further proof of this is the network of water supply canals that were implemented during the Inca occupation.

Along the north flank of the Second Wall, we found several well-preserved sections of a water supply canal that must have come from the Lurín River and have been dated to the Inca Period. This section would be part of a main canal with an east-west direction, since it seems to go to the *acllawasi*, an Inca building that, according to the accounts of Hernando Pizarro and Estete, was the residence of the *acllas*, women whose main tasks were the production of textiles and sacred *chicha* for rituals and offerings.

Likewise, when excavating the first meters of the North Section, we found the segment of a water supply canal that is derived from the canal described above. This segment of the canal crosses the west wall of the street in the direction of the squares of Pyramid with Ramp No. 4. In this case, it was not possible to determine to which point of the plaza or to what structure inside it the canal was directed, since we have not excavated the plaza in question.

It would be interesting to determine where the water was being directed in order to define the activities carried out inside the plazas, which could give more information about the reasons for the reorganization of this space during the Inca occupation (we are working on a project about the use of canals in the sanctuary with the University of Engineering and Technololgy–UTEC, and the first results are quite interesting).

The renovations identified in the Northern Section, together with the findings made inside the plazas of the groups of Pyramids with Ramps nearby, seem to indicate a change in function between the Ychsma and the Inca occupations. The drastic increase in the proportion of remains between the corresponding layers to these occupations (Pozzi-Escot and Bernuy 2010: 41) could be a product of the change in function and/or of an increase in the density of use that would reveal a greater influx of people during the Inca occupation.

Another piece of evidence to suggest a change in the function of the Pyramids with Ramps was recovered by digging inside one of the side plazas of the Pyramid with Ramp No. 7, where we discovered a tomb that was looted during the Colonial Period (Bernuy and Pozzi-Escot 2018).

The chronology of the tomb was defined based on the associated material and the stratigraphic location, as corresponding to the Inca occupation. Due to the discovery of a small glass bead inside a reed sewing kit, it is not possible to determine if the funerary context dates from the Inca Period, the Transition Period, or the beginning of the Colonial Period, because glass beads circulated in South America even before the arrival of the Spanish in the Peruvian territory.

Originally, the tomb must have been on the surface, in a kind of enclosure located at the corner of the south side platform of the Pyramid with Ramp No. 7 and the wall of the North-South Street. The enclosure was defined by the construction of a low wall attached to the facing of the south-side platform.

Using the categories defined by Eeckhout that are based on chronicles, we can classify this funerary context in the category of visible deceased (Difuntos visibles), "that is, those whose mummy was accessible (permanently or occasionally). . . . The visible deceased belonged to the class of important ancestors and lords" (Eeckhout 2004: 41).

In the funerary context, four almost complete adult individuals and part of a fifth adult individual were identified, in addition to five infants. The physical anthropological analysis carried out by Elsa Tomasto revealed that two of the adult individuals were possibly female, between 25 and 35 years old; another was between 35 and 44 years old; and another male, between 35 and 45 years old. The individuals presented very little evidence of having suffered stress during the growth stage compared with other pre-Hispanic Andean populations, and none showed evidence of having carried out tasks that involved high physical exertion, while almost all presented traits that suggest that they spent a long time in squatting position (Tomasto 2013: 35).

As usual in this funerary pattern, the objects must have been inside the funerary bundle. However, due to the looting, the few remaining objects were found outside of them, except for a ceramic bottle found in the central part of the older woman. We consider the most important association found in the tomb a wooden *kero* with an incised decoration of synthesized and geometrized characters and vertical bands of chevrons (see Figure 7.3). Two very similar *keros* are found in the deposits of the Museo Nacional de Arqueología Antropología e Historia of Perú. The finding of the Inca *kero* indicates that at least one of the individuals in this funerary context must have been an elite individual in life.

Unfortunately, the looting that the funeral context was subjected to prevents us from establishing whether there are main and secondary individuals, and we have not been able to reliably establish to which individual the *kero* belonged. However, from the location of the object after the looting, it is possible to assume that it must belong to the male individual. The bundle of this individual was the most damaged by the looting, to the point that the

Figure 7.3. Looted grave and kero. Photo by "Proyecto de Investigación y Conservación de la Calle Norte-Sur Temporada 2010 (PIA CNS 2011–2012)."

Denise Pozzi-Escot and Katiusha Bernuy

body was completely disarticulated, which is why we suppose that it must have been the individual with the best funerary offerings.

Some researchers have found looted funeral contexts in the Pyramids with Ramps. Eeckhout published a photo of a deposit in the Pyramid with Ramp No. 3 in which Late Horizon burial bundles were found (Eeckhout and Farfán 2004: 166, figure 04). The field notes written by Zefarra, who was in charge of the excavations led by Jiménez Borja in the Pyramid with Ramp No. 1, describe the discovery of the "remains of three completely disordered corpses" (Jiménez Borja 1985: 94) in the landfill located in the back patio of the Pyramid with Ramp No. 1. In addition, the notes illustrate a complete bundle found in this area. Furthermore, an intact tomb was found by Squier, probably in a Pyramid with Ramp; according to Cornejo, it would date from the Late Horizon by Chimú-style associations.

Cornejo describes the grave found by Squier as:

> "a multiple tomb" reoccupying a residential area (Squier 1978 [1869]: 216), located beyond the edge of the "ancient city" in the vicinity of the temple (Squier [1978] [1869]: 210). (Cornejo 2004: 805)

In excavations carried out inside one of the plazas of Pyramid with Ramp No. 4, we found a kind of funeral platform attached to the internal part of the northwest flank of the Second Wall.

According to the data described, the evidence seems to indicate, during the Inca occupation, that some Pyramids with Ramps acquired new functions, among which were serving as burial places.

Southern Section

Unlike the Northern Section, the Southern Section does not seem to have existed before the Inca Conquest. The data obtained in our excavations, added to those obtained by other researchers (Eeckhout and Farfán 2008: 107), show that all the exposed architecture was built during the Inca occupation, a period in which there was an intense construction process that turned the North-South Street into the main access road to the sanctuary's nuclear area. The total reorganization of the area should have been linked to the adaptation of the sanctuary infrastructure to the new conditions of use imposed by the Incas, which surely implied restricted and controlled access, in addition to the establishment of entrance rituals typical of the Inca shrines.

When excavating the end of the Southern Section, we found the access to the East and West passageways (Figure 7.4). As Max Uhle pointed out in the drawing he made in 1903, the East passageway borders the Central Hall and leads to the east flank of the First Wall; while the West passageway, which also bordered the Central Hall—apparently—leads to the Pilgrims' Plaza, where two accesses are located that go to the main temple area (Old Temple, Painted Temple, and Temple of the Sun).

The area excavations of the entire final section of the Southern Section allowed us to confirm that there is no other means of communication between the street and the Pilgrims' Plaza, as suggested by the map by Eeckhout and Farfán (2008: 16). Likewise, we have determined that there is no direct connection between the access to the Central Hall and the East and West passageways. Therefore, up to now, we can establish that at the end of the North-South Street there were three possible routes: the first through the West passageway to the Pilgrims' Plaza; the second, the Anteroom to the Central Hall; and the third route, through the East passageway to the East flank of the First Wall, which is closely related to structures associated with Building 47, or Solsticial.

Figure 7.4. CNS end point, access to Pasadizos, and access to the Central Hall. Photo by "Proyecto de Investigación y Conservación de la Calle Norte-Sur Temporada 2011–2012 (PIA CNS 2011–2012)."

On the sides of the access to the Central Room were two post bases and a small receptacle delimited by rectangular stones, which had a kind of stone covering. Although there is no evidence of carving, it is possible that they were idols that flanked the access to the Central Room.

The presence of a series of scattered offerings in front of the posts seems to indicate that it is possible that this is a space where offerings were placed, looted possibly in colonial times, since the entire area shows evidence of huge holes, and it was covered by the collapsed materials caused by an intense earthquake from the Colonial Era. This evidence, together with the presence of the bases of these two posts with clear signs of having been cut, could coincide with the description by Miguel de Estete of the existence of idols in other areas of the sanctuary:

> Por las calles de este pueblo y a las puertas principales de él, y a la redonda de esta casa, hay muchos ídolos de palo, y los adoran a imitación de su diablo [Through the streets of this town and at the main gates of him, and around these houses, there are many wooden idols, and they worship them in imitation of their devil. Translated by authors] (Xerez 1891: 37)

During the excavation of the collapsed walls that make up the Anteroom, we found evidence of plastering on its walls, as well as the presence of a layer of red paint on which different designs were drawn and painted; on the wall that defines the west side of the Anteroom, and at the same time defines the east side of the West passageway, we have been able to establish that the designs correspond to fish and corn plants similar to those registered in the last pictorial layer of the Painted Temple. This data is of utmost importance because the West passageway leads to the Peregrinos Plaza, a large space located at the foot of the main temples, and probably a meeting point for pilgrims who came to worship and consult the Pachacamac *huaca*.

The characteristics of the access to the Central Hall, the large number of offerings found and the evidence that the area was painted with colors and designs similar to those reflected in the last pictorial of the Painted Temple, allows us to affirm that the Anteroom, together with the Central Hall—which also had its walls painted—were spaces with special functions where, perhaps, ritual activities were carried out that would have been related to the cult of Pachacamac.

In addition to the offerings, we found a series of pillow basalts that appar-

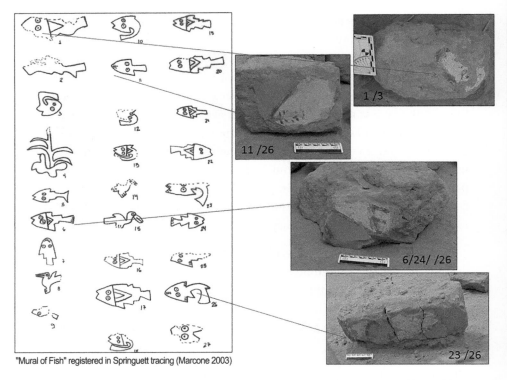

"Mural of Fish" registered in Springuett tracing (Marcone 2003)

Figure 7.5. Evidence of mural painting and similarity of designs with those of the last pictorial layer of the Painted Temple. Photo by "Proyecto de Investigación y Conservación de la Calle Norte-Sur Temporada 2011–2012 (PIA CNS 2011–2012)."

ently came from the south-central region of Peru (Bernuy and Pozzi-Escot 2018: 67–69). These amorphous rocks have also been found in other buildings. We think that the rocks could also be offerings and that they were chosen because of their peculiar shapes, which could have been interpreted as animals or faces.

In the West passageway, the one that leads to the Peregrinos Plaza, we found a series of *chuspas* (bags) and wrappers that contained two golden copper containers; a bracelet of spherical beads of the same material; pigments of green, red, and orange color, in addition to necklaces or pendant beads of various materials, among which the presence of *Spondylus princeps* stands out. This finding indicates how pilgrims revered the Pachacamac *huaca*, asked it for their favors, or thanked it for its concessions, by offering objects of great value and meaning. These offerings are surprising due to their complexity and the quality of some of the objects, which contrasts with the offerings found in areas remote from these temples.

Likewise, among the collapsed material and walls that make up the passageways, the Central Hall, and the Anteroom, we found a series of offerings made at the time of the walls' construction, for example, a fragment of green pigment in its natural state embedded in the mortar used to build the walls. In addition, among the collapsed material we found *Spondylus* sp. and three brushes with traces of paint. These types of constructive offerings have also been reported in the Painted Temple (Pacheco 2014).

An exceptional finding that evidences the practice of constructive offerings was the finding *in situ* of two complete specimens of *Spondylus princeps*, inside of which we found *Nectandra* seeds strung together. These offerings had been carefully located inside the stone segment of the wall that defines the west side of the Anteroom and the east side of the West passageway at the time of its construction. The leaving of offerings within the walls during construction has been reported on several occasions during the emergency conservation work carried out in the sanctuary as part of the Emergency Conservation Program, as well as in the Painted Temple (Pacheco 2014; Pozzi-Escot and Chávez 2008).

We should recall that the practice of offering *Spondylus* with *Nectandra* seeds inside has been recorded in contexts in the north of Peru, both in the Moche and Lambayeque cultures. Specific examples of this practice are those described by Carod-Artal and Vázquez-Cabrera (2007). A similar case of this type of offering was found in a context of mass sacrifice of the Lambayeque culture, in the Sanctuary of Cerrillos; in this context, "dozens of Spondylus princeps shells were recovered, some of them with strings of Nectandra s.p. seeds" (Carod-Artal and Vazquez-Cabrera 2007: 47). Another case, from the Moche Period, is the one reported in Huaca de la Luna; in this case, "The seeds of *Nectandra* sp. were deposited in *Spondylus* seashells" (Carod-Artal and Vazquez-Cabrera 2007: 47). In various late contexts excavated in Pachacamac, objects of Chimú affiliation and even some of Lambayeque affiliation have been reported (Pozzi-Escot et al. 2014).

The finding of a mural painting in this area, the different types of offerings, and the finding of offerings made during the construction of the buildings demonstrate the sacredness of this space and its function as a ritual path that led to the main temple and the area of the temples. Recent excavations allow us to affirm that the walls that delimited the street at the intersection with East-West Street were up to 6 m high; this creates a restricted access from different points of view, as the visitor could only see the temples painted from afar—a notable difference from the public character that the Northern Section seems to have had.

Our excavations at the end point of the street have also allowed us to obtain data that shows a continuity in the use of this access, suggesting that the street does not end at the intersection with the East-West Street. For this reason, we decided to excavate the crossing of the North-South with East-West streets and the beginning of the Southern Section, in order to provide new data to verify the continuity of this circulation area.

With these excavations, it was possible to establish that the slope between both sections of the North-South Street is not as dramatic as it was thought; rather, it is due to the multiple alterations that the area underwent after the Spanish Conquest. In addition to confirming the continuity of the street to the south, we have determined that the west section of the East-West Street had no direct connection to the North-South Street or the east section of the East-West Street. The apparent connection of the west section of the East-West Street with the North-South Street and the west section of the East-West Street was the product of postabandonment alterations, mainly the result of the enabling of a road or carriage trail during the Republican Period, which allowed the city of Lima to be connected with the Lurín Valley and the south coast. That is why it is important to carry out excavations in the west section of the East-West Street, to know its real characteristics and its function in the internal communication system of the site.

Restricted excavation carried out at the beginning and at the end point of the Southern Section have revealed that, underneath the exposed architecture there is pre-Inca architecture with different characteristics, the nature of which must be investigated. This architecture was intentionally buried in preparation to reorganize the space. In order to know the spatial organization of the area currently occupied by the Southern Section during the Ychsma occupation, it will be necessary to carry out excavations in the squares associated with the Southern Section and neighboring squares, since they are the only spaces where it will be possible to go deeper until reaching the levels corresponding to the Ychsma occupation.

Likewise, the mapping and characterization of the walls that delimit and/or are found in the enormous plazas located to the east of the Southern Sec-

Figure 7.6. Crossing streets and evidence of the last level of traffic on the southern street. Photo by "Proyecto de Investigación y Conservación de la Calle Norte-Sur Temporada 2011–2012 (PIA CNS 2011–2012)."

tion, designated by Uhle as Section B, and which he describes as an area "full of tombs, which are, in general, of much earlier date than those of the other three sections" (Uhle 2003 [1903]: 239), will provide interesting data to reconstruct what the site looked like before the Incas reorganized this space.

As we pointed out at the beginning of the article, the research work carried out by the team at the Pachacamac Museum is complemented by conservation tasks, carried out in accordance with current international standards. To complete the vision offered by the study of the North-South Street that we have just outlined, it is important to us to present the actions related to conservation in the sanctuary that will allow us to better understand its spatial characteristics.

Conservation Work in the Pachacamac Sanctuary

Practically since its construction, the sanctuary buildings have suffered serious damage, mainly due to intense seismic movements, since the sanctuary is situated in a highly seismic zone, in the area of influence of the Pacific Ring of Fire. Significant damage has been inflicted on the structures of Pachacamac by vandalism and anthropogenic actions, which, in some cases, has caused the walls to become unstable. All the conservation interventions have been made principally according to the international documents of ICOMOS and UNESCO, which guide the conservation interventions worldwide.

As part of our management plan, a work protocol that includes the optimization of each of the procedures for the conservation of architectural structures within the Pachacamac Sanctuary has been prepared: an adequate archaeological record, the graphic record, and the measurement of damage to the structures at risk; this is combined with the identification of environmental factors that could affect the asset, characterization of pathologies, and identification of damage caused by the anthropogenic factor. The protocol is complemented by the archaeological analysis, the study of the original construction materials and techniques, and finally by the monitoring of the interventions that have been carried out.

To initiate the conservation tasks, a diagnosis of the state of the main structures was prepared (Pozzi-Escot and Chávez 2008), even though this has been refined in recent years with the application of new technologies. This first work allowed us to have an overview of the different conditions and the looting that the different buildings of this important sanctuary had suffered since ancient times.

After this first diagnosis, we divided our intervention into three fronts: (1) conservation of surfaces, minor repairs, repairing of the plaster, and so forth; (2) punctual conservation of some buildings whose walls only needed a minimal intervention such as footings, reintegration, and so on; and finally, (3) interventions aimed at protecting the affected architecture, which required considerable interventions to avoid the collapse of the affected walls. All this allowed us to start conservation work in a systematic way, although conservation efforts began in the sanctuary with the work of Julio C. Tello (an important Peruvian archaeologist) in the 1940s.

The main damage has occurred in the corners of the walls and/or platforms; the partial collapse of structures from frequent earthquakes has caused damage by excessive bending, due to the strong vibrations. Finally, we have noticed the differential settlement of the structures.

Since 2008 the conservation work of the fragile adobe structures has been one of the main aspects of our Conservation Program. We have a classification of the different types of walls that have been improved over the years, and a series of analyses of the composition of the materials used to complete the field work has been carried out (Pozzi-Escot 2018: 210). We have also managed to consolidate and restore structural stability to 103 points or walls of the sanctuary's main archaeological buildings—representing approximately 1,400 m³ of intervention—which were in danger of collapse; this was done with minimal intervention when possible, while respecting the original site's characteristics. Furthermore, the workers were trained in conservation work and in the protection of plaster, and we have achieved a level of quality in the registration of architecture and conservation with the use of new technologies.

In order to have an adequate record of the environmental conditions that allow us to have a successful intervention of architecture-at-risk and mural paintings, the Pachacamac Museum today has two meteorological stations: one located at the Temple of the Sun—that is to say, on the highest part of the sanctuary—and the other at the entrance of the monumental area. To this has been added the construction of test walls in order to check the reaction of the materials and thus have adequate monitoring and control of our proposed work.

Thanks to the support of the Global Heritage Fund, we were able to train a team of young archaeologists in the main conservation techniques, in addition to having the advice of John Hurd, an expert in the conservation of earthen structures, for almost four years, and with the permanent support of Julio Vargas Neumann from the PUCP and Ricardo Morales from Huacas de Moche.

Conservation and Research in the Painted Temple of Pachacamac

Another of the emblematic buildings at Pachacamac is the Painted Temple. A series of analyses have been carried out in order to work on the conservation of what little remains of the mural painting, which went without attention from 1939 to 2009 (Pacheco 2014; Pozzi-Escot, Pacheco and Uceda 2013). The work carried out in the conservation of the murals in the Painted Temple has added first-rate information to the bank of archaeological knowledge.

The installation of a provisional cover (500 m²) over the fragile north front of the Painted Temple, with a windbreaker made of bamboo, constituted an important advance in the preservation of the exposed paintings. In addition to the installation of this roof, the topographic and planimetric survey of the Painted Temple was carried out, which allows us to have a map of the building that consolidates and corrects the information of previous maps. In order to start the conservation work on the mural painting, the faces of the 29 steps of the north façade were recorded: a detailed photographic and graphic record was made to identify the state of conservation of the layers of mural painting and the structure. All this allowed us to register and retrieve designs of birds, fish, human figures, plants, and so forth; we managed to register 27 designs.

With these works we have conserved 42 m² of mural painting on the north façade: consolidating, readhering, and conserving the remains of the mural paintings that had been exposed to erosion and environmental deterioration since 1938. This preserved area corresponds to approximately 30 percent of the mural painting that would have originally covered the front. The cover and the installation of a windbreak protect the wall paintings on the north façade from environmental erosion (winds, changes in temperature, rainfall, and so on), creating a more stable environment for the preservation of the paintings.

The rest of the building—warehouses, north façade, east façade, and the altar in the upper plaza—had also been significantly damaged, and the structures were in danger of collapse; conservation was done to consolidate and protect the structures with techniques like replacing materials, grouting the walls, and anastylosis of the walls.

The research work on the materials used in pre-Hispanic painting include tests with readherents and organic consolidants using different inputs, such as rice, potatoes, and cactus mucilage starches, products that have been monitored on test walls. X-ray diffraction and fluorescence analysis of the pigments in the paintings of this important building are also being carried out (Pacheco and Pozzi-Escot 2018: 198). Currently, we can attest to the fact that the red color would correspond to hematite, and the yellow to goetite. X-ray fluorescence analysis was done with a Bruker Tracer III-SD, thanks to the support of V. Wright and L. J. Castillos, with the following parameters: 45 kV–11,30 µA. Twenty-two samples of mural paintings were analyzed: 10 from the Painted Temple, 6 from the Temple of the Sun, and 3 from the North-South Street.

An interesting fact that helped in our understanding of these paintings was the discovery of several brushes. One of them, from the first step of the east front of the Painted Temple (Pacheco 2014), was analyzed in two areas: on the hair where there were traces of red pigment, and on the reed handle. Both analyses indicate the presence of iron, which possibly corresponds to the hematite (Fe_2O_3) associated with calcium (gypsum or calcite).

The 2017 excavations by Rocio Villar and Sarita Funtes on the esplanade of the northwest façade of the Painted Temple revealed, under three layers of debris, a structure that presents two trapezoidal blind niches on the inside and are associated with constructions of the Inca Era on the Central Coast, the Lurín Valley, and Pachacamac. We have continued studying the pigments and, in collaboration with the team of the Proyecto Inca, have carried out new analyses to determine the elements; this will allow us to reconstitute part of the pictorial process and techniques in the Painted Temple and in the archaeological sanctuary of Pachacamac.

Conservation in the Temple of the Sun

The most imposing Inca building of the sanctuary is the Temple of the Sun, located in the southwest of the site; it is composed of overlapping platforms where, even today, you can see openings and niches with double jambs and trapezoidal forms. Its state of conservation is also quite critical, despite the fact that conservation work has been carried out on this structure since the 1930s (Villar Córdoba 1935). Our interventions seek to reduce damage to the walls in critical condition or at risk of collapse (Pozzi-Escot and Chávez 2008).

Its location on the Pacific Ocean affects the building in a different way: the adobe walls show the disintegration of the joint mortar and seat mortar, leaving grooves, which are going to be affected by wind and humidity, weakening the structure. Nonetheless, once again, it is earthquakes that are the main cause of deterioration of these buildings; the northeast corner has been seriously affected, as well as a large part of the walls located on the terraces to the north of the building.

Carolina Jiménez began research and conservation works in the Temple of the Sun in 2010 on the north front. Her excavations allowed us to define the characteristics of the walls and to propose how to conserve them. We were also able, based on the evidence found, to make a proposal for how the walls were plastered, since a large amount of red pigment and the remains of cotton spots with red paint were found; these served to paint the walls. Later, a series of conservation works were done on the structures-at-risk located along the southern and western façades, and work was implemented for the maintenance of the clay plasters with red pictorial layers at various points on the eastern and northern fronts.

Additionally, the protection of the intangible area is also important since threats of illegal occupation are frequent due to the lack of social housing planning. The architect José Canziani has made a proposal to protect the intangible area, creating more friendly spaces so that the surrounding population can somehow have a link with their heritage. This proposal is for the implementation of a cultural park, with information points on the environment and history of the heritage asset along the perimeter of the archaeological zone. In this way, the concrete fence that isolates/protects the monument would be accompanied by a landscaping proposal that would integrate the community, thus preparing the limits of the sanctuary for its social use.

References Cited

Bernuy, Katiusha, and Denise Pozzi-Escot
2018   Santuario Arqueológico de Pachacamac: Investigaciones en la ruta de los Peregrinos. Museo Pachacamac. Qhapaq Ñan. Ministerio de Cultura, Lima, Perú.
Bueno, Alberto
1982   El antiguo valle de Pachacamac. Espacio, Tiempo y Cultura. Boletín de Lima 4(24): 10–29.
Carod-Artal, Francisco J., and Carolina B. Vazquez-Cabrera
2007   Semillas psicoactivas sagradas y sacrificios rituales en la cultura Moche. Revista Neurol 44(1): 43–50.
Cornejo Guerrero, Miguel Antonio
2004   Pachacamac y el canal de Guatca en el bajo Rímac. Bulletin de l'Institut Français d'Etudes Andines 33(3): 783–514.

Diaz Arriola, Luisa

2004   Armatambo y la sociedad Ychsma. *Bulletin de l'Institut Français d'Etudes Andines* 33(3): 571–594. Lima, Perú.

Eeckhout, Peter

2004   Relatos míticos y prácticas rituales en Pachacamac. *Bulletin de l'Institut Français d'Etudes Andines* 33(1): 1–54.

Eeckhout, Peter, and Carlos Farfán

2004   *Informe final del Proyecto Ychsma: Investigaciones arqueológicas en el sitio de Pachacamac Temporada 2004.* Final report delivered to INC in November 2004. Lima, Perú.

2005   *Informe final del proyecto Ychsma: Investigaciones arqueológicas en el sitio de Pachacamac Temporada 2005.* Final report delivered to INC in Decembre 2005. Lima-Perú.

2008   *Informe final del proyecto Ychsma: Investigaciones arqueológicas en el sitio de Pachacamac Temporada 2008.* Final report delivered to INC in September 2008. Lima, Perú.

Jiménez Borja, Arturo

1985   Pachacamac. *Boletín de Lima* 38: 40–54. Lima, Perú.

Makowski, Krzysztof

2006   *Informe de la temporada de trabajo 2005/2006 del Proyecto Arqueológico—Taller de Campo PUCP—"Lomas de Lurín."* Final report delivered to INC in December 2006. Vols. I and II. Lima, Perú.

2008   *Informe de la temporada de trabajo 2006/2007 del Proyecto Arqueológico—Taller de Campo—"Lomas de Lurín" PATL (antes Tablada de Lurín).* Final report delivered to INC in March 2008. Lima, Perú.

Ministerio de Cultura and Ministerio de Comercio Exterior y Turismo

2012   Plan COPESCO Nacional. Lima, Peru.

Oré, Gabriela

2008   *Aspectos Cronológicos y Funcionales de la Ocupación Inca a lo Largo de la Segunda Muralla: Excavaciones en los Sectores SE-A, SW y SW-D en Pachacamac.* Tesis de Licenciatura en Arqueología. Pontificia Universidad Católica del Perú. Lima, Perú.

Oshiro, Janet

2014   Conservación de Emergencia en Taurichumpi. In *Pachacamac: Conservación en arquitectura de tierra,* edited by Denise Pozzi-Escot, pp. 53–75. Ministerio de Cultura. Lima, Perú.

Pacheco, Gianella

2014   Ponencia presentada en el *II Taller de técnicas Aplicadas a la Investigación Arqueológica.* Ministerio de Cultura y Museo de Sitio de Pachacamac. 10 y 11 de mayo del 2014. Lima, Perú.

2014   Conservación de las estructuras y murales del Templo Pintado de Pachacamac. In *Pachacamac: Conservación en arquitectura de tierra,* edited by Denise Pozzi-Escot, pp. 143–163. Ministerio de Cultura. Lima, Perú.

Pacheco, Gianella, and Denise Pozzi-Escot

2018   Investigación y conservación en el Templo Pintado de Pachacamac. In *La cooperación científica francesa en Latinoamérica: Avances recientes en datación y arqueometría en los Andes,* edited by Iván Ghezzi and Luis E. Salcedo, pp. 189–201. IFEA–Plural, La Paz.

Paredes, Ponciano

1988   Pachacamac: Pirámide con rampa no 2. *Boletín de Lima* 55: 41–58.

Pozzi-Escot, Denise

2018   Investigación y conservación en el santuario de Pachacamac, Lima, Perú. In *La cooper-*

ación científica francesa en Latinoamérica: Avances recientes en datación y arqueometría en los Andes, edited by Iván Ghezzi and Luis E. Salcedo, pp. 203–230. IFEA–Plural, La Paz.

Pozzi-Escot, Denise, and Katiusha Bernuy

2010   *Pachacamac: Calle Norte-Sur. Investigaciones Arqueológicas*. Ministerio de Cultura. 1° edition. Lima, Perú.

Pozzi-Escot, Denise, Katiusha Bernuy, and Isabel Cornejo

2014   Pachacamac y la Costa Norte durante los Periodos Tardíos. Actas del primer y segundo coloquio *Cultura Lambayeque. En el contexto de la costa norte del Perú*. Edited by Julio César Fernández Alvarado and Carlos Eduardo Wester La Torre. Lambayeque, Perú.

Pozzi-Escot, Denise, and Anibal Chávez

2008   Informe Final de las labores de Conservación de Emergencia 2008. Instituto Nacional de Cultura–Museo de Sitio de Pachacamac. Lima, Perú.

Pozzi-Escot, Denise, Gianella Pacheco, and Carmen Rosa Uceda

2013   *Pachacamac: Templo Pintado Conservación e Investigación*. Ministerio de Cultura. 1° edition. Lima, Perú.

Seiner, Lizardo

2009   *Historia de los sismos en el Perú: Catálogo Siglo XV–XVII*. Fondo editorial Universidad de Lima. Lima, Perú.

Shimada, Izumi

2010   *Max Uhle (1856–1944): Evaluaciones de sus Investigaciones y Obras*. PUCP, Lima.

Shimada, Izumi, Rafael Segura, and Maria Rostworowski.

2004   *Informe Final de la Primera Temporada de Campo 2003 del Proyecto Arqueológico Pachacamac*. Final report delivered to INC in March 2004. Lima, Perú.

Tomasto Cagigao, Elsa

2013   *Informe del análisis de los restos óseos humanos del contexto PC02-C3-CF1 de Pachacamac*. Manuscript in the documentary archive of the Pachacamac Site Museum, Lima.

Uhle, Max

2003 [1903]   *Pachacamac: Informe de la expedición Peruana Wiliam Peper 1986*. Serie Clásicos San Marquinos. Translated by Manuel Beltroy Vera. Fondo Editorial UNMSM, Lima.

Vallejo Berríos, Francisco

2004   El Estilo Ychsma: Características generales, secuencia y distribución geográfica. *Bulletin de l'Institut Français d'Etudes Andines* 33(3): 595–642.

Xerez, Francisco

1891   *Verdadera relación de la conquista del Perú*. Tip. De J. C. García, Lima.

Zegarra Galdos, Jorge

1957–1959 *Cuaderno de Campo N° 1*. Manuscrito en archivo documentario del Museo de Sitio Pachacamac. Lima, Perú.

8

Why Pachacamac? When Pachacamac?

Investigating Theories of Environmental, Culture History, and
Late Horizon Triggers for the Development of the Ychsma Capital

LAWRENCE S. OWENS AND PETER EECKHOUT

Waves are not measured in feet or inches;
they are measured in increments of fear.

Buzzy Trent

The current volume can answer no greater question than how Pachacamac
came to be, and when, topics that have generated numerous theories on
the basis of different approaches. Some consider environmental impacts to
be seminal in triggering the transformative steps of the site in what can be
loosely defined as the Deterministic Model [DM] (see Shimada et al. this volume; Winsborough et al. 2012). Culture history approaches take two routes.
The more widely accepted is the Local Chiefdom Model [LCM], in which
Pachacamac was the capital of the Ychsma polity, where elites resided in
monumental buildings and controlled the Lower and Middle Lurín Valley
from the thirteenth to the fifteenth century AD (that is, before the Inca Conquest). A more radical view sees virtually no occupation at the site prior to
Tahuantinsuyu, attributing nearly all visible architecture to the Incas. We will
call this the Imperial Model [IM] (Makowski 2012, 2015, 2017, this volume).

These cases deserve assessment. However, while all have their merits, we
suspect that the DM too strongly diminishes the role of human agency, while
the IM is too selective in its approach, overlooking total morphological pattern and architectural sequencing, methods for which Pachacamac is unusu-
ally well suited. Finally, we assert that bioarchaeology might be turned to in
order to provide alternative scenarios.

To this end we aim to (1) delineate Andean archaeologists' stubborn proclivity for environmental narratives of sociocultural development, (2) undertake a full architectural profile of Pachacamac in order to assess chronology and development of the site and thus differentiate between the IM and the LCM, and (3) undertake a bioarchaeological study to assess whether the tsunami events can be detected in terms of human impacts. We anticipate that this approach will demonstrate the benefit of a unified yet multifaceted foundation for analytical questions of this sort.

Climatic (Meta)Narratives in the Andes

Thompson et al.'s (1985) work on the Quelccaya ice cap spawned a plethora of related studies as numerous Andeanists cited climate as the central (and often singular) cause of everything from Archaic monumental architecture to social stasis, site abandonments, ill health, sacrifice, aberrant burials, population diasporas, ideological changes, and polity collapses (Bourget 1998; Erickson 1999; Williams 2002). Adherents believe (either implicitly or explicitly) in catastrophism—humans failing to adapt to extreme climatic and environmental phenomena—or varying degrees of ecological determinism, whereby humans are forced to bow before progressive and inexorable climatic change (Bawden and Reycraft 2000; Moseley et al. 1981; Sandweiss and Quilter 2012; Segura 2012; Shimada et al. 1991). Yet while this preoccupation reflects the academic zeitgeist—and while acknowledging the vital importance of climatic data in any measured approach to human prehistory—the catastrophism/determinism paradigm has come to be seen as overly simplistic. In a sense it has become the deus ex machina (van Buren 2001: 142) of cultural change, and that important cultural information is being overlooked in a rush for climatic correlation (Ellen 1982; Sandweiss and Kelly 2012). While every human group is subject to climate, environment, and ecology, it is also empowered by cultural, magico-religious, aesthetic, or ritual factors that must be taken into account (Ellen 1982: 16). Human ecodynamic approaches are in the ascendant, assuming sophisticated, dynamic, and ever-changing relationships between climate, environment, and culture, not climatic/cultural Pavlovian responses.

Objections to Climatic Narratives

There is a lack of consensus as to what a disaster is, how much of a climatic change made a difference, and if any modern definition of disaster coincides with ancient perspectives, given that we do not share Andean groups' long familiarity with their environment. In any case, behavior that coincides temporally with climatic events may overshadow more important cultural causes; for example, death of a family member, nightmares, insects, fouling, and social conflict are more likely than climate to cause camp abandonments among the Hadza of Tanzania (Ellen 1982: 4–7). Groups are also likely to attribute environmental phenomena to sociocultural or supernatural factors, so responses may be muted, fatalistic, or socially channeled (Torrence and Grattan 2002: 13). Furthermore, what may comprise "meltdowns" to modern western analysts may have presented positive opportunities to these ancient groups. It should also be noted that the vagaries of the archaeological record make it nearly impossible to accurately establish climate/behavior correlation, much less causation. The very nature of the evidence makes it unwise to be dogmatic about environmental triggers, even assuming that they were considered to be so by ancient groups (van Buren 2001: 145). Finally, reliance upon ice/deep-sea coring makes no allowance for the environmental heterogeneity, microclimates, oceanic currents and local weather systems to which the Andean area is subject (Eitel et al. 2005; Eitel and Mächtle 2009; Flantua et al. 2016; Reindel 2009).

The current chapter aims to examine the rise and rise of climatic phenomena as social drivers in Andean prehistory, and to take lessons from this in an innovative analysis of a claimed tsunami event near the site of Pachacamac, on the Peruvian Central Coast.

Environmental Triggers in Andean Prehistory

El Nino is often seen by archaeologists . . . as a sort of "black box." Human societies enter one end of the box, El Nino occurs, and societies exit the box transformed in some dramatic fashion. (Billman and Huckleberry 2008: 117)

Climatic drivers are fundamental to biogeography and hominid evolution, yet their applicability to cultural, socially sophisticated, and environmentally adaptable modern humans is less certain (Torrence and Grattan 2002: 2). Nevertheless, climatic and environmental regimes have proven to be a deeply seductive skeleton from which to flesh out 5,000 years of Andean adaptation, rooted in two centuries of ethnohistory (Sheets and Cooper 2012: 9). Modern archaeologists have been much taken by sixteenth–nineteenth century reports of volcanic eruptions, earthquakes, storms, floods, landslides and droughts, disease proliferation, crop spoiling, and plagues of insects and rodents (Sandweiss and Quilter 2012: 126–128), resulting in "desperation, death and extreme poverty" (Vallejos 2001: 50), social breakdown, and disintegration (Gaither 2010: 77). The extent to which these can be imposed upon the archaeological record has been a matter of debate since Richardson's (1973) inquiry into El Niño Southern Oscillation (ENSO) effects in preceramic midden structures, and thence to the timing of monumental apogee and decline between 5800 and 3000 cal yr BP (Sandweiss 2003: 31; Sandweiss and Richardson 2008: 100–101). ENSO has since been implicated in the triggering of social complexity in the North Coast Preceramic (and the entire Pacific Basin), the decline of the Moche, coastal political decline in the Initial Period, settlement/irrigation collapse in Ilo, heightened levels of sacrifice, residential pattern changes among the Chiribaya, the development and spread of the Chavín cult, agricultural abandonment in the Altiplano, the final collapse of the Tiwanaku, the genesis of the Chimu, and even human expansion into the Pacific (Arkush 2008: 365; Bawden 1996; Bourget 1998; Binford et al. 1997; Bourget 1998; Clement and Moseley 1991; Erickson 1999; Moseley 1983; Ortloff and Kolata 1993; Reycraft 2000, 2005: 58; Roscoe 2008: 91; Ryan Williams 2002; Sandweiss and Richardson 2008: 101; Van Buren 2001: 143). However, has this been done in haste? Modeling climate/human relationships is reliant upon highly refined data and a robust conceptual framework that measures not only perturbations but also populational structure, governance, resilience, robustness, and the balance of vulnerabilities necessary to reduce the cost of disasters. Yet the means for measuring these factors cannot even be agreed upon for the present day, much less the past. The necessarily vague "the existence of damage to individuals or their property" may serve as a heuristic to guide research (Torrence and Grattan 2002: 5–6), but other factors must be considered. For example, cultural convention rather than resource optimization may dictate the perpetuation of inefficient methods and a "rigidity trap," increasing the eventual human cost (Nelson et al. 2012: 198–214). Voluntary isolation versus incorporation may also define vulnerabilities, playing off high benefits in a time of plenty against mitigation of collapse risk in the long term (Nelson et al. 2012: 213–214). Irrigation can increase carrying capacity and population size, and thus lowers vulnerability to threats from hostile neighbors (Kohler 2012: 231–232). Yet what follows immediately is vulnerability for the loss of mobility and the emergent elites' maintenance of the status quo rather than resource optimization; this creates a status-based risk distribution (Sheets and Cooper 2012: 10–11) that can impact differently according to social structure (that is, the higher burden of environmental impacts suffered by women and children in androcentric social systems [Sultana 2014: 379]). This can in turn affect susceptibility to disease—as COVID-19 has recently demonstrated, diseases differently impact certain age/sex groups, ethnicities, social structures, or socioeconomic groups, reflecting differential genetic immunities, differential robusticity against infection, socioeconomic status, access to education, nutrition, and even differential levels of social obedience that affect the likelihood or intensity of infection (Sheets 2008: 182). Therefore, so long as society, religion, perception, and individual or group idiosyncrasies can be seen to have such an effect on populations in the modern era, therefore, monocausal climatic interpretations of social change in the past cannot be sustained (Richardson and Sandweiss 2008: 68; Roscoe 2008: 87).

Culture as an Agency of Social Change

Natural disasters are human disasters; they are measured as such in terms of human cost, in terms of impacts upon humans, and very often caused or at least exacerbated by humans (Kiracofe and Marr 2008: 160–161). While it is true that "ENSO-related floods, tsunamis, flash floods from highland rains and droughts all have contributed as much as anthropogenic modifications to this evolving landscape" (Shimada et al. 2013: 15), the key word is "contributed"—humans are active, not passive; adaptive, not static; and variable, not homogenous (Ortloff and Kolata 1993: 215; versus Owen 2005). There is a wealth of evidence to suggest that anthropological and archaeological populations simply do/did not consider "disasters" in the same way as we do (Van Buren 2001: 141; Wilkerson 2009). Despite inhabiting marginal environments, the Kuril Islanders and various southern North American groups are seemingly oblivious to volcanism, drought, tsunamis, and climatic fluctuations, concerned instead with human agency, ambitious neighbors, and social networks (Kohler 2012; Sheets and Cooper 2012: 7–11). Modern ethnographic groups treat environmental factors as evidence of human malfeasance and develop social adaptive strategies to deal with them (Ellen 1982: 7; Fairhead and Leach 2012: 95; Rout 2009). For this reason, "natural" events rarely appear in oral histories or mythologies, adversity instead being attributed to social issues (Torrence and Grattan 2002: 13), or divine punishment of the godless (Eeckhout and Peperstraete 2022). For example, bad weather resulting in "a year of much barrenness and hunger" in sixteenth-century Peru was attributed to the local lord having consorted with a female demon (Cavello Balboa 1586/1951: 329). Climatic/ecological events were often used to seize or consolidate power, resulting in regime change, polity expansion, and economic development (Kohler 2012: 231–232; Roscoe 2008; Swenson 2003: 284–285), and even altruistic acts such as the 1980s Ronda philanthropic movement (Billman and Huckleberry 2008: 117).

A further critism of environmental determinism is the means by which the arguments are constructed. Andean environments are so enormously variable (Flantua et al. 2016) that ice/deep-sea coring data cannot be reliably used to accurately pinpoint climatic fluctuations for the region as a whole. Direct proximity to the sites under discussion is thus a *sine qua non* of sensible environment/culture approaches.

Discussion

Analysts' relentless search for environmental triggers for cultural phenomena can obscure the hyper-adaptation Andean groups exhibit to the extreme climates and environments from which they evolved (Billman and Huckleberry 2008: 125; Erickson 1999: 641). This infatuation with biogeographical drivers is augmented by a weakness for metanarratives that account for *vita, universum et omnia* through a series of selected observations and meaningless averages. The question is not whether "natural" impacts affected humans, but that we can't accurately identify the social effect of a climatic cause, nor the climatic cause of a social effect. Climate/behavior correlation is easy, but causation is often too readily assumed (Torrence and Grattan 2002: 2; Sandweiss and Quilter 2012: 121); the 1925–1926 ENSO event can be correlated with the Columbine Mine Massacre, the invention of penicillin, Mickey Mouse, Popeye, Tintin, the Academy Awards, and the collapse of the global economy (Davis 2001), yet to assume causation would be a step too far. We posit that an enduring fascination with matching ancient human groups' rise and fall to an environmental metronome is hindering a holistic understanding of human existence, contorting the topography of the field into gratuitous, climatic correlation rather than exploring alternative analytical routes. Understanding human-environmental relationships, residential patterns, economic strategies, social structures, their affiliations, and the nature of their adaptations to a changing world are both more rewarding and more useful than seeking triggers for their dissolution, decay, and demise (Van Buren 2001: 145).

Earthquakes and Tsunamis in Andean History

The Nazca plate's subduction under South America makes the region a hotspot for seismic activity, and thus tsunamis (Dorbath et al. 1990). While strength and regularity vary from Ecuador to Chile, all coastal groups are thus accustomed to earthquakes. There are no wave references in Inca/pre-Inca mythologies, other than Viracocha's creation/destruction flood cycle, and a tendency for superhuman beings to disappear into the sea (Eeckhout and Peperstraete 2022); this seems to suggest that waves were considered to be a matter of little consequence.

At least 14 major exemplars were recorded between 1535 and 1746. These events happened frequently enough for inhabitants to have direct or social memory of the events, which occurred every 20–100 years and remained vividly in the minds of the populations (Canque 2007: 115). They were often highly destructive. The 1576 flood caused so much damage that it was still not repaired after 10 years (Cavello Balboa 1586/1951: 223–224). The 1586 wave was 25 m tall and ran 10 km into Callao, while the 1746 quake/tsunami (15–20 m tall) killed 6,000 in Lima and Callao in 1746 (Canque 2007: 38–41, 48; Carcelen Reluz 2011; Pérez-Mallaína 2005: 58). The greatest historical earthquake/tsunami struck Arica in 1868, which killed around 25,000 people (Canque 2007; IISEE 2010; Zamudio et al. 2005). Impact was devastating in urbanized areas (while mitigated by the use of indigenous building materials [Walker 2003: 62–3]), although the death toll was increased by high infection rates in the survivors' shantytowns (Carcelen Reluz 2011: 90). In 1746, a briefly philanthropic state of forgiving enemies and seeking confession lapsed almost immediately into social conflict, worsened by the religious elites' calling-in of debts and plundering of silverware from the rubble (Perez Mallaina 2005: 58, 63); this resulted in a religious shift toward a precontact deity (Pachacamac) in the new guise of the Lord of Miracles (Carcelen Reluz 2011: 60). The death toll of the 1868 event was considerably heightened by an earlier mass migration from Lima, in order to avoid yellow fever outbreaks that killed 10,000 Limans and a fifth of Callao's population (Canque 2007: 237–238). The aftermath of the event saw major structural faulting and complete destruction of all large (that is, western-style) buildings; the debris built up into "a horrible mass of debris made up of everything, including bodies of the victims, mounted up to a height of 6 to 10 metres," and a resultant wave of yellow fever that swept through the survivors (Canque 2007: 230, 270, 288). Shantytowns sprang up; the survivors fed and dressed themselves from the city's ruins and the beach, fighting off llama trains of "wild Araucanian Indians" who descended from the Andes to do likewise. Social order breakdown led to inflation, price gouging, and famine, while free access to pillaged alcohol meant "fatal fights broke out frequently" (Canque: 168–169, 231–232, 269, 275).

Perhaps most significantly from an archaeological point of view is the fact that "the most affected populations in 1868 . . . were those whose location did not obey preventive norms that pre-existing cultures had tried to anticipate" (Canque 2007: 312). Indigenous architecture, residential patterns, and populations were attuned to their environment (Sheets and Cooper 2012: 9), suggesting that it was only because of European settlement patterns, architecture, and population size that tsunamis (and, perhaps, other "natural" disasters) wrought as much damage as they have. Arica is a case in point—this large colonial city stands at less than 2 masl, making it excessively vulnerable to flooding (Billman and Huckleberry 2008), whereas the site of Pachacamac (circa 23 masl) and the adjacent sections of the Lurín Valley and the fertile site margins (circa 6–8 masl) were less vulnerable to such a possibility.

Tsunamis as Agents of Cultural Change

Earthquakes/tsunamis have been cited as driving mechanisms for cultural change across the Pacific region, one strength of this approach being the necessary propinquity of earthquake/tsunami indicators to the sites under discussion (rather than regional averages based upon distant ice/deep-sea cores). Oral histories of great waves at Aitape in Papua New Guinea were connected to geoarchaeological indications of a tsunami between AD 1440 and 1600 (Davies et al. 2019), which caused dune formation and site abandonment in New Zealand (Goff and McFadgen 2002). Goff et al. (2017) have suggested that human groups colonizing Papuan coastal areas during the mid-Holocene may have been impacted by a tsunami event, leading to changes in social structure and mobility, innovative risk-mitigation strategies, and the development of tighter intergroup ties (Goff et al. 2017: 8–9). Humans may have thought the risk of tsunamis to be an acceptable tradeoff for desirable coastal environments, for economic purposes, for low malarial risk, and even for the appreciation of pleasant settings (Goff 2004: 178). There is less data for

Peru. The classic example is Bird (1987: 290–291), who postulated that a 12 m tsunami around 900 BC led to the spread of the Chavinoid style, Las Aldas site abandonments, an economic emphasis on maize, military elites, and the first major defenses and weapons on the central/south-central coast. A major flood—likely a riverine event—may have prompted abandonments in the Osmore Drainage around AD 1340 (Moseley and Keefer 2008).

Tsunamis at Pachacamac

The possibility of tsunamis at Pachacamac has been posited on the basis of salt crystals in Early Lima buildings (Franco Jordán 2015: 163–164).[1] This was believed to represent storms and tsunamis in the third century AD, leading to social hardship, building remodeling, ceremonies, and sacrifices. However, the strongest arguments for tsunamis and associated cultural change were proposed by Segura and Shimada (2010), Winsborough et al. (2012), and Shimada et al. (in this volume). Their arguments are based upon reading sedimentary profiles of the Urpi-Kocha Lagoon, situated beside and below the site. Winsborough et al.'s analyses of diatom and pollen data attest to fluctuating salinity, desiccation, and vegetation cover, the result of ENSO and tsunamis (2012) (Table 8.1).

The authors' interpretation of a 9 cm silty sand layer containing marine and brackish diatoms is of a flood event around AD 1010, associated with drought stress indicators, and presaging "a new phase of extensive occupation, ritual offerings and major construction around AD 1100 by the group called Ychsma" (Winsborough 2012: z611–612) several generations later. Below this was a layer containing freshwater/marine diatoms, woody debris, and

Table 8.1. Events from the Urpi Kocha Lagoon

Date	Range	Interpretation
1010 BP	AD 995–1008	El Niño & tsunami
1540 BP	AD 436–651	El Niño & tsunami
1700 BP	AD 260–283	El Niño & tsunami
2018 BP	436 BC–AD 93	River flood & El Niño
2293 BP	398 BC–AD 177	Tsunami

Source: Authors.

pollen (circa 1330 BP), a period of intense irrigation and land use in the MH connected with "shifts in subsistence strategies and corresponding changes in cultural development" (2012: 612–613) throughout the Pacific region. Beneath this was a thick deposit of dark gray muddy sand with rocks and freshwater/marine diatoms, evidence of a tsunami/flood following a prolonged ENSO event around 1540 BP. This coincides with depopulation of the Middle/Late Lima culture, which was stratigraphically associated with freshwater stability to around 1700 BP, a (mostly) freshwater flood at 2018 BP, and continued stability to circa 2293 BP. The deepest stratum is a sand-rich, mixed layer attesting to a probable tsunami, perhaps connected with the EH storm/tsunami reported in northern Peru (Bird 1987).

The ecological profile seems to fit into a general trend of high highland variability and relative lowland homogeneity (Flantua et al. 2016). The sequencing is certainly unarguable and we welcome its substantiation of our previous point concerning the necessary proximity of environmental data to archaeological sites if any environmental/cultural relationship is to be reliably posited. While we concur with the methods employed, the validity of the analysis and the enduring vision of Pachacamac's sanctity regarding its privileged relationship with water, we do find it unusual that it is unsupported by detritus banks or other evidence of catastrophic impact beneath or near the site, given the enormous scale of such debris noted in historical tsunamis (Shimada et al. 2013). We wonder if the format of the Lurín Valley tributary catchment made it less susceptible to flooding than larger, lower catchments such as Arica (Billman and Huckleberry 2008). It is also striking that in over a century of research, no mass burials of mangled bodies have been recovered. It is of course possible that the dead were interred at the main, funeral site, but the standard format of burials dating to this period tends to imply either that lifeways were not greatly affected, or that the tsunami was smaller or less impactive than one might suppose.

We would also like to comment on the role that the tsunami/s are believed to have played as triggers for social evolution at the site and area. The site's 26-masl elevation suggests that the inhabitants were aware of danger from the sea, and were unlikely to have been directly affected by it. Furthermore, the notion that the Late Lima abandoned the site and area would seem to be a rather irrational response, given that the agricultural areas do not seem to have been destroyed, the valley plain was seemingly unaffected, and there was biological continuity between the Lima, their MH successors, and the Ychsma (Vlemincq-Mendieta et al. 2019). These facts make a century of absence post–AD 1010 hard to explain; despite the catastrophic scale of the Arica tsunami, for example, rehabitation of the area was immediate, even attracting external groups intent on exploiting the situation (Canque 2007: 269). It should be remembered that these were urbanized colonial and indigenous cityfolk; the traditional agriculturists of Pachacamac are likely to have been even more resilient. Finally, even assuming wave damage to agricultural grounds, it has been demonstrated that land reclamation takes less than a year (Billman and Huckleberry 2008: 122), and that tsunamic salinization can be reversed in one to four years (Roy et al. 2015), especially if tsunami detritus is not excessive (as seems to be the case for Lurín and Pachacamac). Soil lavage is accelerated by high rainfall, but while the area is quite dry, lavage is promoted by good drainage; the manual irrigation that was probably used at the time would have effectively destroyed and washed away salt crusts that form post-tsunami (Chague-Goff et al. 2013). We suspect that population size was not especially large during this period; this would have limited vulnerability to perturbations, and it was not until population expansion in the LIP that their descendants brought about the development of hierarchical structures and monumental architecture.

Research Questions

We carried out a review of architectural and habitation history at the site. We then studied bioarchaeological data that straddles the time period in question. The questions were as follows:

1. Did the sixth century tsunami trigger the Lima culture's collapse, as suggested in the Deterministic Model?
2. Did the AD 1010 tsunami presage the AD 1100+ burgeoning of Ychsma monumental architecture at the site, as suggested in the Deterministic Model?
3. Do the chronometric, architectural, and stylistic records spanning the sixth–twelfth centuries favor the Local Chiefdom or Imperial Model?
4. Is there any bioarchaeological or funerary evidence to suggest biological discontinuity at the AD 1010 boundary, reflecting reaction— or adaptation—to the aftermath of the tsunami?

The first issue can be addressed with relative ease: Lima culture does not end around AD 600, and thus the tsunami cannot be implicated in its demise.

Recent studies at Pachacamac and the Rímac show that the Lima continued until the end of the eighth century AD (Eeckhout 2018; Lumbreras 2014; Mac Kay 2011; Mac Kay and Santa Cruz 2000; Mauricio 2018; Mauricio et al. 2015; Olivera Astete 2014). Whatever the effect of the tsunami, therefore, it cannot be said to have triggered the dissolution of the Lima. As stated above, we suspect that low population size and density in the Lima—and their familiarity with their environment—made them both flexible and resilient in the face of what probably seemed to be a relatively mild disturbance.

The second claim posits that the AD 1010 wave was followed by an 80-year period of cultural quiescence, then a monumental building phase under the aegis of the Ychsma. However, this springs from a misapprehension, as there is currently no evidence for monumental construction at that point. The earliest Ychsma major works date to around AD 1200—the Central Hall and sections of South Street—but monumental building efforts do not commence until the pyramids with ramps (PWRs) of the fourteenth century (see below). Small/medium multiperiod ceremonial buildings (that is, B15) are also known, but are more the exception than the rule (Eeckhout 2020; Lujan and Eeckhout 2022). While stylistic and temporal frameworks of Ychsma material culture remain a matter of debate (see Dolorier 2013; Eeckhout 2018; Makowski, this volume; Vallejo 2009), ongoing study of Pachacamac material indicates as much continuity as change between the Lima and the Ychsma styles, rather than the abrupt Middle Horizon rupture originally posited by Menzel (1964, 1968). There is therefore no relationship between these phenomena and any known environmental events.

Pachacamac: Basic Structure

It has become increasingly apparent that there is an unfortunate lack of consensus concerning what happened, when, at Pachacamac, meaning that faulty or unrefined data may be used to prop up misleading narratives of genesis, apogee, and decline. The true facts are actually far more complex. What happened during the five centuries of LIP-LH occupation, and how is this expressed structurally and architecturally?

It was under the Ychsma that Pachacamac became a polity capital, and hugely significant to Central Coast cultural development (Capriata and López-Hurtado 2017; Eeckhout 2004a; López-Hurtado 2011; among others). The site is tripartite, the three sectors running from south to north (Figure 8.1). The

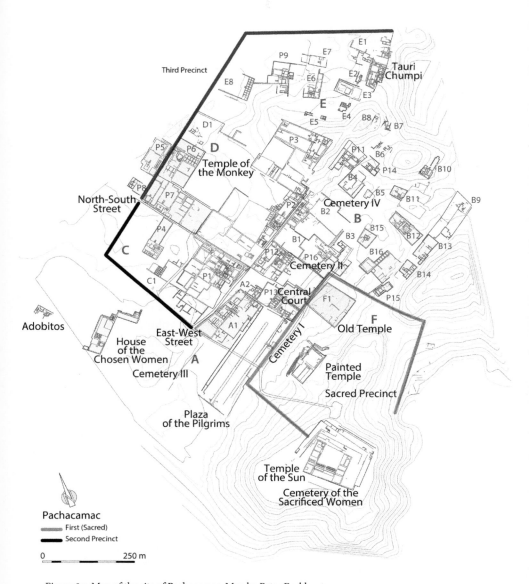

Figure 8.1. Map of the site of Pachacamac. Map by Peter Eeckhout.

first is the Sacred Precinct, with the temples and other religious buildings. The Second Precinct contains PWRs, plazas, streets, and other assorted structures. The Third Precinct is an almost empty, currently unexcavated space (Uhle 2003 [1903]). Sector and structure sequencing is of key importance to understanding how and when the site developed as it did.

The Local Chiefdom Model and PWRs

The tenth–thirteenth centuries AD are noted for numerous collective tombs containing dozens of individuals of both sexes and all ages accumulated through generations (Owens 2017; Owens and Eeckhout 2017; Segura Llanos and Shimada 2010; Takigami et al. 2014). Body treatment, distribution, and skeletal morphology suggest kinship systems and ancestor cults, probably reflecting the growing importance of ayllus (lineages) that were first seen during the EIP (Isbell 1997); this presaged the Local Ychsma Chiefdom in the thirteenth–fourteenth centuries (Eeckhout 2008). This was a gradual process, and was not prompted by catastrophic events or by the arrival of the Incas. Political authority was based in the elite residences of the Second Precinct, while the First Precinct represented the sacred sphere. The Inca destroyed this indigenous system, transforming the site into a pilgrimage center and a node in their imperial network. We define pre-Inca Pachacamac as a local chiefdom.

PWRs are a largely LIP phenomenon, spanning circa 1340 to 1480 (López-Hurtado this volume; Pozzi-Escot and Bernuy this volume; among others), each building having a use-life of 30–55 years (Eeckhout 2003, 2004a, 2013; Eeckhout and Lujan 2022; Lujan and Eeckhout 2022; Michczyński et al. 2003, 2007). The large pyramids construction sequence (PWR No. 1–2–3–7–12) suggests a transition from a centralized to multiple/dual power system, with strong indications of internal succession and abandonment. The building construction sequence has been taken to signify that secular leaders ruled with political comanagement, culminating with the death of the main occupant, the abandonment of their pyramid, the creation of an ancestor cult, and the modification of the building for their successor. This is attested to by settlement pattern analysis and Lurín ethnohistory (Eeckhout 2008; Feltham 1983; Rostworowski 1999), and was a template for the valley's main administrative center. The remaining pyramids were probably elite residences and/or administrative buildings. Their locations—appended to larger structures—have been taken to signify the gradual emergence of high-status officials or minor nobles, thus implying increasing complexity of Ychsma political organization.[2] The Second Precinct monumental buildings developed alongside the North-South Street, which ended at the so-called Central Hall—perhaps a pilgrim assembly area (Pozzi-Escot and Bernuy, this volume). Pilgrimage boomed under the Inca, resulting in major logistical and architectural transformations, including massive fortifications along the North-South Street, modifying the site's internal transit system, and creation of the monumental

Pilgrims' Plaza. This vast open area contained patios, colonnades, private access to the Sacred Enclosure, and an ushnu-with-ramp toward the east (Eeckhout and López-Hurtado 2018). Ethnohistoric and archaeological data agree that pilgrims spent three weeks in a first courtyard and a full year in a second before gaining access to the idol. Burials and intrusive offerings in abandoned administrative buildings suggest that pilgrims may have lived there (Eeckhout 2010; Pozzi-Escot and Bernuy, this volume; Shimada et al., this volume). The reuse of abandoned Ychsma palaces was both convenient and ritually desirable, given the religious and sacred significance with which the center of the site was imbued.

The site's political status is less clear. The Chiefdom of Ychsma was based in Pachacamac's PWRs and dominated the lower and middle Lurín Valley from the fourteenth century (Eeckhout 2003; 2008). Having expelled local leaders—probably from PWRs No. 1 and 7—the Inca seized power and then exploited local authority architecture to their advantage: the palace of Tauri Chumpi (seat of the Inca governor) is in fact a partially transformed PWR (Eeckhout 2004b), while other Inca administrative and storage facilities also incorporated local elements. By contrast, Building E8—standing away from

Figure 8.2. Aerial view of PWR No. 2 at Pachacamac. Illustration by Peter Eeckhout.

Table 8.2. PWR (Pyramid with Ramp) life spans

PWR	Date BP	Interval	Cal, 2 sygmas	Lesser probability	Interpretation	Foundation	Abandonment	Max occup. length	Sector
P02	627	50	1280–1410	1340–1395	1340–1395	1340	1395	55 yrs	D
P04	660	22	1350–1390	1280–1320	1350–1390	1350	1390	40 yrs	C
P12	574	19	1300–1360	1380–1420	1380–1420	1380	1420	40 yrs	B
P14	521	22	1390–1440		1390–1440	1390	1440	50 yrs	B
P08-Early	482	34	1395–1465		1395–1465	1395	1465	70 yrs	3rd Precinct
P07	480	21	1400–1470?		1400–1470	1400	1470?	70 yrs?	D
P03B	514	12	1405–1435		1405–1435	1405	1435	30 yrs	D
P15	467	24	1410–1455		1405–1455	1410	1455	45 yrs	B
P05	483	22	1410–1450		1410–1450	1410	1450	40 yrs	3rd Precinct
P06	482	16	1410–1445		1410–1445	1410	1445	35 yrs	D
P03A	450	14	1425–1455		1425–1455	1425	1455	30 yrs	D
P08-Late	398	30	1430–1530	1570–1630	1430–1530	1430	1530	60 yrs	3rd Precinct
P11	434	18	1430–1475		1430–1475	1430	1475	45 yrs	B
P09	442	13	1430–1460		1430–1460	1430	1460	30 yrs	E
P13	327	19	1480–1650		1480–1650	1480	1650	?	A
P01	?				?	?	?	?	C

Source: Authors.

the elite residences—differs completely from Ychsma designs (Eeckhout 2012; Eeckhout and Lujan 2014). The notion of a local chiefdom partially transformed by the Inca is confirmed by large-scale excavations and research carried out by the Ychsma Project (YP) and the Museo de Sitio de Pachacamac (MSP) (Pozzi-Escot and Bernuy, this vol.).

The Imperial Model (IM)

The IM differs from the LCM in claiming a lack of substantial occupation prior to Tahuantinsuyu, based on small excavations (North Street; the Second Precinct; the Third Precinct) and test-pitting (Temple of the Sun). The model denies the existence of South Street, and claims that North Street was entirely built by the Incas. They then abandoned it following earthquake damage, constructing a new entrance slightly to the west; the fact that it faces PWR No. 1's entrance leads to the conclusion that PWR No. 1 was also built by the Inca, rather than the Ychsma. Under this theory, the Inca also constructed PWRs No. 2, 4, 6, and 7 (located along North Street), and defined the Third Precinct, which contained small structures thought to be workshops and housing for the LH construction team (Makowski 2012, 2015, 2017; this volume). This highly unorthodox interpretation fails to address a range of evidence that we deem to be important, as detailed below.

1. The MSP and the YP have conclusively demonstrated that the North-South Streets existed early in the LIP, with further development in the twelfth–thirteenth centuries (Figure 8.3).
2. The earthquake that was claimed to have triggered abandonment actually dates to the Colonial Era (probably 1687, see above), not the Late Horizon. The abandonment of the street is also colonial (Pozzi-Escot and Bernuy, this volume).
3. The sealed entrance of PWR No. 4 is located on North Street and dates to the fourteenth century (Table 8.2; Eeckhout and Farfán 2004), not the LH; later Inca remodeling in the area can be clearly seen and defined (Figure 8.4).
4. The "new access" to the Second Precinct is a crude hole in the wall, highly inconsistent with Inca monumental modalities, and as there is no street linking it to PWR No. 1, it is more likely to be a colonial carriage access, as seen elsewhere on the site (PWR No. 2 [Franco 1993]; PWR No. 3 [Eeckhout 1999]).

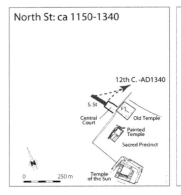

Figure 8.3. N-S Street growth sequence. Illustration by Peter Eeckhout.

5. PWR No. 1 is likely to have originally had a baffled entrance (like PWRs No. 2–3, 5–7, and so on) that was obscured by a route crossing the site in the twentieth century and the later 1950s restoration. This makes the alleged alignment with the "new access" somewhat questionable.

6. There is a secondary formal entrance with stone ashlars to the PWR No. 1 from North Street (Figure 8.5). Its very presence contradicts the IM, since this access would have to be constructed after the streets' abandonment.

7. The contents of PWR No. 1 indicate that it was likely abandoned in the very early LH, if not before (Lanning in Jiménez Borja 1985; Ramos 2011; Rowe 1963). To sustain the IM, the North Street would have had to be constructed, hit by an earthquake, abandoned, the entrance remodeled (with PWR No. 1's construction, use, and abandonment) all within a few decades, at the most.

8. Dates from PWR No. 8 (at the entrance of North Street) indicate two habitation phases: the LIP and the LH (Table 8.2). This is consistent with LH street formalization, but not creation.

9. PWRs No. 4, 6, and 7 have been dated to the LIP, while PWR No. 7's occupation continued into the LH. (Table 8.2)

10. The Third Precinct structures uncovered by Makowski are adjacent to—and closely resemble—LIP buildings excavated by Shimada (2003: 6). The Third Precinct was therefore occupied in the LIP, not only the LH, as confirmed by MUNA's recovery of Early Ychsma burials in the Third Precinct (Owens and Vlemincq, 2016).

Figure 8.4. Sealed entrance of PWR No. 4 in the North Street. Photo by Peter Eeckhout and Lawrence S. Owens.

Figure 8.5. Side access of PWR No. 1 to the North Street. Photo by Peter Eeckhout and Lawrence S. Owens.

What stands out from this short review is that the sequencing, architecture, and spatial arrangements of Pachacamac are incompatible with the IM. As it currently stands, no plausible argument can be made against the LCM, as it is abundantly clear that Pachacamac was a sizable chiefdom well before the arrival of the Incas.

Environmental Impacts, Human Impacts

The issue of the tsunami raises analytical possibilities at Pachacamac. While the issue has been addressed using a range of methodologies, the human impact has not been addressed. If the tsunamis were powerful enough to force polity changes, then surely individuals within those polities would also have felt their effects, perhaps expressed in their soft and hard tissues (Gaither 2010).

Before/after studies of human remains have previously been used to assess the human effects of famines (Antoine and Hillson 2004), economic transitions, and diverse environmental profiles (Larsen 1999). In the Andes, hair analysis was used to study ENSO effects at Pacatnamú (White et al. 2009), dietary effects of imperial breakdowns (Buzon et al. 2012), and changes in activity and social behavior into the Colonial Period (Klaus et al. 2009). To the best of our knowledge, this is the first time that this approach has been attempted in the Central Coast. We are aware that an absence of correspondence on this point is not conclusive proof that a tsunami did not occur. We merely propose it as an analytical stratagem that might be employed to bolster or complement other methods in the archaeologists' repertoire.[3]

The "Osteological Paradox" (Wood et al. 1992) dictates that our observations on the demography of past populations are irrevocably skewed owing to the fact that the patterns of the ancient dead are not an accurate representation of the patterns of the ancient living. The same is particularly true of paleopathology, as those who died from an affliction (or when that affliction was still active) are likely only a subset of those who contracted the affliction yet survived, leaving no trace of its passing in their remains. This is compounded by the fact that many pathological conditions affect only soft tissues, leaving no mark on bones; for example, of the eight physical or pathological conditions cited by Gaither (2010: 77) as major causes of mortality following modern environmental catastrophes, not one leaves diagnostic markers on the bones. The benefits of using aDNA and stable isotopes to this end have been widely noted, and analyses of isotopes are currently under way. Nevertheless, osteologically visible markers do exist

Lawrence S. Owens and Peter Eeckhout

that can provide at least a selective view of illness and physiological issues across this period.

Materials and Approaches

The excavation area lies just outside the Sacred Precinct (Figure 8.6). The density of burials in this area implies that the boundaries of the Sacred Precinct did not denote the limits of the cemeteries. Although not all burials have yet been radiocarbon-dated, there is a clear increase in their number from around AD 1000, suggesting the area's growing popularity as a burial place. The burial ground was reutilized and the bodies reshuffled—seemingly for both ritual and pragmatic reasons—from the tenth to the end of the fourteenth century AD.

We constructed temporal and spatial matrices for cemetery development using cultural data4, superimposition data, and a series of 26 radiocarbon dates (Figure 8.7). The funeral contexts span the MH to the LIP, the latter corresponding to the Epigonal and Early to Middle Ychsma. The latest burials, interred in the ruins of earlier periods in the Second Precinct, date to the fifteenth and sixteenth centuries AD. The total sample is well over 200 individuals; only specimens from well-dated contexts were used, reducing

Figure 8.6. Location of Cemetery I. Illustration by Peter Eeckhout.

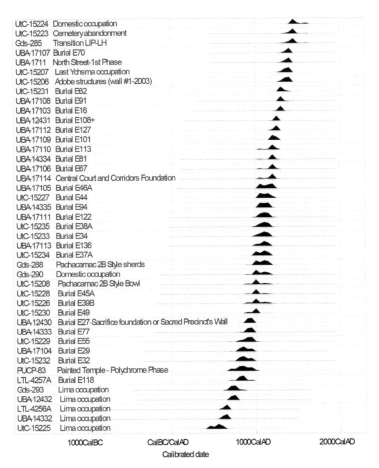

UtC-15224	Domestic occupation
UtC-15223	Cemetery abandonment
Gds-285	Transition LIP-LH
UBA-17107	Burial E70
UBA-1711	North Street-1st Phase
UtC-15207	Last Ychsma occupation
UtC-15206	Adobe structures (wall #1-2003)
UtC-15231	Burial E62
UBA-17108	Burial E91
UBA-17103	Burial E16
UBA-12431	Burial E108+
UBA-17112	Burial E127
UBA-17109	Burial E101
UBA-17110	Burial E113
UBA-14334	Burial E81
UBA-17106	Burial E67
UBA-17114	Central Court and Corridors Foundation
UBA-17105	Burial E46A
UtC-15227	Burial E44
UBA-14335	Burial E94
UBA-17111	Burial E122
UtC-15235	Burial E38A
UtC-15233	Burial E34
UBA-17113	Burial E136
UtC-15234	Burial E37A
Gds-288	Pachacamac 2B Style sherds
Gds-290	Domestic occupation
UtC-15208	Pachacamac 2B Style Bowl
UtC-15228	Burial E45A
UtC-15226	Burial E39B
UtC-15230	Burial E49
UBA-12430	Burial E27-Sacrifice foundation or Sacred Precinct's Wall
UBA-14333	Burial E77
UtC-15229	Burial E55
UBA-17104	Burial E29
UtC-15232	Burial E32
PUCP-83	Painted Temple - Polychrome Phase
LTL-4257A	Burial E118
Gds-293	Lima occupation
UBA-12432	Lima occupation
LTL-4256A	Lima occupation
UBA-14332	Lima occupation
UtC-15225	Lima occupation

1000CalBC   CalBC/CalAD   1000CalAD   2000CalAD

Calibrated date

Figure 8.7. Absolute dates from Cemetery I burials and related structures. Illustration by Peter Eeckhout.

the sample to 147. On the basis of the foregoing, we were able to divide the sample into two groups (Table 8.3).[4]

The first group includes those burials preceding the presumed Mega ENSO (1010 BP) as identified by Winsborough et al. (2012). Date bracketing is either specific (BP in the table) or nonspecific—known to predate AD 1010 (*terminus ante quem*—TAQ in the Table 8.3). It includes eighteen burials, that is, a total of 18 individuals of all ages and different sexes (Figure 8.8).

The second group includes individuals buried after AD 1010 (BP dates, or *terminus post quem* [TPQ in Table 8.3]). They number 99 in total (Figure 8.9). The other 30 burials that could not be accurately dated through either

Table 8.3. Corpus of funerary contexts from Pachacamac

Sample	Individuals (Burial Numbers)
TAQ*	27, 29A, 29B, 32, 37A, 37B, 38, 39A, 39B, 39C, 45, 45A, 49, 55, 69, 77, 113, 115, 116, 118
TPQ**	1 (03), 1 (04), 3, 3 (95), 3 (PWR3), 4 (94), 4 (PWR5), 6, 7, 8, 8 (2), 10 (SK1), 10 (SK2), 10 (SK3), 11 (2004), 14 (PWR3), 16, 17, 18, 19, 20, 21, 22A, 22B, 23 (2000), 23 (2005), 24, 25, 25 (2005), 26, 28, 30, 31, 33, 34, 36, 38A, 38B, 40A, 40B, 40C, 41, 42, 43, 44, 46A, 46B, 50, 51, 52, 53, 57, 58, 59, 61A, 62, 64, 65, 66, 67, 70, 71, 72, 73, 74, 75, 76, 78, 81, 82, 83, 84, 85, 89, 90, 91, 94, 95, 96, 98, 99, 100, 100B, 101, 102, 104, 107, 108, 109, 110A, 110B, 111, 119, 120, 121, 122, 123, 124, 128, 130, 131, 136, 138, 139

Source: Authors.

Notes: * Terminus ante quem.; ** Terminus post quem.

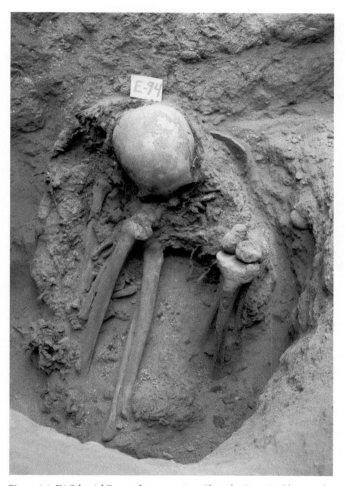

Figure 8.8. TAQ burial E94 under excavation. Photo by Peter Eeckhout and Lawrence S. Owens.

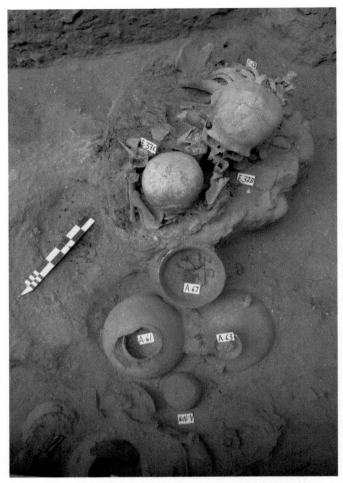

Figure 8.9. TPQ burial E37 under excavation. Photo by P. Eeckhout and Lawrence S. Owens.

method were excluded from temporally based analyses. The differing sample size of burials from before and after 1010 BP reflects the cemetery's growing popularity, the reworking of the cemetery, and the reduced area of the cemetery that could be excavated at depth. This has been taken into account in our analysis (see below).

Our assumption is that disruptions to the status quo at the AD 1010 event would manifest themselves as increases in food shortages; illness prevalence; and general increase in physiological stress, with corresponding increases in osteologically visible pathological and physiological indicators, decreases in stature and body mass (weight), differing age-at-death profiles, and increased levels of trauma reflecting social conflict and strife.

Age-at-Death Structure

Age at death was estimated using dental and osteological development/fusion (subadults) and pubic symphysis, auricular surface, dental wear, and cranial suture closure (adults). The proportion of subadults in the TPQ sample is almost twice as high as in the TAQ sample (34–64 percent). This may reflect increased mortality caused by poor hygiene or poor diet impacting upon physiologically vulnerable children, or breastfeeding mothers unable to sustain their infants (Larsen 1999; Sultana 2014). Conversely, this may reflect sampling error, or greater levels of habitation at the site with the high child death rates that are typically the case in archaeological contexts (Volk and Atkinson 2013).

The ages at death for each sample were pooled and compared (Table 8.4). The results demonstrate a drop in mean age at death from just under 20 to just under 16 between the TAQ and the TPQ, reiterating the increased subadult mortality figures stated above. As the number of children may reflect general population growth rather than plain mortality, the adults were assessed separately. The assumption was that physiological, infective, and nutritional stress as secondary symptoms of resource damage and environmental damage would cause the average age at death to decrease in the latter period. However, while the pre-1010 mean age was 29.6, the postevent age at death was about two years older at 31.5; this difference is not significant. The data were split to ascertain whether either of the sexes demonstrated any differences masked by grouped means. The age differences were in fact almost identical, males increasing from 29.7 to 31.3 years, and females from 29.6 to

Table 8.4. Age at Death

	TAQ*	N	TPQ**	N
Pooled	19.4	19	15.5	98
Adults	31	11	31.9	42
Males	32.1	7	31.5	26
Females	31.5	4	30.5	16
Subadults	2.1	8	3	54

Source: Authors.
Notes: * Terminus ante quem.; ** Terminus post quem.

32 years. The results indicate that the tsunami event resulted in no significant differences to age-at-death profiles. This issue is addressed further below.

Body Proportions

The adults were assessed for stature and body mass, using formulae based on work by Trotter and Gleser (1952) and Auerbach and Ruff (2004). As stated above, it was hypothesized that stature and body weight would decline after the AD 1010 event, in line with reduced economic and environmental circumstances and resulting physiological impacts. The duration of time between the event and the death of the individuals, the accuracy of dating methods, and the amount of time that effects would be felt must be considered, although it is probable that the effects of any truly epic event would still be visible several generations later. The pooled results indicated an average stature of 138.9 cm for all individuals (Table 8.5). When divided by sex, the female mean was 133.3 cm (n = 16),[5] the male mean 143.3 cm (n = 20).[6] The pooled measurements pre-1010 were 139.9 cm, and 138.6 cm post-1010, giving a difference of only 1.3 cm (<1 percent). When the group was split by sex, female stature was almost identical across the temporal divide (133.2/133.3 cm), while male stature decreased by 2.8 percent (146.6/142.5 cm). Neither of these differences comprises a significant change.

The population mean for body mass (weight) was 59 kg; the male mean was 62.2 kg (n = 24) and the female 54.7 kg (n = 18) (Table 8.6). When split across the temporal divide, the males were 8.3 percent lighter after the event (66.5–61 kg), whereas women were 6 percent heavier (52.3–55.6 kg).[7] While the issues of individual variability and sample size limitations should be re-

Table 8.5. Adult stature (height) in centimeters (cm)

	Min	Max	Mean	Median	n
TAQ*_male	144.2	148.3	146.4	146.4	5
TAQ_female	128.3	135.4	131.9	132.0	3
TPQ**_male	132.5	148.3	142.6	142.7	16
TPQ_female	126.5	141.2	133.6	133.7	13

Source: Authors.
Notes: * Terminus ante quem.; ** Terminus post quem.

Table 8.6. Adult body mass (weight) in kilograms

	Min	Max	Mean	Median	N
TAQ*_male	61.6	69.0	66.1	66.5	6
TAQ_female	38.3	59.8	48.9	50.3	4
TPQ**_male	49.3	71.5	61.0	60.3	19
TPQ_female	49.2	59.8	56.0	55.7	14

Source: Authors.
Notes: * Terminus ante quem.; ** Terminus post quem.

membered, that one sex should gain weight at the expense of the other is an unexpected finding. Recent and historical disaster analysis by Zarulli et al. (2018) suggests that women are more physiologically resistant to adversity than men, live longer, and suffer less in extreme conditions. That said, resisting a phenomenon such as that seen at Arica and claimed for Pachacamac is not solely an exercise in physiological robustness, but also a socially bonded process that can favor one sex (or age group) over another as a measure of social structure (Sultana 2014). Certainly, therefore, these results are not a clear vindication of major changes at AD 1010.

Periostitis and Dental Enamel Hypoplasia

Periostitis and hypoplasia are nonspecific indicators of physiological stress that are more common than macromorphological signs of specific diseases, and thus have wider applicability for the addressing of social-oriented questions such as that under discussion.

Periostitis reflects damage to or impacts upon the periosteal membrane overlying the bone and can denote trauma, general overlying soft tissue damage, systemic infections, and nutritional adversity (Ortner 2003). It has previously been used in the Andean area to ascertain impacts of Inca imperialism (Boza Cuadros 2010), as well as in North America, the Near East, and elsewhere (Larsen 1999).

Dental enamel hypoplasia describes textural irregularities in enamel formation, arguably caused by physiological disturbances that interrupt the circadian rhythms of dental growth during development (Hillson 1996). It can be caused by anything that affects the human organism—illness, fevers, starvation, and erratic growth—and is typically used as a general indicator of physiological impacts (Larsen 1999).

Scoring methods vary between researchers and projects; as odontogenesis is well understood, estimating the time at which physiological impacts took place permits identification of the developmental age at which the impact was sustained (Reid and Dean 2006). Periostitis remodels through life and thus reflects a shorter term than does hypoplasia. It can appear anywhere on the skeleton but is particularly common on the tibial crests and skull. As children display periosteal texturing as part of their development, this must be differentiated from the patches of periostitis left by overlying soft tissue lesions, trauma, or physiogical issues. In the current case, a "positive" score was any periostitic or hypoplastic disturbance (that is, per individual). As before, a positive result would see all the indicators increase post AD 1010. A negative result would be any other finding (Dietz 2009; Klaus and Tam 2009).

Table 8.7. Hypoplasia, periostitis, and other afflictions

	Hypoplasia	Periostitis	Treponema	Neoplasms	Osteoporosis
TAQ*_female	3	1	1	0	0
TAQ_male	5	3	1	1	0
TAQ_subadult	0	4	0	1	0
TPQ**_female	10	4	0	0	2
TPQ_male	17	10	1	1	0
TPQ_subadult	6	33	1	0	0

	Tuberculosis	Arthritis	Spondylolysis	Chagas	Rickets	N
TAQ_female	0	0	0	0	0	4
TAQ_male	0	0	0	0	0	7
TAQ_subadult	0	0	0	0	0	9
TPQ_female	0	1	1	0	0	17
TPQ_male	0	3	0	1	0	30
TPQ_subadult	1	0	0	0	2	51

Source: Authors.
Notes: * Terminus ante quem.; ** Terminus post quem.
Additional points: Single trepanation (male); one possible case of leprosy (Late Period male); one possible case of scurvy (Late Period subadult)

The results were conflictive (Table 8.7). Whereas periostitis prevalence increased from 40 to 46 percent, hypoplasia fell from 77 to 53 percent. The significance of this is ambiguous. Periostitis remodels, hence visibility will decrease through time, unlike hypoplasia, which could be sustained before the event and added artificially to prevalence in the later sample. Interestingly, both conditions saw the severity of lesions—and the number per affected individual—almost double in the later period. Despite this, however, it does not appear to signify an epic physiological impact across the population.

Specific Pathologies

Traditional palaeopathological markers—of infectious (tuberculosis [vertebral and joint erosion], treponemal disease [cranial and longbone thickening and lesions]), parasitic (Chagas' disease), nutritional (rickets [longbone bowing], osteoporosis [also age related]), behavioral (degenerative joint disease [DJD]), and neoplastic (cancers) disease—were scored for the same populations.[8]

Prevalence of all these afflictions was low, with the exception of DJD and osteoporosis, which were found throughout the sample and differed primarily by age and sex. Chagas' disease (American trypanosomiasis)—a parasitical infestation characterized archaeologically by a bolus of food waste in the lower abdomen—was uncommon, and only found in the later period (Aufderheide et al. 2004). Low rates of tuberculosis and treponemal disease were present both before and after AD 1010, although more marked forms of the latter were found in the later period. It is also interesting to note that aggressive cancers—including single cases of probable multiple myeloma and carcinoma—were restricted to the later period, whereas TAQ neoplasms were restricted to button osteomata. A single case of rickets occurred in the later period. No single clear pattern appeared from the temporal distribution of these multiple conditions. The only notable difference was increased prevalence and more range of afflictions in the later period, reflecting either the secondary effects of population growth or, perhaps, migrations to the site.

Social Indicators: Trauma

Social unrest caused by natural disasters can manifest itself as interpersonal conflict and osteologically visible trauma (Judd and Roberts 1999), as demonstrated for ethnohistoric tsunamis (see above). Trauma can be "mapped" to

Table 8.8. Cranial and postcranial trauma

TAQ*	Cranial	Postcranial	Cranial +	Postcranial +	N
Females	0	1	1	0	4
Males	2	2	0	1	7
Subadults	0	0	0	0	8

TPQ**	Cranial	Postcranial	Cranial +	Postcranial +	n
Males	4	4	6	7	30
Females	1	5	0	0	16
Subadults	0	2	0	0	60

Source: Authors.
Notes: * Terminus ante quem.; ** Terminus post quem.

differentiate intentional versus accidental wounding, especially with regard to laterality and infra/cranial position. The system is not without its limitations—osteological lesions do not fully reflect actual levels of conflict or trauma, given soft tissue–only lesions, remodeling, and issues with sampling (Waldron 2008). Temporospatial correlates of "malintent" trauma have been comprehensively assessed for the Andean area (Vega Dulanto 2016), while there are various studies of Ychsma interpersonal and sacrificial trauma (Eeckhout and Owens 2008, n.d; Owens and Eeckhout 2015). To our knowledge, this is the first time that trauma has been used to assess the effects of a single natural phenomenon on the Central Coast. One would anticipate elevated levels of cranial trauma in the post–AD 1010 group, although postcranial lesions would be harder to predict. The data, however, were highly inconsistent (Table 8.8). Both cranial (20–12.5 percent) and postcranial (29–19.5 percent) trauma actually decreased with time, to roughly comparable extents. The signal is certainly not clear, although a postapocalyptic burial of people wounded in conflict caused by deteriorated environmental conditions does not seem to be supported.

Discussion

While tsunamis are difficult to detect archaeologically, the social effects thereof are evidently even less clear. We do not dispute the finding of tsunamis/floods at Urpi Kocha, although the magnitude of the event seems open to interpretation given the lack of mixed material and sediment mounds on the floodplain. The absence of evidence for catastrophic death assemblage of tsunami victims could reflect either that they were buried elsewhere—which would be odd, given the site's importance as a place of interment from its inception to the Late Horizon—or that the effects of the tsunami were less injurious than previously imagined.

What is certainly true is that the narrative concerning the fluctuating relationships of tsunami events, the dissolution of the Lima and the rise of the Ychsma are based upon inaccurate evidence that does not adhere to archaeological and architectural sequencing. We suspect that this reflects a longstanding eagerness to attribute climatic and environmental triggers to every aspect of Andean cultural history (Fehren-Schmitz et al. 2014). The Lima saw no catastrophic finale, and they went through various architectural and cultural transformations both at the site and nearby. The fact that they appear to have been genetically affiliated with the subsequent Ychsma group also suggests internal evolution, not disappearance, destruction, or displacement.

The rise of the Ychsma should not be confused with the rise of monumental Ychsma architecture, thus the apparent correlation between the AD 1010 event and the PWRs is more imagined than real. Nevertheless, careful study of the later Lima and earlier Ychsma establishes definitively that the central elements of the site (including the precincts and the main streets) were already in place well before the Late Horizon, affirming the high probability of the local chiefdom model, while contradicting the imperial model.

While the wave may not have had a directly detrimental effect on Lurín populations, it provides an opportunity to test the notion of literal "human" cost by assessing life history indicators at either side of the AD 1010 watershed to see if anything changed in terms of trauma, body proportions, or disease prevalence. None of the variables tested demonstrated any internal consistencies that suggest negative impacts caused by a "natural" disaster. Adult stature was essentially unaffected, while there is a perplexing disparity in terms of male/female weight that may reflect physiological and/or social selection. Hypoplasia and periostitis produce directly contrary results, although multiple/severe lesions increase into the later period. The data from cranial trauma trend the opposite way from what would be expected from an apocalyptic event presaging a social meltdown. The irregular way in which the sexes and age groups are affected by different growth patterns, physical proportions, physiological disturbances, diseases, and trauma precludes a simple causation paradigm.

There are of course limitations on these approaches, in terms of depositional histories, lesion visibility, and chronometric refinement. However, while (1) many of the afflictions that would perhaps be expected leave no bony signs, and (2) patterns of deposition may have removed relevant data from our view, perhaps the most significant finding is that the tombs under study continued to be used throughout the period under discussion, with no evident breaks or directional changes in tradition or status. The larger number of children in the second sample could be argued to represent higher mortality for subadults—reflecting selective physiological vulnerability to childhood diseases and hygiene issues—yet we suspect that this has more to do with population expansion, not erosion. We hypothesize some population growth during this period (Shimada 2003: 6), boosted by local populations coming into the area to exploit new opportunities (perhaps caused by the wave, as seen in the Arica tsunami of 1868). This expanded population may have resided in the Third Precinct; new arrivals may also be responsible for the more diverse range of pathologies in the latter group, as previously argued for the LH pilgrimage population (Owens and Eeckhout 2015). That said, we suspect that population size and density were not high in either the Lima or the early Ychsma, conditions that preclude fast disease spread; the fact that burial traditions continue unchanged also seems inconsistent with an unanticipated disease outbreak. A seeming lack of apocalyptic disturbance to the status quo is also attested to by earlier historical and biological research into coastal and marine resources on the central Peruvian coast between the tenth and sixteenth centuries AD (Eeckhout et al. 2016), indicating negligible change through time up to the present day. Even if there were perturbations, it seems axiomatic that long residence in this region would have led local groups to rely upon the oscillations wrought by ENSO, rather than considering them an "unmitigated disaster" for fish and human populations alike (Bakun and Broad 2003).

Conclusions

The Lima's contribution to Pachacamac did not end with the wave of the seventh century AD, and the genesis of the Ychsma owed nothing to the wave of

AD 1010. Both polities contributed extensively to Pachacamac's site structure, which was established well before the Late Horizon. We assert that the social complexity of the site and the polities from which it sprang are not the result of simple environmental/cultural triggers. While the power of the wave(s) remains uncertain, the relief of the coastline and the absence of catastrophic geological and archaeological detritus make it unlikely that it matched the severity of sixteenth-, eighteenth-, and nineteenth-century tsunami events. It is clear that those most affected by recent events were sustained by those "whose location did not obey preventive norms that pre-existing cultures had tried to anticipate" (Canque 2007: 312); this would not be an issue to the low-density, small populations who were well attuned to their local environment (Sheets and Cooper 2012: 9).

Social narratives that favor environmental triggers as agencies of cultural change have been allowed to color other areas of Andean research. There is nothing to suggest that marine and other resources were adversely affected at this time, and in any case the vulnerability of the Central Coast, less populous than the Northern Coast, made it less vulnerable to environmental catastrophe. The mosaic formats of coastal resources (especially when combined with wide trade networks) also comprise damage limitation in the face of climatic or ecological issues, from Mesolithic Denmark (Rowley-Conwy 1983) to the Caribbean (Cooper 2012). While not insensitive to biome transformations, human groups develop economic strategies, social networks, and domestic structures well suited to a landscape regularly afflicted by challenging environmental impacts.

The danger of post-hoc accommodative arguments is that any cultural material can be molded to fit an environmental storyline. While there may be grounds for certain "scene setting" climatic events over the very long term (Fehren-Schmitz et al. 2014), it is increasingly evident that the same cannot be said of extreme or occasional events (Reindel 2009, 2012). Dealing with repeated events such as earthquakes, tsunamis, and climatic oscillations is built into the cultural DNA of Andean peoples; geological/seismic profiling and ethnohistoric observation tells us that coastal groups have been subjected to at least one tsunami every generation, or, at the very most, every two generations, well within the range of social memory.

The data from this bioarchaeological survey have produced conflictive results. While recognizing the limitations of the methods and the chronometric framework around which it is based, we believe that the ranges we have are sufficient to address whether or not that event was a defining and seminal moment in the history of the site's human population. Clearly, it was not. The crux of the matter is that ancient people were more flexible and accommodating than they are often given credit for. Further, any truly traumatic impacts on their lives would have been handled using attuned social networks that will blur the boundaries of "expected" impacts based upon ethnohistoric studies of people less well adapted to their environments than were the Lima and Ychsma. Finally, the unequal impacts of CO-VID-19 are a salutary reminder of how age, sex, genetic background, social structure, systemic resilience, prosperity, social obedience, traditions, and behavior can temper, hinder, or promote the effects of environmental or pathological phenomena, beyond mere Pavlovian response. While it is certainly true that humans are actors on a climatic and environmental stage, they are not puppets.

Acknowledgments

Research at Pachacamac was authorized by the Peruvian Ministry of Culture. We owe a great debt of gratitude to all the members of Ychsma Project, as well as the ULB, the ULB Foundation, the National Fund for Scientific Research (Belgium), and the Engie Foundation. We would also like to thank Dr. Dennis Ogburn for his invaluable provision of obscure references, Nathalie Bloch (CReA) for illustration editing, Letisha Service for her assistance with referencing, and Jera Boam for her insightful editing and commentary. We would like to thank the editors for inviting us to submit this chapter—and for their patience during its preparation—as well as the anonymous reviewers for their remarks and advice on an earlier version of the manuscript. All remaining errors are, of course, our own.

Notes

1. Henceforth abbreviated as follows: Early Intermediate Period (EIP), Late Intermediate Period (LIP), and Late Horizon (LH).

2. For a detailed discussion of PWRs, see Eeckhout 2004a.

3. While longer term effects are more common for such climatic profiling, it is our intention to be rather more specific in the current study (see below).

4. In order to facilitate comparisons with the palaeoclimatic record, we have used BP dates for the burials.

5. $2.443 \times \text{MAXFEM} + 42.805$ (Males); $2.336 \times \text{MAXFEM} + 44.253$ (Females).

6. Males $(2.741 \times \text{FH} - 54.9) \times .90$.

Females $(2.426 \times \text{FH} - 35.1) \times .90$.

7. For details on the disease definitions and the macroscopic appearance of these patholo-gies, see Ortner 2003 and references therein.

8. There has been increased refinement of archaeological/ecological narrative in the North Coast area, starting with a clear trend toward environmental determinism. It was originally believed that Huaca de la Luna at Moche was abandoned as a result of violent ENSO events in the early 7th century AD, at the end of Moche Phase IV (Moseley 1992: 211). Researchers have since revised this catastrophist scenario, and explored other drivers of social change (Bawden 1996: chap. 9). It has now been demonstrated that the enormous Huaca del Sol was built be-tween AD 600 and 800 during the "Second Moche Period," which saw the replacement of a theocracy by a more secular power base (Uceda 2010).

References Cited

Antoine, Daniel, and Simon Hillson

2004 Famine, the Black Death, and health in fourteenth-century London. *Archaeology International* 8(1): 26–28.

Auerbach, Benjamin M., and Christopher B. Ruff

2004 Human Body Mass Estimation: A Comparison of "Morphometric" and "Mechanical" Methods. *American Journal of Physical Anthropology* 125(4): 331–342.

Arkush, Elizabeth

2008 War, Chronology, and Causality in the Titicaca Basin. *Latin American Antiquity* 19/4: 339–373.

Aufderheide, Arthur C., Wilmar Salo, Michael Madden, John Streitz, Jane Buikstra, Felipe Guhl, Bernardo Arriaza, et al.

2004 A 9,000-year Record of Chagas' Disease. *PNAS* 101(7): 2034–2039.

Bakun, Andrew, and Kenneth Broad

2003 Environmental "Loopholes" and Fish Population Dynamics: Comparative Pattern Rec-ognition with Focus on El Niño Effects in the Pacific. *Fisheries Oceanography* 12(4–5): 458–473.

Bawden, Garth

1996 *The Moche*. Blackwell Publishers, London.

Bawden, Garth, and Richard M. Reycraft

2000 *Environmental Disaster and the Archaeology of Human Response*. Maxwell Museum of Anthropology, Albuquerque, New Mexico.

Billman, Brian R., and Gary Huckleberry

2008 Deciphering the Politics of Prehistoric El Niño Events on the North Coast of Peru. In *El Niño, Catastrophism, and Culture Change in Ancient America*, edited by Daniel H Sandweiss and Jeffrey Quilter, pp. 102–128. Dumbarton Oaks Research Library and Collection, Washington, D.C.

Binford, Michael, Alan Kolata, Mark Brenner, John Janusek, Matthew Seddon, Mark Abbott, and Jason Curtis

1997 Climate Variation and the Rise and Fall of an Andean Civilization. *Quaternary Research* 47: 235–248.

Bird, Robert

1987   A Postulated Tsunami and Its Effects on Cultural Development in the Peruvian Early Horizon. *American Antiquity* 52(2): 285–303.

Blaikie, Piers, Terry Cannon, Ian Davis, and Ben Wisner

1994   *At Risk: Natural Hazards, People Vulnerability and Disasters.* Routledge, London.

Bourget, Steve

1998   Pratiques sacrificielles et funéraires au site Moche de la Huaca de La Luna, côte nord du Pérou. *Bulletin de l'Institut Français d'Études Andines*, 27(1): 41–74.

Boza Cuadros, Maria Fernanda

2010   *The Bioarchaeological Effects of Inca Imperialism on a Maranga Community.* Department of Anthropology, University of Wyoming.

Buzon, Michele R., Christina A. Conlee, Antonio Simonetti, and Gabriel J. Bowen

2012   The Consequences of Wari Contact in the Nasca Region during the Middle Horizon: Archaeological, Skeletal, and Isotopic Evidence. *Journal of Archaeological Science* 39(8): 2627–2636.

Cabello Balboa, Miguel

(1586)1951   *Miscelánea antártica: una historia del Perú antiguo.* Universidad Nacional Mayor de San Marcos, Facultad de Letras, Instituto de Etnología, Lima.

Canque, Manuel Fernandez

2007   *Arica 1868: un tsunami y un terremoto.* Ediciones de la Dirección de Bibliotecas, Archivos y Museos. Santiago de Chile.

Capriata, Camilla, and Enrique López-Hurtado

2017   The Demise of the Ruling Elites: Terminal Rituals in the Pyramid Complexes of Panquilma, Peruvian Central Coast. In *Rituals of the Past: Prehispanic and Colonial Case Studies in Andean Archaeology,* edited by Silvana Rosenfeld and Stefanie Bautista, pp. 193–216. Colorado University Press, Boulder.

Carcelén-Reluz, Carlos Guillermo

2011   La visión ilustrada de los desastres naturales en Lima durante el siglo xviii (The Enlightened View of the Natural Disasters in Lima during the 18th Century). *Cuadernos de Geografía* 20(1): 55–64.

Chagnon, Napoleon A.

1992   *Yanomamö: The Last Days of Eden.* Harcourt Brace Jovanovich, New York.

Chagué-Goff, Catherine, Henri K. Y. Wong, Daisuke Sugawara, James Goff, Yuichi Nishimura, Jennifer Beer, Witold Szczuciński, and Kazuhisa Goto

2013   Impact of Tsunami Inundation on Soil Salinisation: Up to One Year after the 2011 Tohoku-Oki Tsunami. In *Tsunami Events and Lessons Learned: Environmental and Societal Significance,* edited by Yev Kontar, Vicente Santiago-Fandiño, and Tomoyuki Takahashi, pp. 193–214. Springer, New York.

Chepstow-Lusty, A. J., M. R. Frogley, B. S. Bauer, M. J. Leng, K. P. Boessenkool, C. Carcaillet, A. A. Ali, and A. Gioda

2009   Putting the Rise of the Inca Empire within a Climatic and Land Management Context. *Climate of the Past* 5(3): 375–388.

Clement, Christopher O., and Michael E. Moseley

1991   The Spring-Fed Irrigation System of Carrizal, Peru—a Case Study of the Hypothesis of Agrarian Collapse. *Journal of Field Archaeology* 18: 425–443.

Cooper, Jago

2012   Fail to Prepare, Then Prepare to Fail: Rethinking Threat, Vulnerability, and Mitigation in the Precolumbian Caribbean. In *Surviving Sudden Environmental Change: Answers from Archaeology*, by Jago Cooper, edited by Jago Cooper and Payson Sheets, pp. 91–116. University Press of Colorado, Boulder.

Davies, Hugh L., Oliver B. Simeon, Geoffrey Hope, Fiona Petchey, and Jocelyn M. Davies

2019   Past Major Tsunamis and the Level of Tsunami Risk on the Aitape Coast of Papua New Guinea. *Natural Hazards* 96(3): 1019–1040.

Davis, Mike

2001   *Late Victorian Holocausts: El Niño Famines and the Making of the Third World*. Verso, London.

Delanghe, Joris R., Marijn M. Speeckaert, and Marc L. De Buyzere

2018   Iron Status as a Confounder in the Gender Gap in Survival under Extreme Conditions. *PNAS* 115(18): 4148–4149.

Dietz, Michael J.

2009   Diet, Subsistence and Health: A Bioarchaeological Analysis of Chongos, Perú. Graduate School, University of Missouri–Columbia.

Dolorier, Camilo

2013   Cronología, organización social, especialización laboral y género definidos como producto del análisis de los contextos funerarios registrados en los "diarios de campo" de Huallamarca, años de 1958 y 1960. Tesis de Licenciatura, UNMSM, Lima.

Dorbath, Louis, A. Cisternas, and Catherine Dorbath

1990   Assessment of the Size of Large and Great Historical Earthquakes in Peru. *Bulletin of the Seismological Society of America* 80(3): 551–576.

Eeckhout, Peter

1999   *Pachacamac durant l'Intermédiaire récent. Etude d'un site monumental préhispanique de la Côte centrale du Pérou*. British Archaeological Reports International Series, 747. Hadrian Books, Oxford.

2003   Ancient Monuments and Patterns of Power at Pachacamac, Central Coast of Peru». *Beiträge zur Allgemeine und Vergleichenden Archäologie* 23: 139–182.

2004a   La sombra de Ychsma. Ensayo introductivo sobre la arqueología de la costa central del Perú en los periodos tardios. *Boletín del IFEA* 33(3): 403–425.

2004b   Reyes del Sol y Señores de la Luna: Incas e Ychsmas en Pachacamac. *Chungara* 36(2): 495–503.

2008   Poder y jerarquias Ychsma en el Valle de Lurín. *Arqueologia y Sociedad* 19: 223–240.

2010   Las pirámides con rampa de Pachacamac durante el Horizónte Tardío. In *Arqueologia en el Perú: Nuevos aportes para el estudio de las sociedades andinas prehispánicas*, edited by Ruben Romero Velarde and Trine Pavel Svendsen, pp. 415–434. Universidad Nacional Federico Villareal, Lima.

2012   Inca Storage and Accounting Facilities at Pachacamac. *Andean Past* 10: 212–238.

2013   Architectural and Political Dynamics at Pachacamac. Paper read at the South American Archaeology Seminar, Institute of Archaeology, University College, London.

2018   Middle Horizon and the Southern Andean Iconographic Series on the Central Coast of Peru. In *Images in Action: the Southern Andean Iconographic Series*, edited by William H. Isbell, Mauricio Uribe, and Anne Tiballi, pp. 533–569. UCLA Cotsen Institute of Archaeology, Los Angeles.

2020   Farewell to the Gods: Interpreting the Use and Voluntary Abandonment of a Ritual Building at Pachacamac, Peru. In *Archaeological Interpretations: The Meaning within*

Symbolic Activities, Artifacts and Images in Andes Prehistory, edited by Peter Eeckhout, pp. 240–270. University Press of Florida, Gainesville.

Eeckhout, Peter, and Carlos Farfán

2004   Proyecto Ychsma: Investigaciones Arqueologicas y Planimetria en el Sitio de Pachacamac, Quinta temporada (2004). Report to the INC, Lima.

Eeckhout, Peter, and Enrique López-Hurtado

2018   Pachacamac and the Inca on the Central Coast of Peru. In *The Oxford Handbook of the Incas*, edited by Alan Covey and Sonia Alconini, pp. 179–195. Oxford University Press, New York.

Eeckhout, Peter, and Milton Lujan Dávila

2014   Un complejo de almacenamiento inca en Pachacamac. *Revista Studium* 18: 51–80.

2022   Cronología e impacto de la conquista inca en la costa central: una reevaluación crítica desde el caso de Pachacamac. In *Nuevas perspectivas sobre la conquista y ocupación inca en la Costa Central: una mirada desde las comunidades locales*, edited by Camila Capriata. Ministerio de Cultura del Perú, Lima.

Eeckhout, Peter, and Lawrence S. Owens

2008   Human Sacrifice at Pachacamac. *Latin American Antiquity* 19(4): 375–398.

2022   War or Peace on the Central Coast? Questioning Metanarratives of Late Intermediate Period Mobocracies on the Basis of Ychsma Evidence from Pachacamac, Peruvian Central Coast. In *Archaeological and Ideological Manifestations of Conflict in Indigenous Latin America*, edited by Yamilette Chacon. University Press of Florida, Gainesville.

Eeckhout, Peter, and Lawrence S. Owens, eds.

2015   *Funerary Practices and Models in the Ancient Andes. The Return of the Living Dead.* Cambridge University Press, New York.

Eeckhout, Peter, and Sylvie Peperstraete

2022   To the End of the World . . . and Back Again. Perspectives on Apocalypses through Mythological Tales from Mesoamerica and the Andes. In *Post-Apocalypto. Crisis and Resilience in the Maya World: Proceedings of the 18th European Maya Conference*, edited by Harri Juhani Kettunen. Verlag Anton Saurwein.

Eeckhout, Peter, Philippe Béarez, and Luz Segura

2016   Recursos marinos, territorialidad y crísis climáticas en la costa central del antiguo Perú: un estudio exploratorio. In *Crisis y dinámicas territoriales: Movilidades, fronteras y ocupaciones en los Andes*, edited by Nicolas Goepfert, pp. 51–70. Actas y Memorias del Instituto Francés de Estudios Andinos, Lima.

Eitel, B., S. Hecht, B. Mächtle, G. Schukraft, A. Kadereit, G. A. Wagner, B. Kromer, I. Unkel, and M. Reindel

2005   Geoarchaeological Evidence from Desert Loess in the Nazca–Palpa Region, Southern Peru: Palaeoenvironmental Changes and Their Impact on Pre-Columbian Cultures. *Archaeometry* 47(1): 137–158.

Eitel, Bernhard, and Bertil Mächtle

2009   Man and Environment in the Eastern Atacama Desert (Southern Peru): Holocene Climate Changes and Their Impact on Pre-Columbian Cultures. In *New Technologies for Archaeology*, edited by Bernhard Eitel and Bertil Mächtle, pp. 17–37. Springer, Berlin.

Ellen, Roy

1982   *Environment, Subsistence and System.* Cambridge University Press.

Erickson, Clark L.

1999   Neo-environmental Determinism and Agrarian "Collapse" in Andean Prehistory. *Antiquity* 73(281): 634–642.

Fairhead, James, and Melissa Leach

2012   *Misreading the African Landscape.* Online. Cambridge University Press. https://doi.org/10.1017/CBO9781139164023.

Fehren-Schmitz, Lars, Wolfgang Haak, Bertil Mächtle, Florian Masch, Bastien Llamas, Elsa Tomasto Cagigao, Volker Sossna, et al.

2014   Climate Change Underlies Global Demographic, Genetic, and Cultural Transitions in Pre-Columbian Southern Peru. *PNAS* 111(26): 9443–9448.

Feltham, P. Jane

1983   The Lurin Valley, Peru: AD 1000–1532. Ph.D. diss., Institute of Archaeology, University of London.

Fitzhugh, Ben

2012   Hazards, Impacts, and Resilience among Hunter-Gatherers of the Kuril Islands. In *Surviving Sudden Environmental Change: Answers from Archaeology,* edited by Jago Cooper and Payson Sheets, pp. 19–42. University Press of Colorado, Boulder.

Flantua, S. G. A., H. Hooghiemstra, M. Vuille, H. Behling, J. F. Carson, W. D. Gosling, I. Hoyos, et al.

2016   Climate Variability and Human Impact in South America during the Last 2000 Years: Synthesis and Perspectives from Pollen Records. *Climate of the Past* 12(2): 483–523.

Franco Jordán, Régulo G.

1993   Excavaciones en la Pirámide con rampa n°2, Pachacamac. Tesis de Licenciatura, Universidad Nacional Mayor de San Marcos, Lima.

2015   La ocupación Lima Temprano en Pachacamac: una mirada a partir de los orígenes del Templo Viejo. *Boletín de Arqueología PUCP* 19: 145–169.

Gaither, Catherine M.

2010   Bioarchaeology and El Niño: Identifying the Biological Signature of Disaster. *Revista Archaeobios*: 75–84.

Goff, James R.

2004   Natural Disasters and Cultural Change. *Geoarchaeology* 19(2): 177–183.

Goff, James R., and B. G. McFadgen

2002   Seismic Driving of Nationwide Changes in Geomorphology and Prehistoric Settlement—A 15th Century New Zealand Example. *Quaternary Science Reviews* 21(20–22): 2229–2236.

Goff, James, Mark Golitko, Ethan Cochrane, Darren Curnoe, Shaun Williams, and John Terrell

2017   Reassessing the Environmental Context of the Aitape Skull—The Oldest Tsunami Victim in the World? Edited by Siân E. Halcrow. *PLOS ONE* 12 (10).

Hillson, Simon

1996   *Dental Anthropology.* Cambridge University Press.

Huertas-Vallejos, Lorenzo

2001   *Diluvios Andinos: a través de las fuentes documentales.* PUCP, Lima.

Jiménez Borja, Arturo

1985   Pachacamac. *Boletín de Lima* 38: 40–54.

IISEE (International Institute of Seismology and Earthquake Engineering)

2022   Recent Tsunamis. https://iisee.kenken.go.jp/staff/fujii/TsunamiTop.html

Isbell, W. H.

1997 *Mummies and Mortuary Monuments: A Postprocessual Prehistory of Central Andean Social Organization*. University of Texas Press, Austin.

Judd, Margaret A., and Charlotte A. Roberts

1999 Fracture Trauma in a Medieval British Farming Village. *American Journal of Physical Anthropology* 109(2): 229–243.

Kiracofe, James B., and John S. Marr

2008 Marching to Disaster: The Catastrophic Convergence of Inca Imperial Policy, Sand Flies and El Niño in the 1524 Andean Epidemic. In *El Niño, Catastrophism, and Culture Change in Ancient America*, edited by Daniel H Sandweiss and Jeffrey Quilter, pp. 145–164. Dumbarton Oaks Research Library and Collection, Washington, D.C.

Klaus, Haagen D., and Manuel E. Tam

2009 Contact in the Andes: Bioarchaeology of Systemic Stress in Colonial Mórrope, Peru. *American Journal of Physical Anthropology* 138(3): 356–368.

Klaus, Haagen D., Clark Spencer Larsen, and Manuel E. Tam

2009 Economic Intensification and Degenerative Joint Disease: Life and Labor on the Postcontact North Coast of Peru. *American Journal of Physical Anthropology* 139(2): 204–221.

Kohler, Timothy A.

2012 Social Evolution, Hazards, and Resilience: Some Concluding Thoughts. In *Surviving Sudden Environmental Change: Answers from Archaeology*, edited by Jago Cooper and Payson Sheets, pp. 223–236. University Press of Colorado, Boulder.

Kovats, R. Sari, Menno J. Bouma, Shakoor Hajat, Eve Worrall, and Andy Haines

2003 El Niño and Health. *The Lancet* 362(9394): 1481–1489.

Larsen, Clark Spencer

1999 *Bioarchaeology: Interpreting Behavior from the Human Skeleton*. Cambridge University Press, Cambridge.

López-Hurtado, Luis Enrique

2011 Ideology and the Development of Social Hierarchy at the Site of Panquilma, Peruvian Central Coast. Unpublished Ph.D diss., University of Pittsburgh.

Lujan Dávila, Milton, and Peter Eeckhout

2022 Agua y cultural material: hacia una interpretación holistica de las practicas rituales desde el edificio B15 de Pachacamac (with M. Luján). Paper read at the Congress *Water, Technology and Ritual: Function and Hydraulic Cosmology in the Pre-Hispanic World* (2018), Universidad Sede Sapientae, Lima.

Lumbreras, Luis G.

2014 *Jacinto Jijón y Camanó. Estudios sobre Lima prehispánica: Maranga*. PetroPeru and Municipalidad Metropolitana de Lima.

Mac Kay, Martín

2011 Ideología y funeraria Lima. El caso de la Huaca 20. In *Arqueología peruana: homenaje a Mercedes Cárdenas*, edited by Luisa Vetter et al., pp. 177–207. PUCP, Lima.

Mac Kay, Martín, and Rafael Santa Cruz

2000 Excavaciones del Proyecto Arqueológico Huaca 20(1999–2001). *Boletín de Arqueología PUCP* 4: 583–595.

Makowski, Krzysztof

2012 City and Ceremonial Center: Conceptual Challenges on Andean Urbanism. *Annual Papers of the Anthropological Institute* 2: 1–66 (in Spanish and Japanese). http://www.ic.nanzan-u.ac.jp/JINRUIKEN/publication/index.html

2015   Pachacamac—Old Wak"a or Inca Syncretic Deity? Imperial Transformation of the Sacred Landscape in the Lower Ychsma (Lurín) Valley. In *The Archaeology of Wak'as: Explorations of the Sacred in the Pre-Columbian Andes*, edited by Tamara L. Bray, pp. 127–166. University Press of Colorado, Boulder.

2017   Pachacamac y la política imperial inca. In *El Inca y la Huaca. Religión del poder y el poder de la religión en el mundo andino antiguo*, edited by Mario Curatola and Jan Szeminski, 121–175. PUCP, Lima.

Makowski, Krzysztof, and Alain Vallenas

2015   La ocupación lima en el valle de Lurín: en los orígenes de Pachacamac monumental. *Boletín de Arqueología PUCP* 19: 97–143.

Mauricio, Ana Cecilia

2018   Reassessing the Impact of El Niño at the End of the Early Intermediate Period from the Perspective of the Lima Culture. *Ñawpa Pacha* 38(2): 203–231.

Mauricio, Ana Cecilia, Gabriel Prieto, and Cecilia Pardo

2014   Avances en la arqueología de la cultura Lima. *Boletín de Arqueología PUCP* 18: 5–14.

Michczyński, Adam, Peter Eeckhout, and Anna Pazdur

2003   14C Absolute Chronology of the Pyramid III and the Dynastic Model at Pachacamac, Peru. *Radiocarbon* 45(1):59–73.

Michczyński, Adam, Peter Eeckhout, Anna Pazdur, and Jacek Pawlyta

2007   Radiocarbon Dating of the Temple of the Monkey: The Next Step Towards Comprehensive Absolute Chronology of Pachacamac, Peru. *Radiocarbon* 49(2): 565–578.

Martin, Robert

2003   Biochronology of Latest Miocene through Pleistocene Arvicolid Rodents from the Central Great Plains of North America. *Coloquios de Paleontología* 1: 373–383.

Martínez, Kenneth, Joan Garcia, Francesc Burjachs, Riker Yll, and Eudald Carbonell

2014   Early human occupation of Iberia: the chronological and palaeoclimatic inferences from Vallparadís (Barcelona, Spain). *Quaternary Science Reviews* 85: 136–146.

Menzel, Dorothy

1964   Style and Time in the Middle Horizon. *Ñawpa Pacha: Journal of Andean Archaeology* 2/1:. 1–105.

1968   *La Cultura Huari*. Compania de Seguros y Reaseguros Peruanos, Lima.

Moseley, Michael E.

1983   The Good Old Days Were Better: Agrarian Collapse and Tectonics. *American Anthropologist* 85: 773–799.

1992   *The Inkas and Their Ancestors*. Thames and Hudson, London.

Moseley, Michael E., Robert A. Feldman, and Charles R. Ortloff

1981   Living with Crisis: Human Perception of Process and Time. In *Biotic Crises in Ecological and Evolutionary Time*, edited by Matthew H Nitecki, pp. 231–267. Academic Press, New York.

Moseley, Michael E., and David K Keefer

2008   Deadly Deluges in the Southern Desert: Modern and Ancient El Niños in the Osmore Region of Peru. In *El Niño, Catastrophism, and Culture Change in Ancient America*, edited by Daniel H. Sandweiss and Jeffrey Quilter, pp. 129–144. Dumbarton Oaks Research Library and Collection, Washington, D.C.

Nelson, Margaret C., Michelle Hegmon, Keith W. Kintigh, Ann P. Kinzig, Ben A. Nelson, John Marty Anderies, David A. Abbott, et al.

2012   Long-Term Vulnerability and Resilience: Three Examples from Archaeological Study in the Southwestern United States and Northern Mexico. In *Surviving Sudden Environmental Change: Answers from Archaeology*, edited by Jago Cooper and Payson Sheets, pp. 197–222. University Press of Colorado, Boulder.

Olivera Astete, Carlos

2014 La ocupación Lima de Huaca 20 a inicios del Horizonte Medio, Complejo Maranga. *Boletín de Arqueología PUCP* 18: 191–215.

Ortloff, Charles R., and Alan L. Kolata

1993 Climate and Collapse: Agro-Ecological Perspectives on the Decline of the Tiwanaku State. *Journal of Archaeological Science* 20(2): 195–221.

Ortner, Donald J.

2003 *Identification of Pathological Conditions in Human Skeletal Remains*. 2nd ed. Academic Press, New York.

Owen, Bruce

2005 Distant Colonies and Explosive Collapse: The Two Stages of the Tiwanaku Diaspora in the Osmore Drainage. *Latin American Antiquity* 16/1: 45–80.

Owens, Lawrence S.

2017 Los restos humanos de Pachacámac. In *Pachacamac: El Oráculo en el horizonte marino del sol poniente*, dir. by Denise Pozzi-Escot, pp. 238–251. BCP, Lima.

Owens, Lawrence S., and Peter Eeckhout

2015 To the God of Death, Disease and Healing: Social Bioarchaeology of Cemetery 1 at Pachacamac. In *Funerary Practices and Models in the Ancient Andes*, edited by Peter Eeckhout and Lawrence S. Owens, pp. 158–185. Cambridge University Press, New York.

2017 From the Cradle to the Grave: Bioarchaeological Perspectives on an Ychsma Period Monumental Multiple Burial from the Site of Pachacamac, Peruvian Central Coast. *Abstract Volume for the 19th Annual Conference of the British Association of Biological Anthropology and Osteoarchaeology*, Liverpool: 59.

Owens, Lawrence S., and Tatiana Vlemincq-Mendieta

2016 Report on the Human Remains Recovered from MUNA Excavations in the Third Precinct, Pachacamac. Ms.

Pérez-Mallaína, Pablo E.

2001 *Retrato de una ciudad en crisis: la sociedad limeña ante el movimiento sísmico de 1746*. Consejo Superior de Investigaciones Científicas, Escuela de Estudios Hispano-Americanos, Lima.

2005 Las catástrofes naturales como instrumento de observación social: el caso del terremoto de Lima en 1746. *Anuario de Estudios Americanos* 62(2): 47–76.

Potts, Richard

2013 Hominin Evolution in Settings of Strong Environmental Variability. *Quaternary Science Reviews* 73: 1–13.

Pozzi-Escot, Denise, and Katiusha Bernuy

2010 *Pachacamac: Calle Norte-Sur. Investigaciones arqueológicas*. Ministerio de Cultura del Perú, Lima.

Ramos Giraldo, Jesús

2011 *Santuario de Pachacamac. Cien años de arqueología en la costa central*. Municipalidad de Lurín-Editorial Cultura Andina, Lima.

Reid, Donald J., and M. Christopher Dean

2006 Variation in Modern Human Enamel Formation Times. *Journal of Human Evolution* 50(3): 329–346.

Reindel, Markus

2009   Life at the Edge of the Desert—Archaeological Reconstruction of the Settlement History in the Valleys of Palpa, Peru. In *New Technologies for Archaeology*, edited by Markus Reindel and Günther A. Wagner, 439–461. Springer-Verlag, Berlin Heidelberg.

2012   Population Crisis caused by Changing Paleoenvironmental Conditions in Palpa, South Coast of Peru. Symposium on Past Crisis in the Americas: Environment and Socio-Cultural Process. 54th International Congress of Americanists, Vienna.

Reycraft, Richard Martin

2005   Style Change and Ethnogenesis among the Chiribaya of Far South Coastal Peru. In *Us and Them: Archaeology and Ethnicity in the Andes*, edited by Richard Martin Reycraft, pp. 58–66. Cotsen Institute of Archaeology Press, Los Angeles.

Richardson III, James B.

1973   The Preceramic Sequence and the Pleistocene and Post-Pleistocene Climate Of Northwest Peru. In *Variation in Anthropology: Essays in Honor of John C. McGregor*, edited by Donald W. Lathrap and Jody Douglas, pp. 199–211. Illinois Archaeological Survey, Urbana.

Richardson, James B., and Daniel H. Sandweiss

2008   Climate Change, El Niño and the Rise of Complex Society on the Peruvian Coast during the Middle Holocene. In *El Niño, Catastrophism, and Culture Change in Ancient America*, edited by Daniel H. Sandweiss and Jeffrey Quilter, pp. 60–75. Dumbarton Oaks Research Library and Collection, Washington, D.C.

Roscoe, Paul

2008   Catastrophe and the Emergence of Political Complexity: A Social Anthropological Model. In *El Niño, Catastrophism, and Culture Change in Ancient America*, edited by Daniel H. Sandweiss and Jeffrey Quilter, pp. 77–100. Dumbarton Oaks Research Library and Collection, Washington, D.C.

Rostworowski de Díez Canseco, María

1999   *El señorío de Pachacamac: el informe de Rodrigo Cantos de Andrade de 1573*. Instituto de Estudios Peruanos, Lima.

Rout, Hemant Kumar

2009   Cursed Tribals Abandon Village to Witch. https://timesofindia.indiatimes.com/city/bhubaneswar/Cursed-tribals-abandon-village-to-witch/articleshow/4460629.cms

Rowe, John H.

1963   Urban Settlements in Ancient Peru. *Ñawpa Pacha* 1: 1–28.

Rowley-Conwy, Peter

1983   Sedentary Hunters: The Ertebolle Example. In *Hunter-Gatherer Economy in Prehistory: A European Perspective*, edited by Geoffrey Bailey, pp. 111–126. Cambridge University Press, Cambridge.

Roy, Kingshuk, Yurika Kato, Naoki Sato, and Sadao Nagasaka

2015   Post-tsunami Salinity Status of Reclaimed and Nonreclaimed Farmlands in Miyagi Prefecture, Japan. *Journal of Environmental Information Science* 43(5): 19–24.

Sandweiss, Daniel H.

2003   Terminal Pleistocene through Mid-Holocene Archaeological Sites as Paleoclimatic Archives for the Peruvian Coast. *Palaeogeography, Palaeoclimatology, Palaeoecology* 194(1–3): 23–40.

Sandweiss, Daniel H., and Alice R. Kelley

2012   Archaeological Contributions to Climate Change Research: The Archaeological Record as a Paleoclimatic and Paleoenvironmental Archive. *Annual Review of Anthropology* 41(1): 371–391.

Sandweiss, Daniel H., Kirk A. Maasch, C. Fred T. Andrus, Elizabeth J. Reitz, James B. Richardson, Melanie Riedinger-Whitmore, and Harold B. Rollins

2007 Mid-Holocene Climate and Culture Change in Coastal Peru. In *Climate Change and Cultural Dynamics*, edited by David Anderson, Kirk Maasch, and Daniel Sandweiss, pp. 25–50. Academic Press, San Diego.

Sandweiss, Daniel H., and Jeffrey Quilter

2012 Collation, Correlation, and Causation in the Prehistory of Coastal Peru. In *Surviving Sudden Environmental Change: Answers from Archaeology*, edited by Jago Cooper and Payson Sheets, pp. 117–142. University Press of Colorado, Boulder.

Sandweiss, Daniel, and James Richardson

2008 Central Andean Environments. In Handbook of South American Archaeology, edited by Helaine Silverman and William Isbell, chapter 6, pp. 93–104. Springer, New York.

Segura Llanos, Rafael

2012 Dinámicas Hidrológicas y Dinámicas Culturales en la Prehistoria Andina: Una Aproximación a los Modelos y Evidencias de Colapso y Resiliencia en la Costa Central del Perú. Symposium on Past Crisis in the Americas: Environment and Socio-cultural Process, 54th International Congress of Americanists, Vienna.

Segura Llanos, Rafael, and Izumi Shimada

2010 The Wari Footprint on the Central Coast: A View from Cajamarquilla and Pachacamac. In *Beyond Wari Walls: Regional Perspectives on Middle Horizon Peru*, edited by Justin Jennings, pp. 113–135. University of New Mexico Press, Albuquerque.

Sharratt, Nicola

2016 Collapse and Cohesion: Building Community in the Aftermath of Tiwanaku State Breakdown. *World Archaeology* 48(1): 144–163.

Sheets, Payson

2008 Armageddon to the Garden of Eden: Explosive Volcanic Eruptions and Societal Resilience in Ancient Middle America. In *El Niño, Catastrophism, and Culture Change in Ancient America*, edited by Daniel H. Sandweiss and Jeffrey Quilter, pp. 167–186. Dumbarton Oaks Research Library and Collection, Washington, D.C.

2012 Responses to Explosive Volcanic Eruptions by Small to Complex Societies in Ancient Mexico and Central America. In *Surviving Sudden Environmental Change*, edited by Jago Cooper and Payson Sheets, pp. 43–66. University Press of Colorado, Boulder.

Sheets, Payson, and Jago Cooper

2012 Introduction: Learning To Live with the Dangers of Sudden Enviromental Change. In *Surviving Sudden Environmental Change*, edited by Jago Cooper and Payson Sheets, pp. pp. 1–18, 43–66. University Press of Colorado, Boulder.

Shimada, Izumi

2003 Pachacamac Archaeological Project: Preliminary Results of the 2003 Fieldwork. Southern Illinois University, Carbondale.

Shimada, Izumi, Crystal Barker Schaaf, Lonnie G. Thompson, and Ellen Mosley-Thompson

1991 Cultural Impacts of Severe Droughts in the Prehistoric Andes: Application of a 1,500-year Ice Core Precipitation Record. *World Archaeology* 22(3): 247–270.

Shimada, Izumi, Rafael A. Segura, and Barbara Winsborough

2013 Pachacamac and Water: An Empirical Approach to the Origins, Significance, and Resilience of Pachacamac. Manuscript, Winsborough Consulting, Leander, Texas.

Sultana, Farhana

2014   Gendering Climate Change: Geographical Insights. *Professional Geographer* 66(3): 372–381.

Takigami, Mai K., Izumi Shimada, Rafael Segura, Sarah Muno, Hiroyuki Matsuzaki, Fuyuki Tokanai, Kazuhiro Kato, Hitoshi Mukai, Omori Takayuki, and Minoru Yoneda

2014   Assessing the Chronology and Rewrapping of Funerary Bundles at the Prehispanic Religious Center of Pachacamac, Peru. *Latin American Antiquity* 25(3): 322–343.

Thompson, L. G., E. Mosley-Thompson, J. F. Bolzan, and B. R. Koci

1985   A 1500-year Record of Tropical Precipitation in Ice Cores from the Quelccaya Ice Cap, Peru. *Science* 229(4717): 971–973.

Torrence, Robin, and John Grattan

2002   The Archaeology of Disasters: Past and Future Trends. In Natural Disasters and Cultural Change, edited by Robin Torrence and John Grattan, pp. 1–18. Routledge, London.

Trotter, Mildred, and Goldine C. Gleser

1952   Estimation of Stature from Long Bones of American Whites and Negroes. *American Journal of Physical Anthropology* 10(4): 463–514.

Uceda Castillo, Santiago

2010   Theocracy and Secularism. Relationships between the Temple and Urban Nucleus and Political Change at the Huacas de Moche. In *New Perspectives on Moche Political Organization*, edited by Jeffrey Quilter and Luis Jaime Castillo B., pp. 132–158. Dumbarton Oaks Research Library and Collection, Washington, D.C.

Uhle, Max

2003 [1903]   *Pachacamac: Report of the William Pepper, M.D, LL.D Peruvian Expedition of 1896.* Dept. of Archaeology of the University of Pennsylvania, Philadelphia.

Utsu, Tokuji

n.d.   *Catalog of Damaging Earthquakes in the World* (through 2015). IISEE, Tokyo.

Vallejo, Francisco

2009   La problemática de la cerámica Ychsma: El estado de la situación y algunos elementos de discusión. *Revista de Antropología* 19: 133–168.

van Buren, Mary

2001   The Archaeology of El Nino Events and Other "Natural" Disasters. *Journal of Archaeological Method and Theory* 8(2): 129–149.

Vega Dulanto, María del Carmen

2016   A History of Violence: 3000 Years of Interpersonal and Intergroup Conflicts from the Initial to the Early Colonial Periods in the Peruvian Central Coast. A Bioarchaeological Perspective. Unpublished PhD diss. University of Western Ontario, London.

Vlemincq-Mendieta, Tatiana, Simon Hillson, Lawrence S. Owens, Krzysztof Makowski, and Peter Eeckhout

2019   The Muddle in the Middle: Dental Morphological Assessment of Population Diversity onthe Peruvian Central Coast during the Prehispanic Period. *Abstracts for the 88th Meeting of the American Association of Physical Anthropologists (AAPA)*, Cleveland, Ohio.

Volk, Anthony A., and Jeremy A. Atkinson

2013   Infant and Child Death in the Human Environment of Evolutionary Adaptation. *Evolution and Human Behavior* 34(3): 182–192.

Waldron, Tony

2008   *Palaeopathology.* Cambridge University Press, Cambridge.

Walker, Charles F.

2003 The Upper Classes and Their Upper Stories: Architecture and the Aftermath of the Lima Earthquake of 1746. *Hispanic American Historical Review* 83(1): 53–82.

White, C. D., A. J. Nelson, F. J. Longstaffe, G. Grupe, and A. Jung

2009 Landscape Bioarchaeology at Pacatnamu, Peru: Inferring Mobility from Δ13c and Δ15n Values of Hair. *Journal of Archaeological Science* 36(7): 1527–1537.

Wilkerson, S. Jeffrey K.

2009 And the Waters Took Them: Catastrophic Flooding and Civilization on the Mexican Gulf Coast. In *El Niño, Catastrophism, and Culture Change in Ancient America*, edited by Daniel H Sandweiss and Jeffrey Quilter, pp. 243–271. Dumbarton Oaks Research Library and Collection, Washington, D.C.

Williams, Patrick Ryan

2002 Rethinking Disaster-Induced Collapse in the Demise of the Andean Highland States: Wari and Tiwanaku. *World Archaeology* 33(3): 361–374.

Winsborough, Barbara M., Izumi Shimada, Lee A. Newsom, John G. Jones, and Rafael A. Segura

2012 Paleoenvironmental Catastrophies on the Peruvian Coast Revealed in Lagoon Sediment Cores from Pachacamac. *Journal of Archaeological Science* 39(3): 602–614.

Wood, James W., George R. Milner, Henry C. Harpending, Kenneth M. Weiss, Mark N. Cohen, Leslie E. Eisenberg, Dale L. Hutchinson, et al.

1992 The Osteological Paradox: Problems of Inferring Prehistoric Health from Skeletal Samples. *Current Anthropology* 33(4): 343–370.

Zamudio, Yolanda, Jesús Berrocal, and Celia Fernandes

2005 Seismic Hazard Assessment in the Peru-Chile Border Region. *6th International Symposium on Andean Geodynamics*, pp. 813–816, Barcelona.

Zarulli, Virginia, Julia A. Barthold Jones, Anna Oksuzyan, Rune Lindahl-Jacobsen, Kaare Christensen, and James W. Vaupel

2018 Women Live Longer than Men Even during Severe Famines and Epidemics. *PNAS* 115(4): 832–840.

Contributors

KATIUSHA BERNUY

Museo de Sitio y Santuario de Pachacamac, Lima, Perú.

Degree in archaeology from the Universidad Nacional Mayor de San Marcos. She is the author of the book *Santuario Arqueológico Pachacamac: Investigaciones en la ruta de los peregrinos.*

RICHARD BURGER

Yale University, Connecticut.

Professor of anthropology at Yale University. He is the the author of many books, including *Chavin and the Origins of Andean Civilization*; *Emergencia de la Civilizacion en los Andes: Ensayos de Interpretacion*; *Excavaciónes en Chavín de Huántar*; and *Arqueología del Periodo Formativo en la Cuenca Baja de Lurín* (edited with K. Makowski).

PETER EECKHOUT

Université Libre de Bruxelles, Brussels, Belgium.

Full professor of pre-Columbian art and archaeology at the Université Libre de Bruxelles, Belgium. He is editor of *Archaeological Interpretations: Symbolic Meaning within Andean Prehistory* and coeditor (with Lawrence S. Owens) of *Funerary Practices and Models in the Ancient Andes: The Return of the Living Dead.*

ANDREA GONZALES LOMBARDI

Center for Heritage Research and Conservation–Universidad de Tecnología e Ingeniería (UTEC), Lima, Perú.

Assistant professor of the Humanities, Arts and Social Sciences Department at the Universidad de Ingeniería y Tecnología (UTEC), Peru. Her most recent publication is "Piura, un centro bajo sucesivos dominios imperiales (1000–1580 d.C.)" in the book *Un imperio, múltiples espacios; Perspectivas y balance de los análisis espaciales en arqueología inca*, edited by Giancarlo Marcone.

ENRIQUE LÓPEZ-HURTADO

United Nations Educational, Scientific, and Cultural
Organization (UNESCO), Lima, Perú.

Cultural Sector Coordinator of UNESCO in Perú who teaches at the Facultad de Letras y Ciencias Humanas de la Pontificia Universidad Católica del Perú. Among his latest publications are "Pachacamac and the Incas on the Coast of Perú," coauthored with Peter Eeckhout in the *Oxford Handbook of the Incas*, and "La obra legislativa de Julio C. Tello: un hito en la defensa del ejercicio de los derechos culturales en el Perú."

KRZYSZTOF MAKOWSKI

Pontificia Universidad Católica del Perú, Lima.

Krzysztof Makowski is full professor of archaeology at Pontificia Universidad Católica del Perú. He is the author of *Urbanismo andino. Centro ceremonial y ciudad en el Perú prehispánico*, and *Señores de los Imperios del Sol*.

GIANCARLO MARCONE

Center for Heritage Research and Conservation–Universidad de Tecnología e Ingeniería (UTEC), Lima, Perú.

Chair of the Humanities, Arts and Social Sciences Department at the Universidad de Ingeniería y Tecnología (UTEC). Master's and Ph.D. in Anthropology from the University of Pittsburgh, Pennsylvania. Among his publications are *The Inca Presence in the Lurín Valley*, and *Dual Strategies of the Rural Elites: Exploring the Intersection of Regional and Local Transformations in the Lurín Valley, Peru*.

LAWRENCE S. OWENS

Birkbeck–University of London; University of Winchester;
University of South Africa, England; South Africa.

Sessional lecturer at London's Birkbeck College, research fellow at the University of Winchester, and research associate at the University of South Africa. He specializes in Andean and African bioarchaeology and funerary archaeology, and is coeditor (with Peter Eeckhout) of *Funerary Practices and Models in the Ancient Andes: The Return of the Living Dead*.

DENISE POZZI-ESCOT

Museo de Sitio y Santuario de Pachacamac Lima, Perú.

Magister from the University of Paris I Pantheon-Sorbonne. Dr. Pozzi-Escot has been Director of the Professional School of Archaeology and History of the Universidad San Cristóbal de Huamanga. She is also the author of numerous articles and books, among them "Pilgrimage and Ritual Landscape in Pachacamac," an article published in the book titled *Pachacamac, the Oracle in the Sea Horizon of the Setting Sun*, of which she was the main editor.

LUCY C. SALAZAR

Yale University, Connecticut.

Lucy C. Salazar is senior research scientist in the Department of Anthropology at Yale University. She is the editor of several volumes, including *Finding Solutions for Protecting and Sharing Archaeological Heritage Resources*; *The 1912 Yale Peruvian Scientific Expedition Collections from Machu Picchu: Metal Artifact*; *Machu Picchu: Unveiling the Mystery of the Incas*; and *The 1912 Yale Peruvian Scientific Expedition Collections from Machu Picchu: Human and Animal Remains*.

RAFAEL A. SEGURA

Southern Illinois University, Carbondale, Illinois.

Lecturer at the Antonio Ruiz de Montoya University in Lima, and doctoral candidate in anthropology at Southern Illinois University. He is the author of *Rito y Economía en Cajamarquilla* and a coauthor of *Historia Económica del Antiguo Perú*.

IZUMI SHIMADA

Southern Illinois University, Carbondale, Illinois.

Professor of anthropology and Distinguished University Scholar emeritus at Southern Illinois University. He has authored or edited 19 books, including *Pachacamac Archaeology: Retrospect and Prospect.*

BARBARA WINSBOROUGH

Southern Illinois University, Carbondale, Illinois.

Independent researcher and consultant specializing in diatom analysis; has authored or coauthored many publications, including the upcoming coauthored journal article "The Diatom Flora of Hall's Cave, Kerr County, Texas."

Index

Page references with the letters *t* and *f* refer to tables and figures.